The "Industrial Culture Handbook" is simply a reference guide to the philosophy and interests of a flexible alliance of the following *deviant* international artists: *Throbbing Gristle, Cabaret Voltaire, SPK, Z'ev, Non, Monte Cazazza, Mark Pauline, Sordide Sentimental, Johanna Went,* and *R&N.* Most of these artists have been working creatively a decade or longer, in varying degrees of obscurity. The impetus in common is rebellion.

By "industrial" we mean the grim side of post-Industrial Revolution society—the repressed mythology, history, science, technology and psychopathology. By "culture" we mean the books, films, magazines, records, etc. which have been plucked out of the available information overload as relevant and important.

There is no strict unifying aesthetic, except that all things gross, atrocious, horrific, demented, and unjust are examined with black-humor eyes. Nothing is (or ever again will be) sacred, except a commitment to the *realization of the individual imagination.* These are not gallery or salon artists struggling to get to where the money is; these are artists *in spite of* art. There is no standard or value left unchallenged.

The values, standards, and content that remain are of a perversely anarchic nature, grounded in a post-holocaust morality. Swept away are false politeness, etiquette, preoccupation with texture and form—all the niceties associated with several generations of art about other art. Starting on a realigned foundation of "black" history, "black" science and the "black arts," these artists have presented their visions reflecting the world as *they* see it, not the official realities. The problems of morality and critical evaluation are left to the eye of the beholder, and to history—what remains of it....

All art has as its source dreams, the unconscious, and the imagination. And in dreams as in the imagination as in art—nothing is forbidden, everything is permitted....

—Vale, San Francisco 1983

RE SEARCH

C
O
N
T
E
N
T
S

**ISSUE #6/7
INDUSTRIAL
CULTURE
HANDBOOK**

Publishers: Betty Thomas, Scott X. Summerville
Editor: Vale
Assistant Editor: Andrea Juno
Managing Editor: Francisco de Oliveira Mattos
Design Consultant: Rebecca Wilson
Photographer: Bobby Adams/White Line Photography
(Barbara Martz, Ira Schrank, associates)
Cameraman & Film Consultant: Jim Morton
Associate Staff: Paul Mavrides, Nico Ordway, Jon Savage
Special Thanks to: James Grauerholz, Charles Gatewood,
and Ratso
Front Cover Concept & Photography: Bobby Adams
(drawing: Peter Hannan)

Contributors: Mark Austin, Ana Barrado, Nicole
Bengiveno, Mark Berlin, Mark Beyer, Lynda Burdick, Pete
Care, Suzan Carson!, Catherine Ceresole, Ed Colver,
Paula Court, Val Denham, Carol Detweiler, Don Gereux,
Marion Gray, Jonathan Haynes, Andrew Hickinbotham,
Steve Hitchcock, Matthew Heckert, Clay Holden, Anne
Janowitz, Jim Jocoy, Dalia Judowitz, Erich Mueller, Dan
Osborne, Richard Peterson, Peggy Photo, Polyploid Sam,
Marzy Quayzar, Wim Riemens, Janice & Mark
Sangerman, Siegfried, Ric Soloway, Paul Velik

ISBN No. 0-940642-07-7
Library of Congress No. 83-60192

All contents copyright © 1983 by Re/Search &
respective contributors

Re/Search, 20 Romolo #B, San Francisco CA 94133
(415) 362-1465.

BOOK DISTRIBUTION: Subco, PO Box 10233, Eugene
OR 97440 (503) 343-6324. RECORD STORE
DISTRIBUTION: Rough Trade, 326 6th St, San Francisco
CA 94103 (415) 621-4102. GERMANY: Rip-off,
Rambachstr. 13, 2000 Hamburg 11, W. Germany. 040-
313-846.

SUBSCRIPTIONS: $20 for 3 issues ($30 air
overseas/$36 for Australia/Asia).

Back Cover Photo: *Throbbing Gristle*
Photos pp.1 & 136: Bobby Adams/White Line

Industrial Culture—it is a little late, you know. Merely to think in terms of "industrial" is, of course, to admit that a particular phase of activity has passed into the history books. It is not for me to judge whether the subject will constitute a mere footnote or a weighty chapter, but the fact that a series of different, if related, projects can be given such a generic indicates assimilation and eventual supersession. That is not to say that the individual ideas concerned have lost their validity: simply that the conditions of the dialogue between the "avant-garde" and "pop"—into which "industrial" was a brief and vigorous intervention—have changed parameters. Focus has shifted from "the underground" to the "mainstream": our problems are too pressing to permit the ghettoization of possible new solutions.

Mind you, if we talk of expression as disturbance, then "industrial" was rather suited to our time's own particular malaise. Consider Lewis Mumford:

"Between 1820 and 1900 the destruction and disorder within great cities is like that of a *battlefield,* proportionate to the very extent of their equipment and the strength of the forces employed. In the new province of city building, one must now keep one's eyes on the bankers, industrialists, and the mechanical inventors. They were responsible for most of what was good and almost all that was bad. In their own image, they created a new type of city—that which Dickens, in *Hard Times,* called Coketown. In a greater or lesser degree, every city in the Western World was stamped with the archetypal characteristics of Coketown. *Industrialism,* the main creative force of the nineteenth century, produced the most degraded urban environment the world had yet seen: for even the quarters of the ruling classes were befouled and overcrowded." (*The City In History,* 1961).

"The street where Gen and Cosey live is unremittingly grim: 1850's artisan housing—dirty brick facades, gaping wounds stretch the length of the street, broken only by a low railway, almost mathematically. Exactly the kind of street you can imagine Victorian murders of the cruelest, meanest kind committed, and no one ever knowing. Cobbles, grey sky . . . ." (Intro to interview with Genesis P-Orridge, taped Nov 77, printed in *Search & Destroy,* April 78.) "The terrace opposite stops short in the grey air, thick with moisture, revealing vistas of factories, tower blocks, endless tightly patterned semi's . . . hills in the distance. Sometimes the factories work at night—the noise can be heard in the house, *filtering through dreams:* dull, percussive, hypnotic." (Intro to interview with *Cabaret Voltaire, Search & Destroy,* June 78).

In the gap caused by the failure of punk rock's apocalyptic rhetoric, "industrial" seemed like a good idea. Punk's implicit concentration, in its purest form, on situationist theory—the "boredom" of everyday life, and the images that filled fanzines and sleeve graphics—graffiti, "cut-ups of fifties consumer goods and the council block death factories in South London"—had left the door open for an even more comprehensive investigation of capitalism's decay. In the *superheated* atmosphere of London in 1977, when 1984 (if not armageddon) appeared round every crumbling corner; when arrays of dark glasses hid clinical paranoias; when the fabric of English society appeared to have been unraveled, by punk rock, into vicious threads of sectarian in-fighting, fascist and leftist violence on the streets, and financial crises; anything seemed possible, and indeed necessary. Punk, by this time, had not gone far enough: its style had become a pose, window-dressing for packaging and consumption through the usual commercial channels. Something new was needed: what was there?

If "industrial" was the most thorough examination yet of the decaying English environment, both physical and *psychic,* then it was also one very thorough reaction against what "punk" rock had become—good ol' rock'n'roll. Really, there was no option. In November 1977, three writers, Jane Suck, Sandy Robertson and myself—as the three "punk" correspondents on *Sounds*—were asked by the editor to provide another long feature about Generic Punk Rock—or New Wave, perhaps. We refused, forcibly.

Consulting our own overheated imaginations, we independently came up with the same thing. The November 26, 1977 edition of *Sounds* contained the blueprint for what has become Generic Industrial, and more besides: called "New Musick," it contained pieces about *Eno, Devo, The Residents, Kraftwerk,* and, archetypally, *Throbbing Gristle.* Indices were the synthetic disco of Giorgio Moroder, whose "I Feel Love" had been a huge summer hit; the first *Throbbing Gristle* album, *Second Annual Report; Devo* as heard on a live tape from the Mabuhay in San Francisco; and many extra-musical sources, particularly William Burroughs and cut-up theory.

As it happened, our emotional reaction, although imperfect on detail, was correct. The issue brought to light many ideas which had been floating around the Performance Art or Mail Art categories, which later became part of pop parlance; the new styles promoted by the phrase "New Musick" were always intended to be part of a full meeting of pop and what is called, in a phrase usually denoting lack of *access* and cultural impotence, "avant-garde." "The insistent pulse beat makes them accessible to anyone who wants to listen: Tesco Disco....Avant-garde smokescreens can put people off needlessly. The box is in your head...."

Quite apart from the impact on mainstream popular music, "New Musick" had opened Pandora's box. Out flew all manner of ideas and mutations. In England, in 1978, these were best exemplified by *Throbbing Gristle* in London, and *Cabaret Voltaire* in Sheffield, who were also benefiting from punk's protracted regionalism. These two, in particular, used the space offered to them to develop the ideas which I, in my purism, would prefer to call, for the sake of argument, "industrial." These included:

1) ORGANIZATIONAL *AUTONOMY*. The choice to record for their own, or "independent" labels was partly enforced, but mainly voluntary. It was felt that the major record companies were both tainted and unnecessary. This period saw the rise of the "independent" network to its peak of 1980: some independent labels like *Mute* and *Some Bizarre*—who both touch on "industrial" ideas—are still having a commercial success thought impossible six years ago.

2) ACCESS TO INFORMATION. At this time, the phrase "Information War"—meaning that the struggle for control was now not territorial but communicatory—came into currency. With the limited access then available, *Throbbing Gristle* and *Cabaret Voltaire* extended as far as was possible Burroughs' precepts about control into the popular media— the former in particular, as disseminators of information and propagandists par excellence. For example, their *Industrial News* [a periodical] would contain all manner of details about control techniques, among more conventional information and listings. The French magazine *Sordide Sentimental* produced packages which, in a happy marriage of form and content, contained outstanding examples of "industrial" and affiliated music—like *Joy Division's* "Dead Souls"—allied with detailed and illuminatory *philosophical* and *spiritual* treatises, often written by Jean-Pierre Turmel or Yves von Bontee. In this way, music was the key to a level of information and discussion which had not previously existed in this arena. Taboos were being openly examined; control, in a small sphere, challenged.

3) USE OF SYNTHESIZERS, AND *ANTI-MUSIC*. This is self-explanatory. Although music was the means to an end, rather than the end in itself, there was still the necessity of matching form to format. In this, *Throbbing Gristle's Second Annual Report* (1977) with its reliance on synthesizers and non-musical sounds, was prototypical. Punk's predilection for amplified noise—as well as works like "Loop" or "Sister Ray"—was refined into a new approach to "music." This development was taken (and is still being taken) to its fullest extent by the profoundly disturbing and haunting work of certain "industrial" artists, whose occasional records provide perhaps *the* true *soundtrack* to the final quarter of the twentieth century.

4) EXTRA-MUSICAL ELEMENTS. Much of this comes under "Access To Information," but there is more besides. Introduction of literary elements in a thorough—as opposed to typical pop dilettantism—manner: the full debt was made clear only long after "Industrial" had passed, in the Final Academy held in London in October, 1982. Another element was the use of films and videos, simultaneous to musical performance: this last is perhaps the most relevant, as television becomes a far more *powerful* agent of control than popular music. Both *Cabaret Voltaire* and *Psychic TV*, to name a couple, are producing their own television, and will concentrate upon this area more and more.

5) SHOCK TACTICS. A time honored technique to make sure what you have to say gets noticed. Lost in press reaction to *TG* and *CV's* more superficial aspects (and in audience reaction also, as on separate dates I saw both forced to stop a performance because of audience *violence* against them: true Performance Art Success!) was the industrial precept— carried out most faithfully by the *Industrial* label—of self-determination and self-control...to name but a few.

You will, by now, have noticed that the situation has changed. As with punk rock, many of "industrial's" preoccupations have been shown to be fact: as often, these days, art cannot compete with "life." Many of the strands first isolated five or six years ago have been fully unraveled, to the extent where the term "industrial" is now obsolete and useless, except as an example. You will hear cut-ups played freely on the radio, in popular "scratch" and "rap" music; you will hear groups with synthesizers at the top of the American charts. The apocalyptic feelings of 1977 and 1978 have burned out: what has replaced them is a grimmer *determination* to translate that desperation into positive action, in our slide to the depths of decline. The context has shifted: pop is no longer important; temporarily, television is. It is there that the next round in the Information War is being fought.

—Jon Savage, London 1983

THROBBING GRISTLE

Throbbing Gristle, Los Angeles 1981 (Photo: Suzan Carson!) **Previous pages: artwork/photo by Throbbing Gristle.**

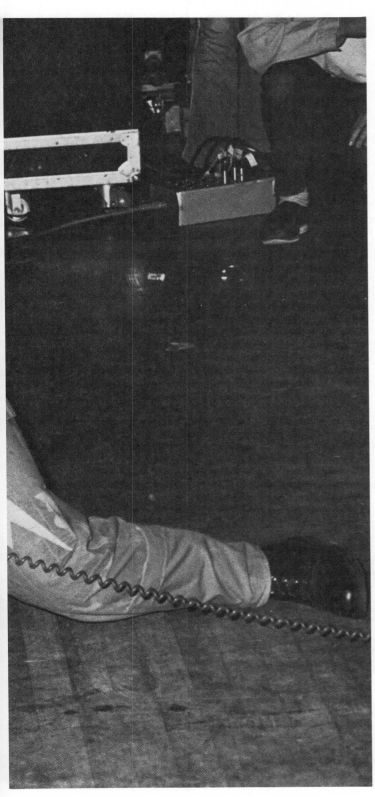

In 1976, *Industrial Records* was founded by *Throbbing Gristle* specifically to explore the psychological, visual and aural territory suggested by the term "Industrial." They demonstrated that with hardly any money they could produce records and cassettes with outstanding graphic standards and *deviant* recorded content—from death threats to factory noise to vanilla-smooth *Abba* tributes. *TG* focused on the *control process*, fighting the *information war* in a general revolt against the obedience instinct. As they put it, "We're just troublemakers, really, 'cause otherwise the world's a very boring place to be . . . ."

Special interests included tortures, cults, wars, psychological techniques of persuasion, unusual murders (especially by children and psychopaths), forensic pathology, venereology, concentration camp behavior, the history of uniforms and insignia, Aleister Crowley's magick, and much more. There were also deliberate attempts to *apply* the cut-up techniques of William S. Burroughs and Brion Gysin.

June 23, 1981: *Throbbing Gristle* split into two partnerships: *CTI* (Chris Carter and Cosey Fanni Tutti's *Creative Technology Institute)* and *Psychic TV/The Temple of Psychick Youth* founded by Genesis P-Orridge and Peter 'Sleazy' Christopherson. Both groups have records available.

What follows are interviews with Genesis, Cosey and Chris summarizing the intentions, means and achievements of *Throbbing Gristle,* as well as some words on *Coum Transmissions,* the performance art group Genesis and Cosey directed from 1969-1976 (Sleazy joined the last year).

> We're interested in information, we're not interested in music as such. And we believe that the whole battlefield, if there is one in the human situation, is about information.

R/S: When you started *Industrial Records* in 1976, what did you have in mind?

GEN: It seemed inevitable, the reasons for it at the time. There's an irony in the word "industrial" because there's the music *industry.* And then there's the joke we often used to make in interviews about churning out records like motorcars—*that* sense of industrial. And . . . up till then the music had been kind of based on the blues and slavery, and we thought it

was time to update it to at least Victorian times—you know, the Industrial Revolution.

Rock'n'roll had been somewhere away in the sugarcane fields of the West Indies and the cottonfields of America, so we thought it was time to try and update it somewhat, towards the world as it is now...meaning *then.* (And it still is like that.)

And "industrial" has a very cynical ring to it. It's not like that kind of romance of "paying your dues, man"; of being "on the road"—rock'n'roll as a career being worthwhile in itself, and all that shit. So it was cynical and ironic, and also accurate. And we liked the imagery of factories—I mean, we just thought there was a whole untapped area of imagery and noise which was suggested when we thought of "industrial."

And then Monte Cazazza was the person who suggested the slogan "Industrial Music for Industrial Peo-

Throbbing Gristle on video. (Photo: Throbbing Gristle)
TG after last show, San Francisco, May 31, 1981. (Photo: Clay Holden)

ple." Funny enough, one of the earliest thoughts was "Factory Records," named after Warhol's Factory and his idea of silkscreening painted pictures and then signing them. But we decided that was too obvious, and that Warhol wasn't really good enough!

That was when we were thinking around an industrial idea, so we thought: use the actual word *industrial.* And there's also *industry,* like *work*—putting a lot of work into it. There's lots of nice connotations—it's far better than *Factory!* A factory's an empty building until people are in it—it's not quite as interesting. I doubt if *Factory Records* even thought that far about it—but they made more money. Then again, a diluted form of something usually does....

R/S: Do you think you started an "industrial culture"?

GEN: There has been a phenomena; I don't know whether it's strong enough to be a culture. I do think what we did has had a reverberation right around the world and back. It obviously revealed that there *were* a lot of people in all sorts of different countries that you wouldn't expect to have a very similar view or vision of what was happening.

There was a market everywhere for that material, and to a certain extent there still is—all our records are still selling. But I don't know how many of those people have actually *analyzed* it beyond a certain point. I think a lot of them got an initial recognition buzz . . . and they also got a novelty buzz, and it made sense to them. It seemed to be relevant to some people, so that they've actually declared that it's changed their lives!

Even graphics have been affected by it—barbed wire and factories are suddenly incredibly acceptable, chic images, when once they were completely ignored.

R/S: Or not even thought of as suitable content.

GEN: It's funny, because in a way it's added a kind of romance to the urban landscape—urban decay in factories has become a kind of romance. I don't like using the word "real," but in a sense we were trying to make everything more real . . . and to portray, the same way that a Cut-up theoretically does: what it's like to be in a house and go along the street and have a car go past or a train and work in a factory or walk past a factory. Just a kind of industrial life, or suburban-urban-industrial life.

When we finished that first record, we went outside and we suddenly heard trains going past, and little workshops under the railway arches, and the lathes going, and electric saws, and we suddenly thought, "We haven't actually created anything at all, we've just taken it in subconsciously and *re*-created it."

The funny thing is, we didn't sit there to make industrial noises, per se. Afterwards, we discovered that one could actually sort of describe in a very documentary way, exactly where we'd created the sounds, in and around Martello Street. Then again, according to our theories of initiated magick, it seemed perfectly reasonable. . . . That's the way it always seems to be—you suddenly realize afterwards that it was very accurate, whereas the initial act is usually *instinct.* . . .

We were also being deliberately perverse by doing the opposite of everything everyone else said was feasible or practical or acceptable. Like everyone else

thought it was an incredible breakthrough for a punk band to do a rock'n'roll single on their own label. So we did a non-rock'n'roll LP. Everyone said we must be complete mental suicides. It turned out not to be....

R/S: Lots of contradictions and ironies—

GEN: And lots of secret information. Just about every record had some reference in it towards one that had gone before or one that was coming next. So there was this strange spider's web building up. And a lot of people weren't sure what it was, but they got this feeling that if they could just get the pattern on the kaleidoscope, it would suddenly all become clear. We used to put in enough red herrings to prevent that!

Assuming that we had no basic interest in making records, no basic interest in music per se, it's pretty weird to think that we've released something like 10 albums, plus bootlegs; 40 cassettes . . . that have had an effect on the whole popular music scene, forever.

> I'm concerned about the human race being stupid right through history. Therefore we use all the archetypes for human stupidity....

Then again, I wouldn't have seen the point of having a group that was just entertainment. I'd only have wanted it to be a group that would remain some kind of cult group like the *Velvet Underground* did—to have that kind of longevity, to be a seminal group. So although I find it on one level irritating or boring that it still exists, at the same time it had to be that way.

But I'm really so disinterested in that now [Sept 1982]—it's got a life of its own now.

R/S: There's a fair number of imitators, imitating the content and tonalities—

GEN: Other people are making their living out of it, existing, releasing these posthumous records. Maggots eating a corpse.... It's the old story, isn't it, of people completely misunderstanding the message. It's like *Joy Division*—to a large extent they evolved a unique sound of their own, a new sound amongst the sort-of progression of musical sound. They had their own recognizable, individual style. And then suddenly there's 50 other groups who, because they like *Joy Division,* use the same style that can't ever have the *content* because they're not Ian Curtis.

Ian Curtis was talking about himself, and it had nothing to do with any separation between his lyrics and the reality inside his head and his emotions. And they might tell you that they are the same—but if they were the same, the sound would be different because they would *have* to have a different sound to describe *their* true individual emotion. The same with us, too—our sound is describing *our* collective and individual emotions and visions. And the sound came from what we thought and saw; it was *second.* To just copy the sound—there's no way anyone can have the same sound as us and be describing themselves in a truthful way. It's just not possible.

Because that sound is completely inseparable from the way we felt at any given moment, which is why we did so much live, and why so much happened live.

11

Whatever happened live was exactly what was going through us all at that time, just like being possessed in a seance. And you can't imitate that or mimic it or copy it....

There we are, trying to say: Go and check and find your individual potential and your own voice...and they don't. If they even looked at the records they would see that the style and the sound fluctuate immensely. It isn't all industrial noise—there's "Distant Dreams" and tracks on *Jazz Funk Greats*—we never felt any style was taboo—there's the Martin Denny one on *Journey Through A Body*.

We had no fear of *having to stick to one style*. We always saw it as a complete entity, and all the records as being chapters of this one big book. And when the book was finished, we stopped. And it's now a reference book.

It's like going into the Louvre and doing a drawing of the Mona Lisa and thinking you're a fucking artist. That's what they're doing. They'd laugh at somebody who came to them and said, "Hey, I'm really original—look at this pencil drawing of the Mona Lisa." Or, "I've done an exact copy of a Picasso—that means I'm a creative, unique artist." They'd laugh...and then they go and do the same thing with sound.

R/S: What you've done has involved a constant manipulation and reassessment—

GEN: Every record we did, we sat back and thought, "Well, what are they expecting now, having done the other one...and how can we manipulate and twist and change things?" There's no way that you can have failed, because you've done the track *you* wanted and that's all you've ever said you are going to do. There-

all the options we wanted to keep. And we were just as able to outrage them by doing something pretty...and yet they weren't even able to understand that that's what we were doing. I hope they go away and never buy our records again!—go and make a tent out of their raincoats, and talk about ax-murderers and....

R/S: You've presented a lot of taboo subjects for listeners to research—mass murders, atrocities, mutilations. What do you think of that?

GEN: It varies. Sometimes, although it's embarrassing, there are exceptions when there's such genuine enthusiasm, and the other person is aware that it's silly. You can't help tolerating it because there is no harm in it—it's not actually doing them any harm, it's a pleasurable hobby, and it's in perspective in their entire life. It's still worrying, but—to do anything to discourage it beyond a certain point would be very cruel, and wouldn't actually be constructive.

But in the vast majority of cases, it's just another example of people totally misunderstanding everything you ever said and did. In its worst cases it's pathologically pathetic. And in most cases it's just a waste of time. I mean, there obviously must be cases where people just genuinely became interested because of being directed toward a subject, and it is a genuine interest—and you were just an accidental catalyst toward something that probably would have happened anyway. But let's put it this way—we get these letters from people who try desperately to write an outrageous, sick letter, and they try and use every swear word they've heard, and mention pseudo-Marquis de Sade scenarios. I don't know if they think it's supposed to be impressive or make us wonder what

There was this exhibition in Canada that General Idea did. Everybody else was doing these arty or witty Fluxus-type things. I sent them a pint of live maggots and, I think, a used tampax.

Skull display, living room of Genesis P-Orridge. (Photo: Vale)

fore, per se, you cannot have failed. So—they either don't like it (which is their privilege), or they don't understand what we're doing, or refuse to *accept* what we are doing.

But I think it's just as bad to not be able to take TG when it's melodic, as it is when it's un-melodic. That's why we did "Adrenalin" and "Distant Dreams"—to make the point that we refused point-blank to give up

they're like or think they're really interesting people, but I just throw them straight into the dustbin. There's a lot of people around who'd be better off dead! Or at least asleep somewhere, out of the way.

R/S: On the other hand, there are hopefully people out there who send you items of interest—

GEN: Two or three. The strange thing is, most of the people who are helpful are people we already knew.

Sleazy, Cosey, Chris, Genesis, 1977. (Photo: Monte Cazazza)

Percentage-wise, it leaves something to be desired! I'm pretty sure we'd have found just as many people we liked and got on with if we'd never done *TG*. I don't think it's increased our circle of lasting acquaintances in the real sense at all.

R/S: How did you happen to study venereal disease and medical texts in general?

GEN: Monte had to do with that. And Sleazy—he was doing all that work with injuries. I think he may have gotten *The Colour Atlas of Forensic Pathology* deliberately for research, whereas when I saw it I thought it was great graphics! But Monte was always interested in medical topics, because he'd done a project on Siamese twins before, and he had books on diseases and amputations and things like that.

Then again, Monte was instantly one of us. It was great when we first met, because he had the same library he used to keep *away* from people in San Francisco, because when they saw the books he had, they'd tell him he was mentally sick and a sadist and a Nazi, and he'd of course go, "Yeah . . . *so what?*" But actually, it did upset him that he couldn't display what he was really interested in . . . freely discuss what he was interested in.

The main reason we got on so well when we met was—there was nothing he could produce that would faze or disturb us. It was like instant rapport—and we were swapping anecdotes about who's got information on what. He had loads of books that I hadn't thought of investigating or hadn't had access to because they were American. And I'd say, "Have you tried reading this, that and the other?" So, it was a very fast cross-fertilization.

And he was very instrumental in the whole concept—he was there when we called it *Industrial Records*. He immediately coined that phrase and did a collage of that; made the big *TG* wooden sign with that flash on it. And he was very involved in *tactics*. He even stuck the labels on most of the LP covers of the first LP, the original white ones, evolving a special template to make it easier. He was very, very involved at the beginning, because he was living here with us for 3 months. The tactics and marketing and propaganda and even the fact of dealing with it as propaganda and tactics was equally as much Monte's as ours. I always have fun when Monte's here—he makes me *more extreme.* It's very healthy.

R/S: You first visited him in 1976?

GEN: He was still living on Shattuck Avenue, in Berkeley.

R/S: You originally met him through the mail art phenomenon?

GEN: Yes. That was one of the few times when I'd written to somebody first. I actually courted him. Anna Banana wrote me this letter that she was living with Bill Gaglione and had met this really horrible, revolting person—the nastiest person she'd ever met in her life, and he was evil and disgusting and vile—she went on and on about how horrible he was. And he was called Monte Cazazza. And the one bad thing about living in San Francisco was the fact he existed. All she did was totally incite my desire to know him more.

So I wrote to Opal Nations (because she wouldn't give me his address) and got his address and wrote more or less a fan letter which said something like,

13

"You don't know me, but you sound pretty good...."
And he wrote back, "I don't usually reply to anybody,
but something about your letter made it seem like you
weren't just another asshole." So we were both very
tentative, really, because we'd both been let down
lots of times.

And then I sent him a dead mouse—I found this
plastic plate with a knife and fork and a dead mouse in
the street, and I stuck it on the plate and sent it to him
as his breakfast so he'd get it...by which time it'd be
pretty stinky. Then it got more out of hand. I started
getting fiberglass resin and making big parcels with
mutant animals made out of bits of rabbits and
chickens and I'd send them in the mail. And at one
point he nearly got prosecuted by the post office for
receiving maggot-ridden, disgusting, stinking parcels!
He got called into the post office—there was this parcel on the desk addressed to him that was just rotten
meat, and they said to him, "Did you ask for this parcel
to be sent?" He had to deny that he knew anything
about it—he had to say that some lunatic in England
had sent it....

Anything dead I found I used to send to Monte. And I
remember him once telling me that some art critic
was trying to chat him up for some reason, so he took
him this jam jar with a rotten dead mouse in it that
he'd received from me...and kept presenting it to this
art critic. It was really foul and smelly. I think he gave
it to him on the bus.

I was going through my maggots-and-meat-through-
the-mail phase then. There was this exhibition in Canada that General Idea did, with lots of perspex boxes
in a big mural. And they wrote to hundreds of people
and you had to send them something to put in one of
these perspex boxes, until there was something in
every box. Everybody else was doing these arty or

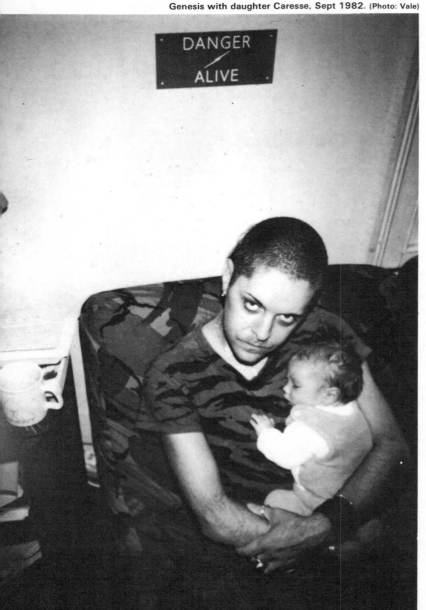

Genesis with daughter Caresse, Sept 1982. (Photo: Vale)

witty Fluxus-type things—I sent them a pint of live
maggots and, I think, a used tampax—but they didn't
put them in (laughs).

I wanted to have something in there that everyone
would go, "Yecchh!" Because for all their so-called
radicalism, they were incredibly conservative and
very moral—they used to get really incensed at some
of my pornographic collages—especially people in
"mail art"—

R/S: They're so smug about being outside the "art estab-
lishment—"

GEN: Because they're not good enough to be in—
they couldn't survive inside.

R/S: There's only a few people you still correspond with that
you met through mail art—

GEN: Monte, Skot Armst, Jerry Dreva, Bobby Bon
Bon, Sergei...and Al Ackerman. Out of hundreds and
hundreds of people I wrote to, honed down to six
people. We got sick to death of mail art people, and just
wanted to do insensitive ugly things to piss them off,
and just get left alone.

We wasted a hell of a lot of money on stamps. And
the novelty of receiving somewhat odd packages in the
post just wore off, because we noticed that the best
ones were always from the same four or five people.
Monte always wrote good letters.

So not long ago I went through my filing cabinets
and burned masses and masses of old "mail art" letters.
It's not worth keeping it just in case one day it's worth
money—it's taking up space. We had a big bonfire—it
was great. All these photos of mail artists curling up,
turning brown and blistering. Xeroxed dada collages...how much better it is!

There was a period when I was really into it very
enthusiastically...and then it kind of got diluted and
plagiarized and misunderstood. What had been a thing
where you just did a really special hand-done letter,
with collages and photos, just for a friend—not as art,
or mail art, but just because it was nice to get a letter
like that. Suddenly there were all these people doing
all these envelopes—xeroxes of absolutely crass, bad
collages with a rubber stamp stamped on it somewhere, and a funny name. And that was their
interpretation—that was their understanding of it.

Exactly the same problem we had with *Industrial Records*—that's why you have to move on quick before it's too late—you get swamped by second-rate misunderstandings!

That's not to claim that everything we've ever done is good, but at least the motivation was correct. I mean, good in terms of—if there is some scale you can mea-

> Real war has become information war. It is being fought by subtle informational media—under cold conditions. Whenever hot wars are necessary these days, we conduct them in the backyards of the world with the old technologies. These wars are *happenings,* tragic games.

sure value of work against. I'm not trying to claim that we are fantastically talented or wonderful, but—we've always had integrity of motive. And whether it has any value beyond that I don't know, but I do always care about the motivation and the integrity and I get upset when I see that being smeared and misunderstood.

And there's not a lot you can do except move on quick to something where there's still a space to move. I mean, there are still people who are locked into those fucking xeroxes *now!* That's like years and years and years after it was obviously a redundant thing to do. Nice letters aren't redundant, but then people who did the nicest letters have been doing them anyway, before they'd heard of mail art, and carried on doing them after they thought mail art was redundant. The best things have come from the people who didn't need to think of it as mail art or correspondence—they were friends!

R/S: What do you think of Mark Pauline?

GEN: What do you mean?—we're friends! He has integrity. I always try to tell people in England about Mark Pauline... I like Neal as well—I see them as the ultimate sort of frontier Americans, the Clint Eastwoods of the art world. 100% reasonable behavior... (Genesis invents a fantasy scenario for a Mark Pauline feature film a la *Mad Max* or *The Cars That Ate Paris*). **He's one of the good guys.**

R/S: I didn't know you knew Z'ev?

GEN: Yes, he's one of the good guys too. I like him. There's not many people around; you've got to take them when you can! When I like somebody, I don't really care what they do—when I do, it's a bonus. He's another kind of *individual.* He's weird—highly intelligent and very weird. I see people like Z'ev and Mark Pauline—to me they're like modern alchemists. All the best people are like that, in that alchemical tradition. I said that to Z'ev and he agreed...wisely nodding.

I'm always flattered when people like Z'ev and Mark Pauline bother to stay in touch, because I know they don't bother to unless they really want to. Z'ev played with *TG* at the Lyceum. I met him through Rod Pierce (of *Fetish* Records).

Boyd Rice is good—I like him a lot. I wanted to release an LP of Boyd on *Industrial* but.... We did

manage to get him on with us a few times—we put him on the first time he ever played England, at the London Filmmakers Co-op. And it was at that gig that Daniel Miller saw him and then signed him to *Mute.* I even mixed for him—some people said it was the loudest they've ever heard Boyd. I had it up loud—it literally made people move. It moved their stomachs like they had been hit. See, Monte told me that we should put Boyd up—that it was the best dance music he'd ever heard. I thought Monte was being ironic, but when I heard it the first time I understood what he meant. Because it was so *physical*—

R/S: When he can get the volume he requires—

GEN: And he played with us in Berlin two nights, and at the Lyceum. So we played with him four times.

R/S: You place extremely high value on work—don't you work all the time?

GEN: Yes. But then you get somebody like Crowley— who wrote all those bloody books! And he goes mountaineering, and has lots of sex; he does paintings, he travels, he does magazines, he gets books published as well as writing them, he organizes magickal societies, he has political in-fighting going on, he's drugging it—how the hell did he do it all? How on earth is it possible?

R/S: Plus he wrote journals—

GEN: That have never yet come out—I know. Reams. It takes all my time to write half a page of a diary every day—and it's not even particularly interesting to read! And this bloke has spewed forth masses of provocative stuff, and he could speak all those languages, and he was a very good mathematician—an amazing mathematician. And it makes you feel really pathetic.

R/S: Maybe the more writing you do, the faster it gets?

GEN: I've gotten slower. I used to be able to write really fast—now I take *ages.*

R/S: Yes, but you were writing more letters then, whereas now you're writing more philosophical, compressed essays.

GEN: It is more compressed. But it's much more laborious.

R/S: Somebody said that writing is the only way to learn anything....Incidentally, does Sleazy write?

GEN: Sleazy is a big tactician; he's been much more seminal in what we've been doing than a lot of people realize. He's very very particular in every sense, and is always checking out tactics and responses. He's very much the head of graphics and design, and is equally involved in the philosophy. He's very much a purist— always trying to make sure we never strayed from our pure directions. It was usually Sleazy whom I would turn to, to have a very long analysis/rap session, about the essential nature of what we're all really doing....

> The more you tell the truth, the more camouflaged it is.

When we shifted from *Coum Transmissions* to *TG,* we were also stating that we wanted to go into *popular* culture, away from the art gallery context, and show that the same techniques that had been made to operate in that system could work. We wanted to test it out in the real world, or nearer to the real world, at a more street level—with young kids who had no education in

THROBBING GRISTLE

art perception, who came along and either empathized or didn't; either liked the noise or didn't.

A little mini-Dada movement, eh?

R/S: Possibly, with the power to affect people lacking a sophisticated art background.

GEN: Well, that's something we've always tried to do. Now we're going to try and do that with a sort of philosophical, mystical magick, so non-dogmatic and non-authoritative—people who've been brought up to despise anything that smacks of "religion"—maybe we can remind them that there *are* useful structures; that spiritual values aren't necessarily to be despised or ridiculed; that there are certain individual attentions which, when used in a mystical way, actually are quite beneficial.

I'd like to be able to present whatever we do so that somebody with no training can get into it as easily as somebody with training. Quite often it is the people without training who get into it quicker. And often it is the people with training who are most antagonistic. And to do it without simplifying it, without taking any of its power away, so that you're not being patronizing—you're merely trying to take away the mystique and the vested interest in trying to sound like you've got to be special to understand this. It doesn't have to be a bastardized version to be understood by a lot of people. I'd like to try and find a form that treats *everybody* as being intelligent, at least potentially....

You assume initially that people want a bit more content, some project which has a lot more depth to it, and that the fact that everyone says "Oh, everyone just wants trivia and superficiality" isn't true. People are actually pleased to be given a bit more credit for a bit more intelligence. I think it's far better to make something on the assumption that people *will* work to understand it...

And, there's no fun if there isn't risk... Sometimes I think we've given birth to a monster, uncontrollable, thrashing, spewing forth mentions of Auschwitz for no reason. It's funny, because when I really think about it, the original half-dozen who started it all off are still the best ones, like the *Cabs* and Boyd—the first wave. I suppose that's inevitable. It's the old story, like in the 60's—Zappa was completely different to Beefheart, who was completely different to the *Doors,* who were completely different to the *Velvet Underground.* And we were completely different to the *Cabs,* really. And Boyd Rice was totally different, and *Z'ev* is different. Monte's different in his way. And we've all got a quite clear individual style linked to our individual lives. Whereas now they all sound like each other, and more than each other they sound like weedy fragments that they've honed in on, of one or the other people. The way they can even not notice that every one of the original industrial groups and people was totally different from each other—they've even missed *that* fact. That Mark Pauline does not sound like "Slug Bait," that Boyd Rice doesn't sound like "Nag Nag Nag," and so on. They don't even seem to be able to take *that* information in.

R/S: And Boyd is capable of doing a totally pop song, totally opposite in an unrecognizable direction...

GEN: These youngsters are less interesting on every level, aren't they? It is worrying.

R/S: It's the old problem—they can't grasp the spirit behind the material forms.

GEN: All of us were working before it became "industrial," and discovered each other and recognized that kindred spirit, that driving force, and that's what made us all, if you like, "industrial culture." It's just that we wanted to have some kind of alliance, because we felt like we were all a kind of outlaw—but we all had some basic motivation and drive in common.

None of us were worried whether we sounded stylistically the same. It never even—I mean we were all quite happy that we didn't! It didn't even matter whether we thought each other was *good*—that had nothing to do with it. Or whether we liked everything that each one did. What was interesting was *the people involved*...and that we'd arrived at the same alienated, cynical point, and somehow found a way, a method to rationalize it and integrate it back.

Like we've often said—I can't really like a lot of records or a lot of things unless I like the people who do them. I don't know the *Velvet Underground* and I enjoy their records, but that's actually an exception. But then it gets funny, because it goes one stage further—if I like the people, it no longer matters whether I ever listen to what they do. It's got beyond that point now—I just trust the reason they're working. I think the reason they're working is valid—that's the crux of the matter. And I don't need to keep checking up on what they're up to!

The other thing that is quite staggering is that "industrial" has become a word that is used worldwide—there are record sections in shops in Japan that say "Industrial Music." And journalists now use "industrial" as a term like they would "blues." It's become part of the vocabulary. And I'm sure most of them have totally forgotten where it came from and don't even realize how it appeared—I think they just write as if it always was a term they used! If we had a royalty for every time the word "industrial" was used, we'd be doing all right! Luckily you don't really think of it like that; if you did, it'd become really scary. Will "psychic" become a trend next? Where will it all end?

R/S: You can feel another occult revival just around the corner.

GEN: Sandy Robertson did a 2-page feature on Aleister Crowley in *Sounds,* and the photo we gave them had lots of psychick crosses added to all of the regalia. It was credited: "Photo courtesy of The Temple of Psychick Youth." And it brought more mail than they've had in 2 years!

The propaganda war has begun! It's time for optimism and hope! And love, with a bit of naughty sex thrown in for good measure....

(I'm sure we were misdirected—but we've seen the error of our ways, dear public! We understand now; Leonard Cohen was the answer. Leonard Cohen and Ennio Morricone had the true image of reality, and violins and cellos definitely play their part. In fact, we might say acoustic music is the thing. Oh, sad day that we decided the machine was somehow relevant!)

Cosey with 2 cats, Chris with Abba picture disc, 1982.
(Photos: Andrea Juno)

THROBBING GRISTLE INSTRUMENTATION:
(from a May 28, 1981 interview with Chris and Cosey just before the last *TG* concert, San Francisco)

R/S: What are your instruments?

COSEY: Cornet and lead guitar, usually with a slide. I prefer that sound because of all the other noises that are going on—it *comes through* then, otherwise it's just a muddy sound underneath everything else.

R/S: Did you teach yourself?

COSEY: I just bash it around—I don't play it sussed. I just get what I can out of it; I could never use it as a melody instrument which most guitars are used as. I use it as a rhythmic instrument.

R/S: Chris, you devised the rhythmic tracks?

CHRIS: (nods.) Some of the rhythms are quite old, from 2 years ago. They're all on cassettes.

R/S: Did you build a lot of the equipment?

CHRIS: I built Sleazy's keyboard. It's a one-octave keyboard; each line is triggering 3 Sony stereo cassette machines, loaded with cassettes with prerecorded noises on them. He makes tape loops with constant noises on them—shortwave noises, a tape loop of a piano, screaming voices, and other things. He had a Jim Jones tape but it was like a subliminal.

He just has all the outputs running through his keyboard, and he can play with the output. He's got a little sequencer built in that can override the keyboard, that can build up a rhythm if he wants to. And he's got a little harmonizer—for pitch changing—and we've all got little Roland micro-monitor amplifiers.

R/S: It's all very compact, suitcase-sized—

CHRIS: Gen's is the biggest—he's got a bass guitar so he's got to have a bigger amp, a Cube. He's got a pedalboard in the lid of his box, so he takes the lid off and all his pedals are on. And Cosey's got the same sort of thing. I've just got a small Casio keyboard, the slightly bigger model, with all sorts of pedals—a harmonizer, phaser, flanger, etc. And I've got a cassette machine which I play all the rhythms on.

And we've got a small box, a chorus echo, that we put all the vocals through, so I can speed them up and slow them down, repeat them, and things like that.

R/S: *You* modify the vocals live?

CHRIS: Yes. And Cosey's got her cornet as well which she puts through her box. That's it! Very mobile.

COUM TRANSMISSIONS 1969-1976
(The performance art group Genesis and Cosey developed with other collaborators; Sleazy joined the final year. Watch for a coming history of *Coum Transmissions* by Gray Watson: *Power, Sex and Magick.*)

GENESIS: I used to do things like stick severed chickens' heads over my penis, and then try and masturbate them, whilst pouring maggots all over it. . . .

In Los Angeles, in 1976, at the Institute of Contemporary Arts (LAICA), Cosey and I did a performance where I was naked. I drank a bottle of whisky and stood on a lot of tacks. And then I gave myself enemas with blood, milk and urine, and then broke wind so a jet of blood, milk and urine combined shot across the floor in front of Chris Burden and assorted visual artists. I then licked it off the floor, which was a not-clean concrete floor.

Then I got a 10-inch nail and tried to swallow it, which made me vomit. Then I licked the vomit off the floor and Cosey helped me lick the vomit off the floor. And she was naked and trying to sever her vagina to her navel—well, she cut it from her vagina to her navel with a razor blade, and she injected blood into her vagina which then trickled out, and we then sucked the blood from her vagina into a syringe and injected it into eggs painted black, which we then tried to eat. And we vomited again, which we used for enemas.

Then I needed to urinate, so I urinated into a large glass bottle and drank it all while it was still warm. (This was all improvised.) And then we gradually crawled to each other, licking the floor clean ('cause we don't like to leave a mess, y'know; after all, it's not fair to insult an art gallery). Chris Burden, who's known for being outrageous, walked out with his girlfriend, saying, "This is not art, this is the most disgusting thing I've ever seen, and these people are sick."

In Amsterdam we did a performance in the red-light district. The people in the theater asked, "What kind of lighting do you want?" and we said, "Oh, just put on all the red lights." Then we played tapes of Charles Manson's LP, *Lie,* cut-up with soundtracks of trains going through thunderstorms, and we went through all different kinds of fetishes. Sleazy cut his throat and had to kind of do a tourniquet on his throat, and Cosey and I did this thing of spitting at each other and then licking all the spit off, and then licking each other's genitals, and then having sexual intercourse while her hair was set on fire with candles. There was an audience of around 2,000 people.

And each day it got heavier, so that on Easter Sunday I was crucified on a wooden cross, whipped with 2 bullwhips, covered in human vomit and chicken wings and chicken legs, while I had to hold burning torches—people in the audience could hear the skin burning on my hands. And then I urinated down Cosey's legs while she stuck a lighted candle up her vagina, so there was flames coming out of her vagina. Just ordinary everyday ways of avoiding the commercials on the television. . . .

Poem for Uncle Bill

UB who UB
supposedly an evil power
yet
    an old man
sometimes it showed
drinking whisky
till it slurred

E am E
we agree it was inevitable
Uncle Bill

''in search of an alternative universe''

Passing a Rolls-Royce
E promise to buy one
complete with chauffeur

he promised night
such a sickness
never known

''this planet rotten''

some future some futility one future

how ridiculous
a name becoums
a dream becoums
a card becoums
a conversation

we agree to eradicate
a few phenomena and parted

    —genesis p-orridge
    (after meeting Bill Burroughs, 1973)

COUM Transmissions performance. (Photo: Coum Transmissions)

SOME BOOKS

LIBRARY OF GENESIS P-ORRIDGE

The Passionate Years/Caresse Crosby
Funeral Rites/Jean Genet
Black Sun/Geoffrey Wolff
Shadows of the Sun/Harry Crosby
Shock Value/John Waters
Naked City
Murderer's Who's Who/Gaute & Odell
Surrealist Art/Sarane Alexandrian
Surrealism/Patrick Waldberg
Sex Life of the Foot & Shoe
Dada & Surrealism
Seven Dadaist Manifestos/Tristan Tzara
Arsenal of Democracy/ed Tom Gervasi
Law Enforcement Bible/ed R A Scanlon
Camouflage (2 titles)
Army Uniforms of World War II/Mollo
Post-Mortem Procedures/Gresham
  & Turner
Venereology/Wisdom
Forensic Pathology/Gresham
Syphilis/U.S. Public Health Service
Anatomy of the S.S. State
Uniforms, Organization & History of the
  Waffen SS (4 vol/Bender & Taylor)
Things That Matter/Rubenstein & Block
Heavily Tattooed Men & Women/
  Spider Webb
Murders of the Black Museum
A Century of Murderers
Feelings About Childbirth
Design Motifs of Ancient Mexico/Encisco
Very Special People/Frederick Drimmer
All About Iguanas/Roberts & Roberts
Keep The River On Your Right/Schneebaum
Trip Trap
Dowsing/Tom Graves
Book of the Damned/Charles Fort
Witch, Spirit, Devil/A.E. Scott
History of Magic, Witchcraft and
  Occultism/W.B. Crow
The Alchemists/F. Sherwood Taylor
Dictionary of Gynecological History/
  Berkeley & Sonney
Ascent of Man/Bronowski
Songs of Gods, Songs of Humans/
  Slava Ranko aka Donald L. Philippi
Fluxshoe
Grotowski's Laboratory
Milton's Poetical Works
I Ching
Ritual in the Dark/Colin Wilson
Swingin' Dors/Diana Dors
A Scanner Darkly/Philip K. Dick
Now Wait for Last Year/P.K. Dick
Cosmic Trigger/Robert A. Wilson
Dada Almanach/Hülsenbeck
Art et Communication Marginale/
  Hervé Fischer
Autobiography of a Yogi/Yogananda

Across Poland
Prostitutes/Denise Winn
The Underground Film
A Crystal Age/W.H. Hudson
Dictionary of Contemporary
  American Artists
Life Star/Hermine Demoriane
Contemporary Artists/ed P-Orridge/Naylor
Infamous Murderers
The Rise of Communist China
Requiem For A Dream/Hubert Selby
National Suicide
The Home Birth Handbook
Breast Is Best
Magic of Tone & the Art of Music
Nuclear Survival Handbook/B Popkess
The Third Wave/Alvin Toffler
None Dare Call It Conspiracy/Allen
None Dare Call It Treason
The Beat Scene
Heartbeat/Carolyn Cassady
Visions of Cody/Jack Kerouac
Visions of Gerard/ ''
Kerouac/Ann Charters
Kaddish/Allen Ginsberg
The Tin Drum/Gunter Grass
Novovision
Dead Souls/Gogol
Diary of a Madman/Gogol
The Government Inspector/Gogol
Overcoat & Other Tales/Gogol
Intimacy/Jean-Paul Sartre
The Age of Reason/JPS
Being & Nothingness/JPS
Nausea/JPS
No Exit & 3 Other Plays/JPS
Malleus Maleficarum
Dagon/H P Lovecraft
At the Mountains of Madness/HPL
The Lurking Fear/HPL
The Tomb/HPL
Case of Charles Dexter Ward/HPL
The Shuttered Room/HPL
Orgasm/Helen Bishop
Fall of the House of Usher/Poe
Tales of Mystery & Imagination/Poe
Harry S Truman/Margaret Truman
The Agatha Christie Mystery
Through Music To The Self
The Books In My Life/Henry Miller
Hitler's Mein Kampf
Technology & Human Affairs
I Was Hitler's Doctor
Human Societies
Inside the 4th Reich/Erdstein & Bean
Number of the Beast/Heinlein
Identity Papers
Drums, Tom Toms & Rattles/B S Mason
Aleister Crowley & The Hidden God/
  Kenneth Grant
Commandant of Auschwitz
Magical Revival/Kenneth Grant
The Magician/Somerset Maugham

REFERENCE

Magician of the Golden Dawn/Roberts
The Magicians of the Golden Dawn/
　Ellic Howe
The Magical World of Aleister Crowley/
　Francis King
Outside the Circles of Time/K. Grant
Cults of the Shadow/Kenneth Grant
The Golden Dawn/Israel Regardie
The Golden Dawn: Inner Teachings/
　R.G. Torrens
The Great Beast/John Symonds
Key of the Mysteries/Eliphas Levi
Legend of Aleister Crowley/Regardie
Secret Rituals of the O.T.O.
Ritual Magic in England/F. King
The Star in the West/Capt. Fuller
Book of Sacred Magic of Abra-Melin
Lesser Key of Solomon: Goetia/
　de Laurence
Le Mystere de Cathedrales/Fulcanelli
The Fulcanelli Phenomenon/K.R. Johnson
Rosy Cross Unveiled
Sword of Wisdom/Ithell Colquhoun
Transcendental Magic/Eliphas Levi
Ceremonial Magic/Israel Regardie
Vril/Bulwer-Lytton
Ritual Magic: An Occult Primer/
　David Conway
Dictionary of Occult, Hermetic &
　Alchemical Sigils/Fred Gettings
Alchemists and Gold/Jacques Sadoul
Crystal Magick/Carlyle A. Pushong
Deadly Magic/Eric Maple
Drum and Candle/David St.Clair
Flight From Reason/Berninghausen
The Psychic Mafia
Ritual Magic/Francis King
Satan Wants You/Arthur Lyons
The Satanic Mass/H.T.F. Rhodes
Sex in Witchcraft/Lauran Pajre
Voodoo-Eros/Bry
Images & Oracles of Austin
　Osman Spare/Kenneth Grant
The Manson Murders/Cooper
Five To Die
The Killing of Sharon Tate
Witness to Evil/George Bishop
Blood Family
Cults in America/David Hanna
The Family/Ed Sanders
Son of Sam/George Carpozi Jr
Ted Bundy: The Killer Next Door
Great Crimes of San Francisco
The St. Albans Poisoner
Urge to Kill
Anatomy of a Psycho
The Denial of Death/Becker
Hitler's Secret Life/Glenn B. Infield
The Dark Side of History/Edwardes
The Berlin Bunker/J.P. O'Donnell
Satan and Swastika/Francis King
Hitler: The Fuhrer and the People
KKK/Haas

Soldier's Handbook/Col Anthony B Herbert
House of Dolls/Ka-Tzetnik
Children of the SS
The Knights of Bushido
The Scourge of the Swastika
The Third World War
Zanoni/Bulwer-Lytton
Truly Murderous
Bad Blood
The Yorkshire Ripper/Roger Cross
Complete Jack The Ripper/D Rumbelow
I'm Jack
The Monsters of the Moors
Beyond Belief
The Killer/Colin Wilson
Wanted! The Search for Nazis in America
Breakthrough/Constantin Raudive
Japan At War 1937-1945
Day of the Triffids/Wyndham
120 Days of Sodom/de Sade
Life & Ideas of Marquis de Sade
Gods & Beasts: Nazis & Occult
Nazi Propaganda/Z A Zeman
Schoolgirl Murder Case/C Wilson
Myth of the Master Race

BOOKS by ALEISTER CROWLEY:

Book of Lies
Book of Thoth
Book of Wisdom or Folly
Commentaries of AL
Complete Astrological Writings
Confessions
Crowley on Christ
Diary of a Drug Fiend
Equinox/10 volume set
The Eye in the Triangle
Gems from the Equinox
I Ching
The Law Is For All
Liber Aleph
Magick in Theory & Practice
Magickal Diaries of A. Crowley
Magickal Record of the Beast 666
Moonchild
777
White Stains
Yoga & Magic
The Vision and The Voice

SOME CASSETTES
LIBRARY OF GENESIS P-ORRIDGE

Alain Presencer Live
Mongolian Gongs
Moroccan Music
Velvet Underground
Master Musicians of Jajouka
New Guinea
New York Poetique
Kraftwerk
Ed Kemper
Gary Gilmore (2)

Manson
Richard Chase
Aleister Crowley
W.S. Burroughs (many)
Brion Gysin (many)
Raudive Voices
Hitler Speaks
Gay Chickens
P.T.V. lectures

SOURCES

TEMPLE MAIL ORDERS, 10 Martello St, London E.8 England. For *Throbbing Gristle* LPs, remaining *Industrial* records including the rare William Burroughs LP *Nothing Here Now But The Recordings* (£7 air mail). Inquiries only send 2 IRCs.

ROUGH TRADE, 326 6th St, San Francisco CA 94103. $1 for catalog. (415) 621-4307, 1-800-272-8170.

ROUGH TRADE, 137 Blenheim Crescent, London W11 England. 01-221-1100. Send 2 IRCs for information. (Also contact address for *Chris & Cosey*.)

SYSTEMATIC. 729 Heinz Av, Berkeley CA 94710. (415) 845-3352. $1 for catalog.

MICHAEL SHAMBERG. Videos. 1050 6th Av, NYC 10018. (212) 840-0659.

NANAVESH. *TG* Magazine, $10 airmail. Dave Farmer, 48 Markwell Close, Longton Grove, Sydenham, London SE26 6QG, England.

GEFF RUSHTON. 1) *Nothing Short of A Total War*. 2) *Assume Power Focus*. LPs & cassettes, £7 airmail each. 14 Beverley Rd, London W4 England.

RIP-OFF. Rambachstr. 13, 2000 Hamburg 11. 040-313846. Send 2 IRCs for catalog.

VOX Magazine. Back issues on *TG*, £2 each. Dave Clifford, 449A South Circular Rd, Rialto, Dublin 8, Ireland. 753-768.

PSYCHIC TV c/o Some Bizarre, 17 St Annes Court, London W1 England. Send £5 for Information.

CLEM (good source for updated *TG* info, current issue $2). PO Box 86010, North Vancouver, B.C., Canada V7L 4J5.

NOTE: A comprehensive discography of *Throbbing Gristle* was printed in *Re/Search* #4/5 (still available). For updated availability of records, cassettes and videocassettes by *Throbbing Gristle*, *Psychic TV*, and *Chris and Cosey*, write Rough Trade.

MARK PAULINE

**Mark Pauline in the indoor assembly room at the original SRL headquarters, San Francisco. CO² laser apparatus in background. (Photo: Bobby Adams)
Previous pages: serial photos of Nov 13, 1982 show by Mark Austin/portrait of Matty and Mark in action by Bobby Adams.**

Mark Pauline manufactures maniac machines with personalities . . . then turns them loose on people in parking lots and other public sites amidst dynamite detonations, spurting blood, rockets on cables, dead animal-robot mutations, mechanical flipping men, huge blowers, giant paintings of public figures being mercilessly mocked and tormented—the general atmosphere of a rusty carnival in hell exuding sweat, fire and poisonous fumes. Often machines battle each other to the death, fall on each other from great heights, and in other ways demonstrate the follies of impersonal power and injustice. Hieronymus Bosch come to life in the graveyard of the Industrial Revolution . . . .

No two performances have been (or can be) alike, as constant destruction requires constant replacement. (Gone are the guitar-copulating cat, the pigeon-eating centrifuge, the mechanical scorpion, the bloody claw, the face-stabbing conveyer blades, and other memorable monsters.) In their place are newer beasts of mayhem whose iron limbs often display fur and flesh from hapless creatures. As well as technically sophisticated perversions of the missile launcher, the helicopter and the laser.

The most exalted values and hazards of assembly-line civilization are paid tribute in Mr. Pauline's cargo cult-like celebrations. In a theater of simulated warfare, machines run free and amok in all directions, expressing very specific ideas of destruction and confusion.

Each show requires extensive preparations. All details of construction (ranging from large backdrop paintings which will be destroyed, to placement of xenon lighting, to carefully spliced ambient soundtracks, to pre-planted explosive charges, to multiple warhead targeting—as well as the invention of the principal machines themselves) are supervised and implemented by Survival Research Laboratories: Mark Pauline, with assistants Matthew Heckert, Eric Werner, Mary Svirsky, Neal Pauline, Jim Storm, Mark & Janice Sangerman, Monte Cazazza and other souls with morticians' smiles.

In these interviews, Mark Pauline recounts events directing him toward his present state of obsessive morbid inventiveness . . . .

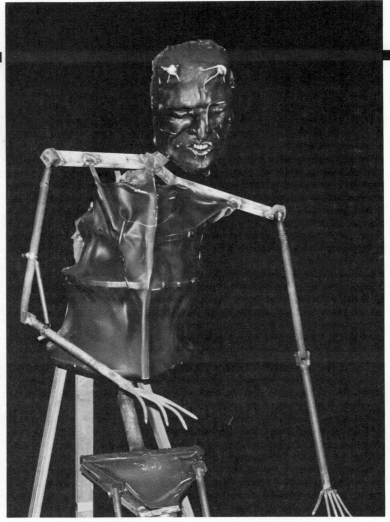

The mobile Mr. Satan hangs from his radio-controlled vehicle at the Nov 13, 1982 spectacle. (Photo: Mark Sangerman)

R/S: When did you first realize you could make things?
MARK: I think the real revelation came when I went to the Police Museum at Fort Charlotte, Florida, and saw zip guns. I took at least a whole year out of my life perfecting the zip gun. I just learned how many permutations the zip gun could come in, all the different kind of loads you could put in. I used spokes from Harley Davidsons, pipes, anything you could imagine. I used shotgun shell powder, auto weights, nails. . . .
R/S: Did you go to stock car races??
MARK: As a family activity we were pretty much restricted to three things: we either went out to the parks or the woods or we went to the horror films that showed a lot in the South, every weekend at all the theaters. If it wasn't those two it was the stock car races.
R/S: So you learned early how to work on cars?
MARK: Not really—the people I hung around were more interested in motorcycles. You couldn't drive a car till you were 16 but you could drive a motorcycle when you were 14. We used to buy Harley Sportsters and drive them around when we were 14 and that's when I first learned mechanical things—I spent many hours of astute study in the art of repairing motorcycles. I spent all my time and in shop classes in high school working on my motorcycle. Making them faster, then wrecking them, then fixing them up and then wrecking them 'cause they were too fast, and then

fixing them up and selling them because they were too fucked up to fix!
R/S: You also went hunting?
MARK: I never really went hunting, just shooting at anything. We used to play the numbers game—we would hunt with our pellet guns and .22's. We used to go out and see how many birds we could kill a day because these blackbirds would be flocking and we'd get up to 100 birds apiece. We'd see who could kill the most birds first. There were lots of offshoots of that game.

Before we had rifles we hunted rabbits with bows and arrows which was a real favorite 'cause if you shoot them with an arrow they run through the bushes and you could always track them down— they'd rustle the bushes and you'd find them struggling with an arrow stuck in them. Of course we had wrist rocket slingshots from a very early age—you'd go to a surgical supply store and get the extra extra thick surgical bands to give it a little boost—those were good. They were good for shooting turtles that used to be under bridges—we'd shoot them with big pieces of lead.

> Then there was the stabbing arm which was blowing up the faces of those unfortunate people who presumably were tortured souls. . . tortured by reactionary thought.

That was the main kind of hunting that we did—we just hunted anything that moved. Back then you could be 11 years old and carry guns around and no one would say anything.
R/S: I suppose you went fishing as well?
MARK: We used to *hunt* fish—we used to shoot fish with rifles, that was another hunting game. We'd hunt fish with bombs—we used to tie M-80's and throw them down into the water. They would blow up and the fish would float to the surface and you could jump in and get them while they were stunned. We experimented with that a lot.
R/S: Where'd you get the M-80's?
MARK: When I was a kid you could send away for the powder. Another place wouldn't ship you the powder but would ship you all the components, the M-80 casings and the fuses, and you would just mix them together. That's how you could get around the ban on fireworks in the state.
R/S: Did you ever try to make a Super M-80?
MARK: Well—that's what it was all about! You'd buy the powder and instead of using the casings you'd walk around behind the department stores and get the big thick cardboard rolls from adding-machine paper, pack the powder in there with a little epoxy and wrap it with a half pound of packing tape. Then you figure out what to do with it. We used to blow up picture windows and do all sorts of things—make time bombs. . . .
R/S: With a clock for a fuse?
MARK: With cigarette fuses.
R/S: 2½ minutes.
MARK: Right. Everybody did that kind of stuff.

BOYD: But not everybody got 100 birds in one day.

MARK: That was exceptionally good—me and this guy would get up really early and go out to where these birds would flock. They would eat these palm berries and get really drunk, and you could just sit there and go Bam! Bam! Bam! until they finally went (Mark gives a confused look), "Hey, let's get outta here!" These birds were so stupid, incredibly dumb—drunk, that you could just kill and kill again.

R/S: How did you transition out of all this? When did you cross the line and start making your machines?

MARK: I made that decision in stages, pretty much. In the first place I decided (like anybody else who really thinks) that *obviously the ideas that are supposed to be right are just lies.* And once I realized that they were lies I realized I didn't have to quit all the fun things I did when I was a kid. So I pretty much kept doing them—I just worked on *different* things. 'Cause I knew it was OK to have fun, but you had to *work* on things because there was more to life than having fun.

So I worked on things like learning how to *really think.* I tried to learn how to think in the classical sense of thinking. I went to school, I went to college—of course I still did pretty much anything I wanted to—but by the time I was done I was pretty well versed in the art of *thinking up things* and taking ideas, getting your own ideas, understanding what ideas were yours, sifting them out from all the other trash that you're surrounded by...and being able to make some kind of communication of them. The machines were

just a connection between my teaching myself to use my hands and make all these gadgets, which I did early on...and learning how to think things out. And then *just doing what I wanted to do.* This just all coalesced with all the machines ... ending up being a natural and powerful vehicle for me to get across ideas that I always had and had never abandoned, never grew out of.

R/S: What are some of these ideas?

MARK: Well, I've always liked to think that I can stir up trouble. It excites me to think that I can cause trouble. It's a very exciting thing and it still continues to make me excited: to think that I can make trouble and annoy people. Not just annoy people, but in more of an open-ended way annoy people in a way that confuses them. There's a big difference between that, and the kind of thing I did when I was 11 years old and would break half the windows in the block and steal cars and run them into poles just for fun. If you continue to *think* about what you're doing—all the ramifications of what you're doing—you eventually realize there are other ways....

R/S: Well, you also attacked billboards. I've always hated those insults and lies on billboards, but you did something about them....

MARK: Well, that just fits in with the idea: *I like to make trouble and I like to work hard.* I think it's really good to work hard. It's something I've always thought was good: to try to make the distinction between working really hard and getting nowhere...and working

Close-up showing a confrontation between two mummies on the Mummy-Go-Round, November 13, 1982 show. (Photo: Mark Sangerman)

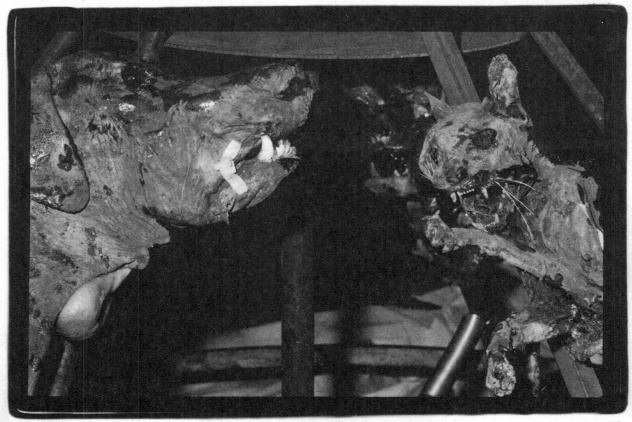

Mr. Pauline posing with the rabot, one example of SRL's experiments with organic robots (makes the dead rabbit walk backward). Sept 1981 show. (Photo: Carol Detweiler)

really hard and accomplishing something that's hard to do. That's the easiest point to get confused on: wasting time or not wasting time. If you spend too much time doing things, then you'll inevitably get confused and start repeating meaningless things over and over again and just waste your time.

R/S: How did you get to the point where you realized you could do a performance?

MARK: I just had all this stuff—I would go into all these factories and collect all this stuff. I'd been thinking about six months before, "God, I've got to do *something;* I've got to take advantage of my training." I had all this training in all these areas that I didn't use anymore.

So I started doing things like randomly going around and breaking into all these industrial places, just because I didn't really know what to do with myself—I was just looking around for something else to do. (I always do that—when I want to come up with something different, I just start snooping around.) I started breaking into all these places, and I saw all this cool stuff and I brought it home...and started getting a lot of it. And after awhile I was doing those billboards...but I started thinking I should do things with machines.

You can make an object and inevitably it falls into the category of sculpture...and becomes just another part of the art world that I was not interested in having to deal with. So to keep it out of that category I put it into the scheme of the performance: I'd spend months and months making this equipment and do a show that lasted only 10 minutes—which makes the whole thing more absurd and ridiculous and pointless. I wanted to see if you could spend all that time and distill it down into those few minutes and—would it still be worth doing? It worked okay for *me,* and I continued to make more sophisticated devices as well as cruder devices, and bigger things.

Now I'm trying to make more sophisticated things that are smaller and have more possibilities for output. I'm trying to make more of a technology breakthrough and do things that are a little bit more complicated and see if it could still work out. Anytime you work on a real technical level with machines, there's always this danger that you can go overboard and come up against the wall of wasting time. You've really got to watch it. I've sort of played that card of increasing complexity and it's worked out and it also hasn't—it's taken a lot of time. But then again, if you don't do it then you're still doing the same things you were doing before. Then you might as well just forget it.

You look at the paper and see someone who's been doing jazz for 30 years—why would you want to go and see him? Or a Country & Western singer who's been singing the same songs for 40 years—why would you want to go see someone do the same things for so long? That's just awful. Writers or scientists don't work on the same projects for 50 years. But in entertainment and the arts, it all gets wrapped up in that game of repetition, because repetition is like money—you can print it. If you can print enough of the same thing, then you can get some value out of it.

Anyone who does anything original never repeats themselves. And if you're really original and clever you can do the same things and change them enough so they don't have the same repeated effect...so it's not a copy of what you've done before.

R/S: Can you describe what you do for someone who's never seen you?

MARK: I use all these different *tangible* devices to conjure up, for anyone who's going to come in contact with it, *very specific ideas*. Every show is pretty much just a collection of *extremely specific ideas* acted out, with very specific promotion. I've come to the conclusion that if you pack enough *very specific ideas,* and can generate enough preconceived notions in people's minds, then they come to a show, the show starts going, and...if you can throw as many specific and defined images and ideas in as short a time as you can, you can end up having a real profound effect on people. And that's pretty much what all these shows and all the equipment is geared to.

> My mother was puzzled, not so much that we would steal things, but that we used a blowtorch—I think that really puzzled her— and then just took *gum*.

The machines have a lot of advantages in that respect: you can get across ideas in a background of incredible power and endurance that you can't do otherwise. If you start having human performers you're very limited, because there are too many preconceived notions. By using machines you can escape that; by throwing up a lot of very specific ideas and images at people you can confuse them.

If you try to impose enough order and organization and throw it out at people, they're going to reject all of it consciously, but *subconsciously* they can't reject it because they're there in the midst of it and it's all happening around them. And that's the area I'm always aiming at to have an effect, because I'm just not a firm believer in the transmission of any specific ideas—I don't have any specific ideas I want to communicate. I don't have any specific dogmas I think anyone else should believe in, but I like the idea of throwing up a lot of information and having it affect people any which way it can, as Clint Eastwood says.

R/S: What was a specific idea of your Fort Mason performance?

MARK: Specifically *Mysteries of the Reactionary Mind: an exploration of the mechanics underlying reactionary thought.* Everyone likes to think they have specific ideas about things like religion and politics, so naturally, if you promote something on the basis of politics, people are going to be thinking of what you do in those terms. Whether it has anything to do with that or not, people are going to try to read into it. Then, all the images in it were just devil and horror images pretty much, like a reactionary horror movie.

There was the devil on a moving platform with the bags of brown and black liquid that had bombs behind them—he was moving into position, jockeying, fighting against the radio car with the big claw that was stabbing at him, firing rockets at him. Then there was the clawing arms getting dragged across the ground, smashing after it went up a ramp and then fell. Then there was the stabbing arm which was stabbing pictures and blowing up the faces of those unfortunate people who presumably were tortured souls...tortured by reactionary thought. Then there was the BB machine firing at the glass....

R/S: Whose huge face was that?

MARK: Oh, that was Lucretia Borgia's father in Fritz Lang's film...her father was really mad at her because she poisoned some people. That was a picture of him really mad. He had his face ripped off by a spitting spike ball and then brown stuff squirted out from it.

That was what it was. I don't know what connection it had to the poster, but those were some of the ideas and images you could have seen.

R/S: What about the *Unfortunate Spectacle of Violent Self-Destruction?*

MARK: That was a little more thematic and consistent throughout; I'd been thinking all along that this should be a show about accidents. That's kinda what it was about. There was a lot of equipment there that had accidents; a lot of equipment was destroyed. I tried to make sure that the things that were destroyed were as helpless as possible. Things were really tied down, roped up, like the big skeletal man, Flippy Man, that got hauled way up in the air and then crashed...and the robot thing whose heads kept blowing up...and the catapult firing at the huge face. Just all these things, like the guy getting hit in the head with a rock who tried to sue me...breaking the girl's windshield with the ball-bearings that got thrown into the blower ...accidents. I emptied a five-pound bag into this big blower; the bearings went past where people were and broke the windshield of a car.

10x10′ face-prop with moving jaw prior to its destruction, televised live on network TV, 6-26-81. (Photo: M. Pauline)

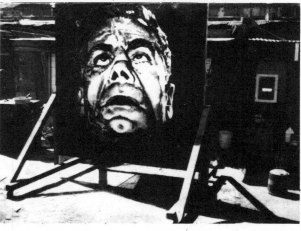

R/S: What about the organic robots?

MARK: That's just another phase. Dead animals— things that are dead—make people feel funny. Then I thought, Well if things that are dead make people feel funny, then what are people going to think if they see things that are definitely dead, but are moving around and look like they're alive? When we first made the little robot for the Night of the Succubus, that's when me and Monte Cazazza started on a new trend.

R/S: That robot elicited a rather strong reaction—someone attacked it with a chair—

MARK: That robot became a big star—he was in theater, TV, in the paper one time. Monte wanted a prop for this show he and *Factrix* were doing. He had made a dart gun already; we were talking about it and I said, Why don't you make a robot with meat parts? And he goes, Yeah! So we got all these meat parts and sewed them onto this robot. We used pigs feet, pig hide, and a cows head and bolted it onto this little fellow who kinda looked like a pig—it had a motor on it and when you turned the motor on it would just vibrate and shake like he was sick, like he maybe had a fever. His little paws were hanging down in front and kind of drawn up in back and his back was twisted in a funny way. One of his paws had a little cable attached to it, and if you've ever seen an animal that's been injured (like hit by a car) that's the motion we got. Then his arm would hit his head and make his head turn to the side. We had him wrapped up in butcher paper on the stage—I cut the butcher paper off with my butcher suit on, and Monte started shooting it with exploding darts. *Factrix* and Monte made a good videotape of that.

R/S: Did anything unusual happen at the *Mysteries of the Reactionary Mind* show?

MARK: When I first went there to put up posters, G. Gordon Liddy was walking towards me and I looked at him and said, "Hello, Mr. Liddy. I'm a real big fan of yours," and I gave him one of my posters. And he said (with a quizzical smile), "Thank you." I couldn't believe it.

G. Gordon Liddy's so funny, such a little macho guy. But he's a cool guy—he doesn't say anything stupid, he's not a jerk. He gets a little carried away sometimes. I like his stories. Like the first thing he did when he came into prison was find the biggest guy in there and get into a fight with him—he said, Then no one will bother you anymore, they'll think you're crazy—no one bothers a crazy person.

R/S: How did you blow apart your right hand?

MARK: I was preparing a rocket motor for a show. I had a pretty good instruction manual, and was finishing one of the processing stages which involved mixing the propellant, casting it, and then removing the mandrill which is a cylinder of metal that you put down the center of the propellant—you have to take that out after it cures. I'd tested the propellant by hitting it with a sledge hammer—it didn't seem too sensitive. To get this rod out of the center, I thought I'd tap it out with a hammer. I went outside, made a little wooden dowel to fit on top of it, and started tapping on the dowel with a hammer. Then it got stuck, and I said, Oh fuck, and then I hit it a little harder, and it moved some. Then I hit it again, and it just *blew up,* and it really blew up—blew me back about 2 or 3 feet away. I

Piggly-wiggly: the first attempt at mating meat with machinery. Equipped with one fully articulated right foreleg and a shuddering mechanism. Photo shows subject impaled by darts fired by Monte Cazazza. "Night of the Succubus," Ed Mock Dance Studio, 1981. (Photo: Jim Jocoy)

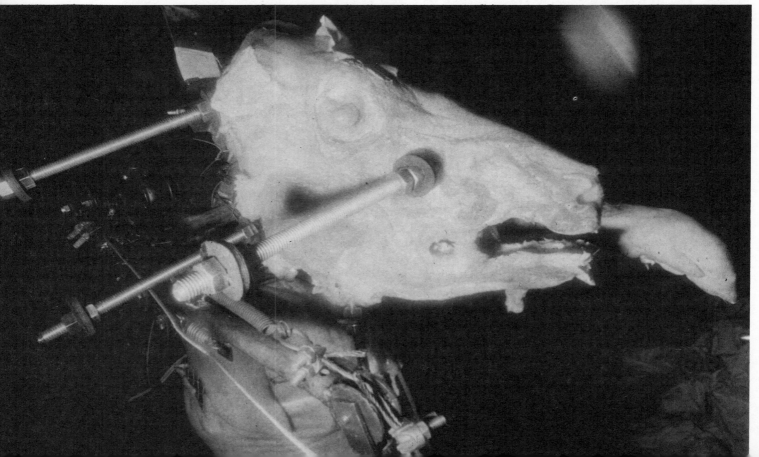

looked up and I was laying on the ground and blood just went in a sheet of red over my eyes. And then I shook it out of my eyes and looked at my hand, 'cause my hand felt funny, and all I could see was just the bones on my hand; there was no skin on any of the bones. Then they took me to the hospital and put me out and that was *it*.

None of the shrapnel hit me, so all I lost was a few fingers. More than anything I had lost *time*—all that time spent in the hospital, having to learn to work again with one hand. I had to think about what kind of state I was in that allowed that to happen. I don't really consider it an accident, it was just a stupid mistake. Why do you do things that are really dumb? You just get in a funny mood and these things start to happen....

In terms of microsurgery, it turns out that some of the best surgeons are in San Francisco General Hospital just two blocks from my house. Over a period of 7 or 8 months they're in the process of assembling what they can of my hand, to give me the basic functions: to pinch, to grasp. Those type of operations are basically experimental. They've done a real good job. It's still hard to climb fences; it's hard to carry five-gallon buckets, you know. But it didn't take as long as I thought it would to be able to do things again. Like, I drove my motorcycle over here.

R/S: How'd you do that?

MARK: I hitched up the front brake and the back brake to the footpedal so you can stop fast, because you can't with just the back brake.

R/S: What day was the accident?

MARK: June 12, 1982.

BOYD: Haven't you already been water-skiing?

MARK: Yeah. And welding too—I've made about four hundred bucks this week. You can work almost as fast.

R/S: The last time I saw you, you were pretty worried about how you'd make money.

MARK: Yeah, but then I got all these jobs and I just had to do them. So I guess I decided that I could do it. I was just having self-pity for myself when I talked to you. But you can't do anything when you think those things—that's a *mental* handicap.

I worry more about having accidents. I don't want to have any more accidents, but I've *always* really worried about accidents. I've always spent a lot of time thinking about all the awful things that could happen to me—I thought about it all the time. I either thought about doing awful things to other people, or the awful things that could happen to me. Every day I spent about an hour thinking about that, for years, ever since I was 7 or 8. You know, the things you daydream about—well, that was the 2 things I daydreamed about.

Now that I've had an accident, I still worry about things like that. But I never had an accident before, I never got hurt before, ever, in any way. I never got sick. I almost got hurt hundreds of time but nothing ever happened to me, it was just *almost*. It was just always a close call—more exciting than anything else.

But after it *happens* to you, it just teaches you that some things really are dangerous, and some things aren't. It doesn't mean that you can't do the same things you did before, you just have to know that there are better ways to do things, to keep yourself from getting surprises. But how you can think about: How am I going to avoid having a bad thing happen to me? It's really stupid to spend a lot of time thinking about that. You don't *prevent* those kind of things, you just don't let them happen.

The accident hasn't changed any of the kind of things I would do—I certainly don't think I'm going to do any safer things than I did before. I just won't do *stupid* things. Making this rocket motor was just stupid. I just went out and bought 3 rocket motors yesterday, and 3 of those together would have been almost as powerful as one of these big motors I was making. I just wanted to make one, it was sort of like a dare, you know—"I can make helicopters, I can make other stuff, I ought to be able to make a rocket motor." And I was wrong. Because those kinds of chemical combinations are far too dangerous—they're just totally unpredictable.

You occasionally read in the papers about how rocket motors blow up just spontaneously. Rocket motors basically consist of an oxidizer—some kind of chemical that has lots of free oxygen atoms that are very easily released by any kind of heat; and very, very densely saturated fuels; and catalyzers that make the fuels burn even faster when they mix with the oxygen. And that's what I made—I made a whole concoction like that, and it just doesn't take much to make it go off.

When a company makes a rocket motor, they have a whole system—all their buildings are spaced very far apart, and everything that can possibly be done

A palm reading featuring Eric Werner's (of SRL) fully automated mechanical arm. (Photo: Bobby Adams)

remotely is done remotely. That's kind of what you have to have....

R/S: Do you think of yourself more as an inventor than an artist?

MARK: Thinking of yourself as anything, but specifically thinking of yourself (say, as an artist because that's what everyone wants to think anybody who tries to get across ideas is) in terms of what other people think of you is just a demoralizing thing. So I try not to think of myself as an artist—no doubt about it, I am a commentator. I process information that comes my way, and control what information comes my way to a certain extent, as much as anybody can, and make a comment based on what's been coming around...just because that's something I like to do. People like to do things that are fun for them to do. At least it's a fun thing for me to do; it's a good game to try to communicate, just to make some kind of a comment on what you've been thinking about. Collecting information, trying to verify it, and writing up some kind of a conclusion. In my case it just happens to be with machinery, performance equipment, whatever it is.

R/S: So the accident didn't do anything to really discourage you?

MARK: I don't think so. I just feel really bad that it's been such a long time since the last show; that just kind of makes me feel sick when I think about it. You don't really get stopped unless you have a *really bad* accident. It's just one more annoying thing to think

interesting—it's not any different than any of the other things that bother me—it's like they bother me but I can still do whatever it is I want to do. It's not any worse than any of the other things, and in a way it's not any more real than any of the other things—I mean any more real in the sense that it stops you from getting what you really want to get.

R/S: What limits your shows?

MARK: Money. Before, when I needed something, I could always just find it somewhere for free, but when I started doing more technical things there was just no way—I started having to *depend* on other people—that was very bad, and I've definitely moved away from that. But, limitations—I would always have liked things to go more perfect. I'd like to have lots more time to set these shows up—3 or 4 days. And that goes back to money—if I had more money it would be more possible to have that kind of time to set up, but I don't.

I just bend limitations that have come up. Once all the machines had to stay in one place and none of them could really move around, so I made machines that could drive around. Then I ran into the problem of too many cords to control the things that moved around, so I made machines that could move around by themselves—radio-controlled equipment.... Then I did a lot of work with things hanging from cables, to sort of bring a more three-dimensional feeling to it. I guess the latest things are a more technical approach—the burning laser, and now I've gotten into

Matthew Heckert fires his hand-held flamethrower at a roomful of imaginary assailants. See schematic drawing of flamethrower elsewhere in this publication. (Photo: SF Examiner/Nicole Bengiveno)

about. I'm the kind of person that's just annoyed, anyway—I'm an annoyed person. Everything bothers me, all the time. Now I just have another annoyance, and it's turned into just something else that bothers me.

I look at my hand and I just say, "Oh, man, what the fuck?" But it doesn't really bother me—it's

flying machines—having aerial robots that can fly around. It can go on from there—I have millions of ideas if I could do them; there's enough ideas where you could keep doing more or less the same thing for years, or at least as long as I live....

R/S: Why did you make the helicopter?

MARK: I wanted to make a big flying, hovering thing

since I was about eight years old...a saucer I could sit in, that had propeller blades with a little pusher prop in the back. I wanted to make one really bad...then I gave up and just made a boat in shop class instead. I couldn't have ever done it before, because I didn't have the equipment. But I ended up with a full-enough machine shop where I could make something like that and have it function effectively.

R/S: What are you going to do with this helicopter?

MARK: Maybe the first time it'll just be a bomber. It'll have a bomb rack underneath; it'll be able to drop powerful explosives, one at a time, on different targets. Eventually I'd like to have a claw underneath, so it can descend on an object, pick it up, and then drop it from fifty feet and wreck it—that kind of thing. I've thought of having spikes as landing gear—a big set of spikes so it could hover and then just drop on something and spear it with all these spikes.

Physically, it makes so much noise, so much wind and air blast, that if you want to move people's attention from one side of the show to another, you can just move the helicopter and everyone will look at it.

R/S: Where'd you get the helicopter blades?

MARK: From Oklahoma. I talked to this guy on the phone and he goes, "Well, I got a whole barrel of these blades out back in the yard, lemme go look." And he goes and looks and says, "Yeah, I got a whole barrel of Hughes 500 blades—you wanna buy some of those?" I said, "Oh...kay." He says, "I'll sell 'em to you for

twenty bucks each. You're not gonna use these on a *real* helicopter now, are you?" I said, "No, no." He said, "Well, I don't have any papers on 'em—you can get in a lot of trouble for usin' those on a helicopter. Those were used in the military but there's no papers on any of 'em—I would never put 'em in a *real* helicopter." I said, "Okay; you mail 'em to me." The biggest helicopter graveyard in the United States is in Alva, Oklahoma—miles long like a big auto wrecking yard, but all helicopters, I guess.

R/S: How did you happen to get a laser?

MARK: This doctorate student at Stanford had just seen the Folsom show, and he figured I could maybe use some help. He called me up and said, "How would you like to make a laser? It'll be real easy." He got me all the parts, but it just wasn't easy. That took a long time.

R/S: How could you take your act to, say, Europe?

MARK: If I was going to try to do something in Europe, I'd approach it differently. I'd probably just bring over a lot of radio-control equipment and get people to give me some big pieces of equipment like bulldozers, stuff like that. And maybe I could put rocket launchers on them so they could have fights with each other. That's how I'd try to get around it—just use things there. That's a lot to ask, but people do funny things for art in Europe—they'll do things they would never do here. I mean, if you tell that to the mayor of some town, maybe he'd just think, "Oh yeah—*kunst!*"

I think that people in Europe at least have some kind of an idea that they should support the arts; that the arts are a good thing, and that the artists aren't just like bums who can't work because they're too lazy. They

think there's something that's probably good about art. And people don't think they have to *understand* the arts—all they have to do is support them.

I think people in the United States feel like they're obligated to *understand* art whenever they see it. And if they don't understand it, it just makes them know that they don't like it because they don't understand it. The problem, of course, in the first place is them thinking that they have to understand it—it's something that has nothing to do with them, basically...or something that has too much to do with them. Art usually has too much to do with what people think, or nothing to do with them—either way, it doesn't work out very well!

BOYD: I think it was good at Project Artaud where you had films of your other machines—because you got the complete impression of the machines but you didn't have to move those big huge things there—

MARK: Yeah....You know, nobody ever calls up and says, Will you do a show here? Ever. Anybody who makes you an offer makes a stupid offer, and then they never call you back again. I have to withhold hope for that kind of thing.

R/S: Who makes those loud soundtracks at your shows?

MARK: I made just the real simple ones; I have no

> How would you like to make a
> laser? It'll be real easy.

pretensions about being able to do anything in particular in sound. If I do it myself I just end up borrowing it—maybe I'll listen to the TV and record the things that appeal to me, and then organize them in a tape and play the tape back real loud. That's one way.

Monte helped me work on a couple soundtracks, and *Factrix* did one soundtrack, and Matty made a couple of the soundtracks up, and I've worked with Matty on some of the soundtracks, and Matty's worked with Bond—you know, just different people. I don't ever try to do anything fancy, because it's just not my cup of tea. I think the sound is really important but I don't ever want people to think that I have any pretensions about being a band or something. So I avoid the situation by being very crude.

R/S: Did you do the art on your walls?

MARK: Sure. I went to school and majored in Visual Arts and Experimental Literature. I read a lot of weird books and did weird things in the more established formats—graphics, drawings, films, theater—but always with the same type of attitude—the attitude has not really changed ever, for me—it's always been pretty much the same bad attitude. It's just that—you're older, you figure out what's better, I guess.

R/S: Do you think money would ultimately just make you conservative?

MARK: You look at people who were supposed to be unconventional; when they got a lot of money they became conventional. Because they just got too close to the people with money—you get too close to those people and they destroy you. But it's not the *money* that made people change, it's their *association with people who are really conservative* who are handling

Posing with the Mr. Satan robot, L to R: Mark Pauline, Eric Werner, Matthew Heckert.
(Photo: Bobby Adams)

I use literature to maintain
a certain sort of order in
my mind. If I don't read literature that has something to do
with my interests, the kind of
cynical ideas I have,
the structure of my mind
starts to fall apart, and I
can't think effectively anymore.

this money. *That's* what makes people change.

Look at the movie industry; look what happens when somebody like Tobe Hooper *(Texas Chainsaw Massacre)* or Wes Craven *(The Hills Have Eyes)* starts to get money—then they make these really stupid movies. And they even say in print, "Well, this is the kind of movie I always wanted to make." They become like zombies, you know; they just get influenced too much by those people.

R/S: What books influenced you?

MARK: I just read *The Lost Ones* by Samuel Beckett. Odd literature has always been the most influential thing in my mind's development, definitely. I've read pretty much all the American avant-garde writers—of course, Burroughs—I read all his books when I was in college. J.G. Ballard, I've read all of his books. Thomas Pynchon; Barth; Walter Abish—he's pretty funny. All kinds of weird science-fiction books—*Kill Test*—any kind of unusual literature—Beckett; Marguerite Duras—all her books.

I use literature to maintain a certain sort of order in my mind. If I don't read literature that has something to do with my interests, the kind of cynical ideas I have, the structure of my mind starts to fall apart, and I can't think effectively anymore...my own ideas. That's what I do—I read and pretty much strip the structure out of books—I use it to shore up my own faulty system. For some reason I need that; I have to have literature to be able to function correctly. That's how I trained my mind to work in the first place: through reading, and analyzing what I read.

I started reading weird books when I was 10 or 11—that's what made me realize there were other ways of looking at things. My mom started bringing these weird books home from the bookstore she worked at and said, "Well, why don't you read *The Crying of Lot 49?*" when I was like, 11½ years old. Or she'd bring home Kurt Vonnegut books: "These are good for you—you'll like *Mr. Rosewater.*" I started reading these books and came to the conclusion that there was a whole different set of values that had nothing to do with anything I'd ever seen—I'd always only seen horror movies and real straight stuff. I didn't know there was anything different that people really thought. That there was, like, a real voice of dissent.... Some people I like more—the tendency is to like the literature that strikes more chords in me, you know. They're probably the writers people would expect me to say, so I won't. But I read a lot.

If I don't read, bad things happen. It probably has something to do with this accident—that I wasn't reading enough. I think that's definitely true—I was working too much and not reading enough. So I got into a wrong state of mind.

R/S: Well, the accident then forced you to read a lot—

MARK: It did, I read a lot in the hospital.

R/S: How do you think horror movies have influenced you?

MARK: Well, I started going to them...and eventually I really started to understand what *fear* was. Like, I'd see Red Skelton on TV and everybody in the whole room would be laughing at him and I'd just go, *Why are they laughing? He's not funny. This is really stupid, it's not funny.* And then I'd watch and see all the comedians, and everyone'd laugh at them and people would

say funny things on TV, and then they'd have that canned laughter, and I'd go, *Why did they think that's funny? That's not funny.*

But then I saw this show on Black Humor, and I realized that Black Humor is like when really awful things happen to people. Like someone breaks their leg, and you think it's funny. And then I realized that horror films were *comedy.* I used to be really scared of horror films, but when I was about 8 I realized that horror films were like comedy for some people. And I watched them real differently after that—I'd just laugh when I'd see the really bad things, instead of cowering, Like someone would get their head cut off and it'd just be like *Ha! Ha!* Horror films became a real form of entertainment for me—they sort of made up for my not thinking that other things were funny.

But then I used to get confused, because really bad things used to happen to people and I'd laugh at them, but then I'd feel bad that I laughed at them. Like one time there was this big pile of logs...and I said to my brothers, "Let's give Bruce a ride in this shopping cart!" And they went, "OK!" So we totally stuffed him in this shopping cart and pushed him down this big log, and then he fell about 15 feet down to the ground and the shopping cart fell on top of him and knocked both of his front teeth out. And I just laughed! I laughed and laughed and laughed. Our brothers laughed a little bit, but then they kind of flipped out. And then I felt so bad that I'd laughed at him, but it was so funny that it had knocked his teeth out.... It really used to confuse me when things like that happened, because I knew that they were funny...but it seemed bad to laugh at them....

R/S: Your drawings look almost like photo-realism.

MARK: Yeah, I wanted to learn how to draw real fast, so I learned how to in a few months. I just learned how to look at things.... I never ever did any abstract stuff, because that just seemed so stupid—that's what you think of as "artists"—just kind of a joke; I thought that was really bad. I only drew things as real as I could—that's the only way I ever did graphics.

I just did really weird drawings, sort of surreal drawings, more conceptual things, not even surreal, just more ideas—one idea or another idea done in that mode. Because I didn't really have any particular modes of my own at that time; to pretend that I did would have just been a lie. So I just used modes that I knew about, and tried to get original ideas.

R/S: So you painted those huge faces and other targets used in your shows?

MARK: Yeah, I can draw them really fast. I can draw one of those 10x10' paintings in about 3 or 4 hours. I project an outline up against a canvas or cardboard, and then I just fill it in.

R/S: With an *overhead projector?*

MARK: It's much faster.

BOYD: *Norman Rockwell* uses them!

MARK: *Everybody* uses those; if you're in a hurry, how else can you do it? I *used to* always look at things and draw them, but after I realized...I just said, *Forget it*—that's just another ruse.

BOYD: Yeah, there's this weird idea people have about "cheating." *How can you cheat?*

MARK: I know, it's just a joke. Who cares about the

means?

R/S: How did you deface that huge billboard with Telly Savalas advertising Black Velvet?

MARK: I just drove around and then I saw that billboard—it was a hand-painted one so I knew that they weren't going to change it for a long time. And it was on the freeway, too. I just saw it, and it said, "Feel The Velvet, Baby" and I looked at it and I said, NO! Not Feel The Velvet, Feel the *Pain*. I knew that Feel The Pain was the hidden meaning—you had to drink the scotch because you're in pain, right, so you wouldn't feel pain anymore. So I wanted to say that you shouldn't *not* feel the pain, you *should* feel it.

So I just changed Telly's face around, made all these parts up so he would look more convincing, so he would look more like he *would be* saying that, and then threw in a few other odds and ends, like some weird little monster dog jumping out of the picture—I pasted that on. And had some guy with a gun in the corner, and then gave Telly one of those mouths from dental school *opening wide*.

R/S: Didn't you have to climb up high?

MARK: We had to climb on top of a building, and use a ladder to get up to the billboard. We used ropes to hang off the billboard and change it. *Fetish Times* printed a picture of it because of the S&M connotations.

The first night we went there we got about half of it stuck up and then the cops came, because I guess they thought we were trying to break into the building. We tricked 'em and got away from them, and then I went back the next night by myself and stuck the eyes up and some of the mouth and finished it up. It was in the *Chronicle* the next day. And I had a warning up there saying that they couldn't take it down before "x" number of days. They left it up, I guess, 4 or 5 days.

They took down one of the other billboards that we did 'way before they were supposed to, so we went around and filled up fire extinguishers with red paint and painted KILL! on about twelve billboards all over town, in letters about twelve feet high. And then my neighbor flipped out that week and killed somebody! He killed some guy he didn't even know; the guy was leaving work next door and he shot him in the back with a .357 magnum right through a window—he didn't even open the window. And the window still has a hole in it.

R/S: He just shot the guy randomly?

MARK: I think he thought he was someone else he had gotten in an argument with about his dogs, a week before. He flipped out and killed the guy. . .'cause he kinda had the same color hair.

R/S: . . .A lot of your machines are constructed from useful machines that really were abandoned, that were not being used by the people who originally had them—

MARK: Temporarily abandoned—just no one was around when I got 'em—let's just put it that way! But yeah, that's definitely a part of it, too: taking equip-

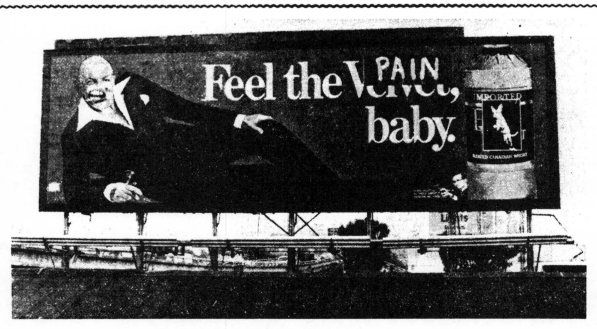

Telly With Teeth

Someone has defaced a billboard visible from the Central freeway near the Bay Bridge. Among the changes, television's Kojak — Telly Savalas — got new teeth. And the message was changed from 'feel the velvet' to 'feel the pain.'

ment and remanufacturing it, turning it against its engineers' better wishes. Making things out of it it was never intended to do. I think there's a nice form of justice there: turning something into something it shouldn't be. It confuses an issue of these things in the first place, because any time you take something that's *so* utilitarian, and do something non-utilitarian with it, it's just confusing—it just blurs the reality of what you're doing even more. Just makes it harder to pin down.

R/S: Have you ever been caught?

MARK: Not really. A few months ago they kinda caught us with all this weird stuff we got from this big factory. Like a gallon of pure sulphuric acid, tons of laboratory equipment, tools, chucks, glue guns, some chemicals, thermometers, metal shears—all sorts of weird stuff. We piled it into my truck. These railroad cops saw us leave, but they didn't see us pile it in there, and they followed us and pulled us over. They looked in the truck and said, "Where'd you get all this stuff— YOU STOLE THIS STUFF!" "No, we didn't steal it, it was in the truck the whole time." So they called the real cops who took us in to the station, and all the guys

> I hated hippies. Hippies were for peace, and I wasn't for peace, I was for death & destruction.

there thought we were really weird—they kept asking me and Matty if we were in the Hitler Youth, because we had really short hair.

They were nice to us; they just joked with us the whole time. All these guys were going, "Ah, they're not guilty, let's let 'em go! These guys are all right. Let's just get these guys outta here; we got enough trouble—we don't need to fuck around with guys like these." They were looking at all the stuff in the boxes, going, "Wow, what are you going to do with *this?*" We just said we used it for our experiments....

The railroad cops kept trying to trick us into signing these confessions. But when they walked out of the room, the other cops came up to me and Matty and said, "Hey look, don't pay any attention to what those guys say. They're not even real cops—you saw when they came in, we made 'em take off their guns. We're just going to let you go. You can get your stuff back if you call this place in five days."

And then the railroad cops tried to trick us again! We just said, "Look, we didn't take this stuff, it's *our* stuff. We own it, we didn't break into anywhere." They kept trying to do these Hawaii-Five-O cop tricks on us.

Then a cop took us back and said, "Look, we're real sorry about this; we're sorry that we had you in here so long. If it would have been us, we would have just let you go, because even if you did steal that, it's just weird stuff, and we just don't care about it—we got better things to do." My truck wasn't registered, and Matty had warrants out for him—they didn't even say anything about it.

Five days later we called up and the detective assigned to the property said, "This stuff is yours." But

then he goes, "Well, the engineer at that brewery over there seems to think that some of the stuff might have come out of there." And Matty says, *"Look.* It didn't come out of there. It's ours, and I want it back." The guy goes, "Well, I have to call this guy back and check with him and see what he thinks." The guy calls back five minutes later and says, "Well, I talked with the engineer out there and he says that some of that stuff *might* have been his, but *he wasn't sure.* So, you can have it back." So we went down there and got it back. We had picked stuff that didn't have any identifying marks on it, so they couldn't prove it was theirs; they just had to let us go.

That was the closest we came, but it was still nothing. You just have to be kinda careful, but that's like one time out of a thousand—at least seven or eight hundred times I've gone out and got stuff and got caught once. We've done things a lot crazier than that, in broad daylight.

INTERVIEW WITH MARK PAULINE
by Anne Janowitz

R/S: What events in your childhood appear as turning points?

MARK: Well, there are several that have really always haunted me, that have led me to believe they're important. When I was four or five years old, I was out in the backyard playing with these little stemmed flowers that you could spin around—they had like little propeller blades that would float to the ground. I started thinking about them, and thinking about spaceships, and I realized they were like spaceships. It scared me, because I thought, "Wait a minute—I never thought about that before." I thought that someone put the idea in my head. And from then on, whenever I would think anything that had to do with outer space or spaceships or monsters—I thought that someone else was making me think about this.

When I used to see horror movies, I'd sometimes have nightmares afterwards. And I thought that the monsters were making me afraid of them, making me think about them. My mother gave me this clay, and I started working with this clay, making little things out of it. I came to realize that I *had* to do it, because these monsters, these beings that I was representing, were *making* me represent them. I realized that I had to do it because I was serving them. So from about the age of five till I was ten years old, every day I had to—and then it became connected with taking a shit, somehow.

I just started putting these clay things on the back of the toilet—monsters, and making these very detailed models of other planets, grapefruit-sized, with mountains on them, etc. I invented this whole universe—I knew it was to pay tribute to these people who were always watching, watching everything I did. I had to please them.

At that point I was confused with like, religion, because they told me what religion was and that god was like these things that were making me do this. But then I learned that god was really evil, and that I hated him, because I started blaming him for anything bad that happened to me. Then I realized there was a difference between god and these other beings from other planets—that they were good, and that god was evil, because he made things happen like the wind blow against me when I was riding my bicycle to school, and he made me get hurt, and it was his fault and I hated him. Then I quit believing in god.

I never told anybody about this; nobody ever knew about it—but these were the kind of things that were important to me when I was young, because it made me do things. Instead of being like other kids and going out and fooling around, I really thought that there was something I *had* to do, that they were making me do this, and that it was really important that I do this. There was no point in telling anybody about it—it just contributed to my thinking that people were really different than me.

The kids in the playground, I didn't like to play with them because they weren't like me. So I just hung around with my brothers, almost always. I liked feeling that these beings were in control of me.... It still seems kinda like that—I didn't become an artist because I wanted to become one—it wasn't like, "I'll become a mechanic." I just sort of ended up doing it, and then I couldn't really stop doing it. I did it because there was nothing else I could really do; there was nothing else that made me—not happy, but made me feel like I was doing the right thing. There's not really such a thing as achieving happiness—that's just like a lie, but you can, like, do the perfect thing. It's possible for people to achieve a perfect function, to achieve total efficiency as a human being. That's what's important.

R/S: When you were a kid, were there things that bothered you?

MARK: There were things that bothered me a lot! I was involved in my own world. It wasn't like I hung around with really bad kids until I got to be about 11. In junior high school I was in a gang, the Fuckers Island Gang. We had boats 'cause none of us were old enough to drive. We had these souped-up boats; we used to wear Nazi helmets, stuff like that, and go around and have wars—throw rocks at each other from these boats. We used to have military-type maneuvers against each other, and against other people in boats. On our own island we had these wild parties—one time some kid called a girl in our gang a whore, and we went over and broke every window in his parents' house, every window. About 30 kids. We were the only gang that had a name in our whole town. We were like really bad—*I* wasn't that bad. I stole anything—a lot of cars, stuff like that, but there were other kids we hung around that were *really bad*—they were like, incredible. We just did total mindless destruction.

R/S: Did you have any ideas of what you wanted to be?

MARK: I didn't really think about what I wanted to do until I was pretty old—until I started doing it, really.

R/S: Did you have any political notions then?

MARK: Yeah. I became really violent and extremely destructive after I got out of Catholic grade school and realized that they had been lying to me all this time, and that I had kind of believed it. That made me really mad. So then I got in with these really bad people and

Flamethrower scorches 4x8′ sheet of glass triggering its explosion. From *Noise,* a performance in Golden Gate Park opposite the King Tut Exhibit, Sept 21, 1979. (Photo: Janice Sangerman)

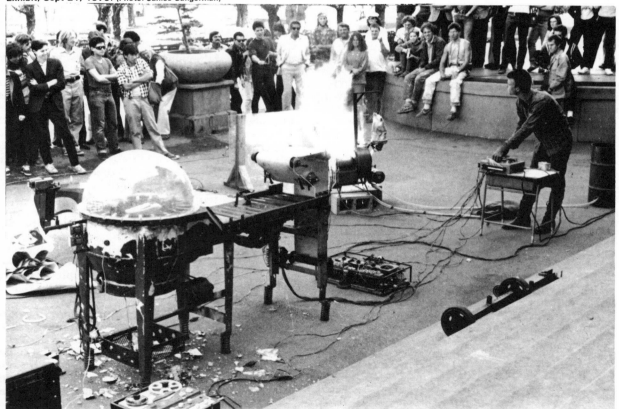

we went around terrorizing anybody we could—to throw *off* the way things were working.

When I was 12 or 13 I became more involved with ideas—that's when I really started to come to an understanding about the people that were running the world—the people that were doing what they wanted to to other people. I realized that *I* was one of the people who was supposed to do what the other people wanted me to do. And when I realized that, I just immediately knew that it was really bad, really evil, that there could be people like that that wanted me to do such *banal* things.

> At least seven or eight hundred times I've gone out and got stuff and got caught *once*.

R/S: Were you against the Vietnam War then?
MARK: I liked war! But I thought anybody who went was just a *dope*.
R/S: What did you think of hippies?
MARK: I hated hippies. Hippies were for peace, and I wasn't for peace, I was for death and destruction. We didn't dress flower power—no way, we were like heavies, biker kids, more like that—tight pants, mean.
R/S: What kind of music did you like?
MARK: *Jimi Hendrix, The Fugs, Frank Zappa,* stuff like that. Kind of sleazy music. *The Doors.*
R/S: Do you still feel connected with your adolescence?
MARK: Yeah, totally. That's all it's been. It's been like one scene to another scene—they're all the same. After I became about 17 I never paid any attention to things like music, because I hated all the music that happened after that, until I was about 19—then I liked the Motown music.

Now I like people who have intentions that correspond somewhat to mine—like *Factrix, Z'ev*—especially now that there isn't much going on that has any connection with *me,* with what *I* do.
R/S: What do you think the "industrial scene" is about?
MARK: It always seemed to me about people who take forms, and deal with them in a way that perverts them, somehow. It's the choice of the things as well—almost always things that have some kind of connection to high technology, to the trappings of modern civilization.
R/S: Have you ever been attracted to Eastern philosophy?
MARK: Not at all. It's just too passive. I just think it's a waste to think of existence in terms of being passive about it. It's a waste of life. I just think that too much of it looks towards death as like, a good thing, and equates it with something that's *better* than life...regardless of how much it goes on to say that death is like an equal thing to life, and that death leads to life. I just think that's a cop-out, a ruse. The actual fact is, it's like a passivity that just doesn't work—it's ineffective, it's wrong for this day and age. It doesn't lend itself to modern society, existing in the world as it is now, as maybe it used to in an agrarian kind of world. So that's why it's never held much of an interest to me, other than the fact of the obvious connotations of hippies being into it—it *must* be wrong if they were interested

in it!
R/S: Back to your childhood—did you have any pets?
MARK: Me and my brothers used to collect a lot of animals; we never had too many pets. There's a lot of animals in Florida, and the pet stores would buy them from you. So we used to have tons and tons of animals in our garage, and sell them to the pet stores. I never got too attached to any of them. We had 30 to 40 hamsters around; we'd breed 'em. We always had lots of different kinds of snakes, iguanas; lots of weird turtles. We used to raid birds' nests and steal the babies and try to raise them.
R/S: What was growing up in Florida like?
MARK: There's lots of weird places in Florida, because in the '20s they really built it up. Before the bust came, they had so much money they put a lot of money into these really weird places. You'll find incredible buildings—the Coral Gardens, castles built out in the middle of nowhere, covered with vines. A lot of places were abandoned when they took a highway and re-routed it into an Interstate. Hundreds of houses are abandoned. We used to look through a lot of houses and find some cool stuff....
R/S: What's your earliest remembered crime?
MARK: I broke into the house next door. I used to break into houses a lot when I was little. I think one of the earliest ones was: me and my brother broke into our neighbor's house (I was about three-and-a-half years old) and just walked around. I knew it was really bad to do that, and he knew more than I did—he was afraid, but I told him that it was okay. We just walked around and looked at stuff, never did take anything. I just remember the clock by the bed.
R/S: When was the first crime you got caught for?
MARK: Hmmm. I was about ten years old; me and my friend took a propane torch and we used it to burn through the plastic on a bubble gum machine, and we stole all the bubble gum. We got caught by the police, and they took us to jail. The police had to chase us for hours; we almost got away from them so many times, and they had all these squad cars. My mother didn't really understand why; she was puzzled, not so much that we would steal things, but that we used a blowtorch—I think that really puzzled her—and then just took *gum*. We had to melt it because it was a kind of plastic you couldn't break—it was impact resistant.
R/S: What were your favorite TV shows?
MARK: *Outer Limits* and *Night Gallery*.
R/S: What about now?
MARK: Monster movies, and the news. I like ABC because it's more sensationalized; I like the guy with the funny haircut, Ted Koppel.
R/S: What were your favorite comic books?
MARK: The horror ones, like *Eerie* and *The Swamp Monster. Metal Men* was really good.
R/S: What was the first important sex experience?
MARK: Probably the most interesting one was this girl who really wanted to have sex with me. We were 15. We kept trying to fuck all the time but it was really hard—her pussy was too tight and stuff like that and it was really weird because we wanted to do this really bad, it wasn't like we thought that it was wrong—we just wanted to do it. It took us two or three times, and then finally we did it. It was interesting, and then it

became definitely more exciting soon afterwards.

R/S: What's your sexual orientation now?

MARK: I like girls. Totally, I'm definitely heterosexual. I'm not bisexual, and never really have been, or homosexual. I especially dislike clones...homos as they are these days. They were interesting in the '70s because they were part of the counter-culture, but now they're certainly very dull, *middle-class,* and I don't like that.

R/S: Ideal relationship?

MARK: Just to have a girl to be really good friends with, and hang around with, and have wild sex with and—just mostly have a companion that I can count on, that's of the opposite sex, that you have sex with.

R/S: What's your social life now?

MARK: I really only hang around with the people I work with on the shows. I spend a long time working—I don't really have much of a social life. Occasional parties. Most of the time I spend at home with my equipment.

R/S: Do you write down ideas for your performances?

MARK: Not really, I just think of them and remember them. I have like a photographic memory for any ideas I think of. I remember all of them. I never lack ideas; now I'm certain there's an endless supply.

R/S: Did you ever play an instrument when you were a child?

MARK: Never. I never was interested in music. I never tried to play a musical instrument; I never wanted to.

R/S: Any hobby?

MARK: The only hobby I have that doesn't directly connect to the kind of shows I do is probably shooting guns. I like to shoot guns a lot. I go out shooting quite often.

R/S: How would you describe where you live?

MARK: It's a junkyard, naturally. It's just a place at the end of its rope, that was once a thriving industrial site where they made scaffolds for the Bay Bridge—it's just gone downhill from there.... I like to live by myself; I have to have my own place. (Matty comes in with a flamethrower and demonstrates it.) I made the cylinder and the tank; he made the electronics.

R/S: If you could make a model that was about ¼ that size and sell it to the women's movement—

MARK: We were thinking about marketing it: *Burn your attackers beyond recognition!*

R/S: I'd feel really safe if I had one of those—

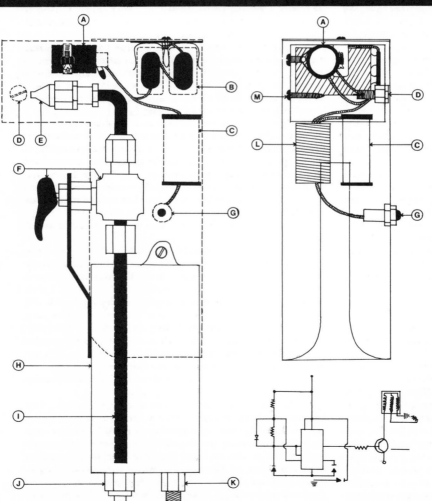

The device detailed here is basically a hand-held flamethrower. It will produce a blazing flame up to 25 ft. A prototype has been test-proven to be reliable, effective, and safe when handled properly. Fuel requirements are satisfied with gasoline, ethyl ether, glo-fuel, or any variety of flammable liquids. Fuel cell pressure can be achieved with any compressor, tire pump, or aerosol can.

Functioning is as follows: after filling the fuel cell, it is pressurized to approximately 100 psi (actual pressure will depend on nozzle diameter, fluid viscosity and the type of flame desired). Depressing ignition switch G activates Timer circuit C which through the use of a switching transistor allows power from batteries B to pulse through high voltage coil A which produces its discharge across the gap between D and M directly in front of fuel discharge nozzle E. Upon working lever F, pressurized fuel is released from nozzle E and is thus ignited by the spark between D and M.

—Matthew Heckert

Note: A *complete* set of plans with detailed schematic can be obtained by sending $20 payable to S.R.L. c/o this publication.

A) High Voltage Coil
B) Batteries for HV Coil
C) Ignition Circuit
D) HV Discharge Mount
E) Fuel Discharge Nozzle
F) High Pressure Needle Valve
G) Ignition Switch
H) Fuel Cell
I) Pick-up Tube
J) Fuel Insertion Point
K) Fuel Cell Pressurizing Fitting
L) Battery for Ignition Circuit
M) Ground Point for HV Discharge

Flamethrower schematic: Dan Osborne.

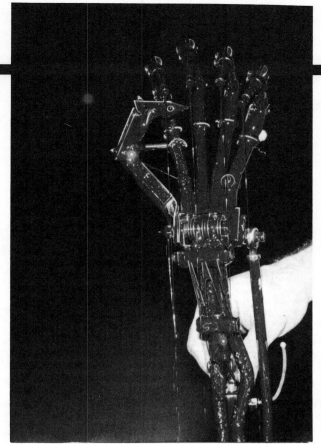

Eric Werner's mechanical hand emerges from its oil-filled aquarium only to serve as an object of worship for three genuflecting, mechanically-activated rabbits. (Photo: Bobby Adams)

MARK: **It's a good terror weapon. I think it's illegal, though.**

R/S: Would you ever make devices for a terrorist group if they approached you?

MARK: **I know what would happen—if they got caught they'd all say that I gave them the stuff, and then *I'd* get put in jail, while they would all get off easy like Patty Hearst. . . .**

R/S: Do you make any money off your performances?

MARK: **Not really—think of all the time, and the stuff.**

R/S: How do you make money?

MARK: **Sometimes I weld for a union—you make a lot of money, twenty bucks an hour, almost, doing that kind of work. In one week you can make seven or eight hundred dollars. I have all these tools here and do little jobs, get a couple hundred dollars here, a hundred dollars there.**

R/S: On the average, how much time per week do you spend doing straight work?

MARK: **Not very much, about six or seven hours. I don't need much to live on, and I don't pay for any of that stuff—I just get it all.**

R/S: Have you traveled much?

MARK: **I was in England for awhile, Italy. . . . There wasn't much going on in England in 1974, but it was kind of fun anyhow. I stayed in a Cornwall Terrace squat, that giant one they had right next to the park. We were about the first twenty people to break into there—somebody who was English told us we could live for free there. No one would move in right at first because they thought the police were going to kick them out, but we just went in and took over a whole apartment building, with free electricity and water for about eight months. It was really cool. There were**

about six hundred people in that squat in the end.

R/S: Where would you like to live if you could live anywhere?

MARK: **I think this is a good place to have a headquarters. I'd like to live in the desert, though. The absence of life appeals to me—I like the idea that everything has to struggle to exist there. . . .**

R/S: What are your sleeping hours?

MARK: **I sleep about eight hours a night, usually from about 12-1 to about 8 in the morning. Sometimes when I work on these shows I don't sleep very much for about two weeks.**

R/S: What's your favorite foods? Are you a vegetarian?

MARK: **I don't really go out and buy meat—it's okay, but I don't go out of my way to buy it. It doesn't really thrill me that much. I like fish; I like seafood the best. I'll eat just about anything.**

R/S: What kind of clothing do you usually wear?

MARK: **Second-hand. Used clothing. I have never bought new clothing, since I was about 11. I haven't worn underwear either, since I was 10 or 11.**

R/S: Did you have a discussion about it with your mom?

MARK: **No, I just told her I couldn't wear it anymore. She said, "That's good, then I won't have to buy it anymore for you."**

R/S: Do you wear the same clothes for a performance that you would any normal day?

MARK: **Uh-huh. Sometimes I wear my dirty clothes; they're my work clothes.**

R/S: What do you think about your physical appearance?

MARK: **I don't know. It's okay. I think that I look weird, though. When I look at myself in the mirror, I just think it's weird that I look that way, it's strange. I don't really think of myself as "looking good"—it appears to me that I look weird. When I'm talking to people I don't know, straight people especially, I always feel that they probably think I'm crazy, just because of the way I look and the way I act. The combination of those two things and my mannerisms probably convinces most people that I'm strange and not normal.**

R/S: Can you talk about the origin of *Survival Research Laboratories?*

MARK: **Sure. In an early *Soldier of Fortune* there was an ad for a real fly-by-night organization—they only had that one advertisement, and after that I never saw an ad for them again. A couple months later, I was given a free page in a local magazine. I thought, OK, I'll do an ad, but what am I going to call myself? Because there were people helping me do activities— modifying billboards, that kind of thing. So I thought, I'll just call it Survival Research Laboratories—I'll take their name. So I made an ad for Survival Research Laboratories, and ever since then that's just what it's been.**

I don't do all the work, obviously; there are other people. And it's good to have a name like that when you're dealing with companies (which I have to do a lot), and for publicity. I don't like the idea of people saying, "Well, it's all Mark Pauline." I think it's better because it makes it more confusing, plus it's just more industrial—it's more in the spirit of the industrial theme—of having a company, the whole mystique of the organization. . . .

A remotely-activated rocket launcher opens and fires, searing the heads of an army of cardboard soldiers; then violently impacts into a large unfortunate face situated thirty yards away, as another radio-controlled rocket launcher prowls in the background. Kezar Pavilion, Dec 3, 1980. (Photos: Mark Sangerman)

CHRONOLOGY/MARK PAULINE

1966) J.H.S. Member *Fuckers Island Gang.* Initial drug experiences, severe delinquency.
1967) J.H.S. Member *Fuckers Island Gang.* Increasing drug use, juvenile delinquency.
1968) J.H.S. Drugs, vandalism.
1969) Same, involved in group *Goethe Gang* headed by charismatic J. Goethe. Belief network included accepting/assuming death at early age, extremes of drug use, hatred of any other approach to existence.
1970) H.S. Motorcycles, drugs.
1971) Grad H.S. Worked on Harley Choppers, rode motorcycles. Drugs.
1972-3) Worked various machine shops, factories, aerospace work for Eglin AF Base in FL. Constructed F-III aircraft target robots, missile launchers, unidentifiable parts. Worked oilfields in Santa Barbara, CA as fabricator-repairman.
1973) Began attending Eckerd College, St. Petersburg, FL.
1974) Attended college in London, England. Lived 6 mos in Cornwall Terrace squat.
1975) Attended college, Italy. Film, still image generation.
1976) Attended college, same as above.
1977) April: Art Exhibition. Invitations were State of FL Grand Jury Subpoena Forms complete with embossed stamp. Lighting was directed at viewers' faces; static from wide-band radio used as soundtrack.
   June: Nearly halted college graduation ceremony due to violently shredded gown exposing black bikini, & boots & hair grease mixed with fluorescent hot pink paint.
   Sept: Arrived in San Francisco.
1978) April: Participated in SF's first *Punk Art Show,* occurring at SFAI, featuring the *Madonna.*
   July: First billboard modification of Pizza Advertisement at Columbus/Vallejo Sts.
   Sept: Pasted up a 6x7' drawing depicting a woman in bondage.
   Oct: Installation of threat billboard at Columbus/Vallejo Sts. Collected "donations" at anonymous PO Box.
   Nov: Bank threat posters installed on Bank of China, Columbus/Green Sts, and Wells Fargo Bank, Geary/Arguello Sts. Due to violation of warning, mixture of urine/nitric acid poured into safe deposit box at Wells Fargo Bank.
   Dec: Third bank threat poster installed on First Federal Bank in Sarasota FL during family visit.

PERFORMANCE EVENTS

- **MACHINE SEX** (Sunday Feb 25, 1979 2 pm, Chevron Station, Columbus/Green. Pigeons play the part of martyrs in a gas station to a musical accompaniment based on Camus' *The Stranger.*
- **FOOD FOR MACHINES** (Sunday, May 20 1979/2pm, United Nations Plaza). Food is consumed in all the wrong ways for all the wrong reasons.
- **NOISE** (Sunday, Sept 21, 1979/3pm, Golden Gate Park Bandshell). An assault on leisure promenades complete with exploding glass. Videotape available from S.R.L.
- **UNTITLED** (Friday, Oct 20, 1979/11:30pm, Mabuhay Gardens). A mechanical ritual of violent abuse for certain rival candidates in 1979's local elections.
- **ASSURED DESTRUCTIVE CAPABILITY** (Saturday, March 11, 1979/12:30pm, Union Square). An omni-directional slap in the face at Soviet Premier Leonid Brezhnev, to which the Consulate General of Red China was invited. Videotape (banned by govts of East Germany & Czechoslovakia) available.
- **USELESS MECHANICAL ACTIVITY** (Saturday, Feb 9, 1980/2pm, Palace of Fine Arts rotunda). A running commentary on the psychology of acts of military aggression and their consequences. Color video available.
- **PORNOGRAPHY, VIOLENCE & WOMEN** (Sunday, April 30, 1980/9pm, Studio Erasmus at Project Artaud). A mechanical cabaret filled with detonations and shock waves. Also featured were *Non, Factrix,* and *Z'ev.*
- **ELEMENTARY SCHOOL NIGHTMARE** (Saturday, June 7, 1980/8pm, Cabrillo Elementary School amphitheatre). Show included premiere of *SXXX-80,* a sex education/alienation film by Monte Cazazza and Tana Emmolo. "Raised serious questions about the school districts monitoring of private organizations renting public school property." Filmed by KQED Ch 9, aired on John Rozak's *Art Notes* program. Videotape available.
- **MALE/FEMALE RELATIONS** (Friday, Aug 28, 1980/9pm, Eureka Theatre). Sentimental rhapsodies of the state of male-female relations, with unexplained overtones of violence. Also on bill were *DNA* and *Minimal Man.*
- **PEARL HARBOR DAY** (Saturday, Dec 3, 1980/8pm, Kezar Pavilion). Terrifying scenes from the battlefields of tomorrow, enacted live. Unique in its extensive use of rockets. Also performances by Monte Cazazza, Tana Emmolo, and *Factrix.* Color videotape available.
- **MYSTERIES OF THE REACTIONARY MIND** (Sunday, April 5, 1981/3:30pm, Fort Mason Center). An examination of the underlying mechanisms that characterize reactionary thought. Nervewracking special effects led to some uncomfortably close calls for the audience. Color videotape available; also a Super-8 film by Andrea Juno from *Re/Search,* 20 Romolo #B, SF CA 94133.
- **LIVE ON 4** (Friday, May 5, 1981/4:40pm, Myrtle Street). A wild 120-second robot drama of predator and helpless prey. Aired live on Ch 4 with narration by anchorman Evan White. Videotape available.
- **A SHORT EXCURSION INTO THE BOTTOMLESS PIT OF EVERLASTING FIRE** (Friday, June 26, 1981/7:40pm, Cadillac Lot, 1000 Van Ness Av). Eleven minutes of hellish fury are unleashed on Ch 4's *SFO with Steve Jamison.* Estimated viewers 500,000. With special guest Monte Cazazza on exploding dart machine, soundtrack by *Factrix.* Videotape available.

REFERENCE

- AN UNFORTUNATE SPECTACLE OF VIO-LENT SELF-DESTRUCTION (Saturday, Sept 6, 1981/8:30pm, Parking lot at Folsom/2nd Sts). Most complex and dangerous show staged to date, in which a wide variety of equipment (organic robots, dart guns, laser-aimed explosive rockets, land mines, and a catapult) interacted to effect a frightening illusion of ultimate misfortune. SRL's first audience injury. Videotaped by Ned Judge, Ch 4 News (6 minute condensed version aired Sept 16 on Ch 4 *Live On 4*).

- A FIERY PRESENTATION OF DANGEROUS AND DISTURBING STUNT PHENOMENA (Friday, Oct 30, 1981/11:30pm, parking lot at 950 Columbus). SRL machine operators ride through flaming tubs of gasoline, detonate bombs attached to their bodies, fire handheld flamethrowers, as a robot fuck machine with an expanding and deflating rubber head mates with a huge black bag in its flaming pen and a radio-controlled buzz saw-equipped tank careens out of control, threatening and finally assaulting the audience and Target Video crew. Sound by Bond Bergland of *Factrix* and Matthew Heckert (also main stunt driver). Videotape available. Staged in connection with SF International Video Festival; aired on KQED Ch 9 Videowest.

- A CRUEL AND RELENTLESS PLOT TO PERVERT THE FLESH OF BEASTS TO UNHOLY USES (Saturday, Nov 13, 1982/9pm, outdoor lot at 934 Brannan St). A parable of re-animated flesh, highlighted with fires of varying origin. The most technically advanced show yet, featuring the huge Billy Graham robot (with Billy Graham sounds), real robotized mummies, a military type CO^2 laser, a mobile Mr Satan, the rabbit Kow-Tow, a fully automated mechanical arm, stink dogs, a squirming rocket target, a 400-lb mechanized tick, and the Mummy-Go-Round. Major destruction of show equipment at the end of event by the Integrator. Mechanical hand built by Eric Werner; Soundtrack and Mummy-Go-Round by Matthew Heckert. High (broadcast) quality videotape available. Staged as part of the *National Offense* Show.

SOME RECORDS

Here are a few classic records that should never be forgotten but already have been. They can be found at thrift stores or garage sales for 10¢-75¢. Certainly there's another 1000 that should be on this list. Don't get discouraged when you snag a whole batch that turn out to be all dogs—in time you'll learn to like them, too.
—Matthew Heckert

The Three Suns
  Warm & Tender
  Twilight Memories
Alfred Hause & His Tango Orchestra
  Time To Tango
Steve Allen
  Bossa Nova Jazz

Joe Vento
  Golden Hits vol. 1 & 2
  The Many Moods of JV
Ferrante & Teicher
  Soundproof!
Perez Prado
  Havana 3 AM
  Mucho Mambo (rare EP)
  Exotic Suite of the Americas
  Latin Dance Rhythms
Barry White
  Greatest Hits
Edmundo Ros
  Latin Carnival
  Sambas
Astrud Gilberto
  The Astrud Gilberto Album
  A Certain Smile A Certain Sadness
Les Baxter
  Skins
  Ritual of the Savage
  Jungle Jazz

SOME BOOKS

All Books by JG Ballard
Prefer Cut-up Novels by WS Burroughs
Locus Solus/Raymond Roussel
Impressions of Africa/R Roussel
A Canticle For Leibowitz/Walter Miller Jr
Hunger/Knut Hamsun
Là-Bas/Huysmans
Maldoror/Lautréamont
Extraordinary Popular Delusions
  & The Madness of Crowds
Ice Pick Slim
Ice/Anna Kavan
Mutant 59: The Plastic Eaters/
  Kit Pedler & Jerry Davis
No Brother, No Friend/R Meredith
Vestiges of Time/R Meredith
The Iron Dream/Norman Spinrad
The Dead Father/Donald Barthelme
All Books by Marguerite Duras
All Books by Walter Abish
All Books by Thomas Pynchon
Armada magazine (Zurich)
Armed Forces Journal
Aviation Week & Space Technology
Perspectives

SOME FILMS

All Films/Herschell Gordon Lewis
Most Films/David Cronenberg
Most Films/George Romero
  (except Creepshow)
Doctor Butcher/Frank Martin
Blood Red/Dario Argento
Twins of Evil/John Hough
Asylum/Roy Ward Baker
The Hills Have Eyes/West Craven
Last House on the Left/   ''
Don't Look in the Basement/Brownrigg
Witchcraft Through The Ages/Christensen
Mark of the Devil/Michael Armstrong

PUBLICATIONS

- Primary Sources (UK, v 1)
- Damage magazine (#1)
- Vacation magazine (#1,3,4)
- Slash magazine (vol 3 #5)
- Fetish Times (#66,67)
- Another Room magazine (vol 2 #4)
- Re/Search (#2, still available)
- Artbeat (May-June 81, Spring 82)
- City Arts (vol 3 #6, vol 4 #5)
- High Performance (Summer 81)
- Artweek (Nov 15, 81)
- Trashola (Vol 1 #7)
- Art Com (Fall 81)
- Storms of Youth/High Performance
  (#3, Fall 82)
- NO magazine (Winter 82)
- HIP magazine (Japan, May 82)
- SF Chronicle (Jan 25, 79/Nov 25, 82)
- SF Examiner (June 10, 80/July 25, 82)
- Ego #5, #6 (Dec-Jan, Feb-Mar, 83)
- Brutus (Japan, March 83)
- Bomb (NYC, March 83)
- High Times (March 83)
- Video '83 (March 83)

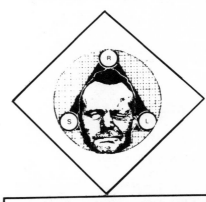

Survival Research Laboratories

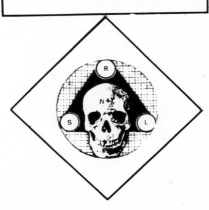

CABARET VOLTAIRE

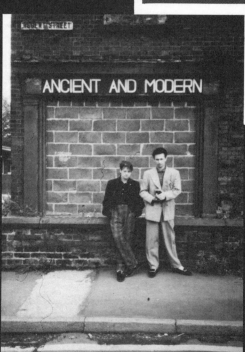

Previous pages: performance photos by Erich Mueller; Sheffield portraits by Vale. Above photo of Mal and Richard by Pete Care.

Cabaret Voltaire are a band of genuine outsiders, by choice isolated from London. In Sheffield over 10 years ago, Richard Kirk, Stephen "Mal" Mallinder and Chris Watson began exploring electronic sound territory with ideas and attitudes inspired by the Dadaists and William Burroughs. In their first gig they were attacked and physically forced to stop (Mal had a bone in his back broken)—the audience wanted "rock'n'roll." They continued to experiment with Cutups, subliminals, noise, non-instrumental sound sources, chance, accident, news recordings—gigs were scarce and they had plenty of time to work out ideas on tapes as well as paper (they've done numerous collages and writings).

A turning point came in 1977 when *Rough Trade* put out their first single, *Extended Play,* including the first song to immortalize the desecration of the bodies of Mussolini and his mistress by *former* avid supporters. They also released the first song alluding to the faked suicides of the Baader-Meinhof. Subsequent record titles have included "The Set-Up," "Control Addict," "Silent Command," "Split-Second Feeling," "War of Nerves," "Spread The Virus"—obviously indicating their interests. Right from the start their records sold well around the world, enabling them to quit their day jobs and experiment full time in their Western Works studio.

Since the Fall 1981 departure of Chris Watson (for a position with Tyne-Tees Television), Richard Kirk and Stephen Mallinder have continued to develop their propaganda war against the *propaganda war.* Their newest tool is video, their newest venture a video company, *Double Vision* (thanks to a high-speed duplicator). Their first videocassette release directly turns images of oppression against their originators, utilizing music to give impact while avoiding the Number One political pitfalls—the facile slogan and the pat statement....

In this interview Richard, his girlfriend Lynn, and Mal converse about motivations and meanings. Questions by Andrea Juno and Vale....

R/S: Do you think your message has changed since you began?

MAL: I think the *methods* have changed—the instrumentation, the way we use the tools, the channels available to us and our approach, but those are superficial—I don't think the *basics* have changed.

R/S: Long ago you stated that you were journalists reporting on issues of importance rather than musicians—

MAL: I think that's still the case. We still don't see ourselves as being technicians—that's secondary. But we are becoming more aware of discipline—of the need to articulate more precisely.

R/S: The visual information level has been expanded—

MAL: Now our visuals have video as an outlet. And the use of video means that we can document a lot easier. I don't think we're neglecting the music side, but you've got to be aware of the age that we're in. The visual side is a much more potent form of feedback that's becoming more and more obvious in people's daily lives.

R/S: With video you can present more of your total vision—

RICHARD: I think the advent of video in our *price range* has brought the 2 sides of what we do together.

R/S: Before, you had to do collages on paper, but now you present them in rhythm—living time—in video.

MAL: I think in people's senses there is a hierarchy, and the visual side is a lot more spontaneous—people react a lot more immediately to a visual image than to an audio image. Visuals tend to have a greater immediate impact—I'm not saying it's longer lasting. Audio can be a lot more subconscious, more subliminal, but audio doesn't have the immediacy of the sense of sight.

RICHARD: People have said that after seeing the video, our music makes a lot more sense! Maybe that's because of a lack of imagination on their part. . . .

MAL: There's a lot more crossover if you see and hear something together—it seems to be a more complete experience. We should do a smellorama video—thank god we can't!

R/S: Video can leap more language barriers than just audio—

MAL: We found that particularly in Japan, our success was more international than a lot of other music groups who were more colloquial. Because it's not so specific and its limits not so defined, our music is a lot more of an international language. I'm not saying we're the only ones, but—

RICHARD: We've always taken our source material from all over the world, not just Britain.

R/S: Have you consciously tried to evolve a philosophy of color in video?

MAL: Not really. We've used the notion of equating black and white with certain moods in music, as opposed to color, but not in terms of evolving a color philosophy. I know about people like *Whitney* who've worked on that. But we've never wanted to get bogged down in rigid sort of structures like that and lose a lot of the chance element we work with. It's intriguing to do, but not in terms of an overall approach.

R/S: Do a video in all army colors—

MAL: It'd be interesting—I'd love to know more about the whole range of the color spectrum, the sound spectrum. I do know a bit from video mixing

It's funny, you don't realize how quickly the media pushes things out of your mind. We've got videos of Afghanistan and Iran—unless you actually record it, the media immediately sweep it under the carpet next week!

and editing—

R/S: What kind of video editing set-up do you have? Isn't video editing really expensive?

MAL: We have a rough editing facility—3 decks for mixing down from video to video. It's not unsuccessful but it is crude to an extent. Synchronization of soundtracks is pretty impossible; just working on image editing is easy enough to do. The master editing for our video was done in Manchester at *Factory's* editing suite.

R/S: These days, I think a lot of people are imitating form without supplying content. We've met people who think innovation means adding a little noise when they play their rock songs, or who think they're making an "industrial" film by just filming sewer pipes or factories. They don't realize the deeper sense of rebellion—they've never felt what it's like to do something original *in spite of great social rejection.*

MAL: It's strange, because it's somewhat flattering to have people copying us and *TG* and other groups, but the whole point was you *didn't* want people to copy you. The reason you were doing it that way was because it was individual, because you had something basic you were working on which was your own—which you'd come to terms with.

R/S: Now that you've moved over into video, it seems you're in a territory you can exploit until you're at least 80 years old. The youth culture/pop music province seems to have built-in limitations to artistic development. At the same time, people like to feel rhythmic power and drive. But in this culture rhythmic power seems exclusively confined to young people's pop music, whereas in a culture like Jajouka, you can have 60-year-old men drumming like demons. . . .

RICHARD: Well, we don't intend to do this forever—we don't want to be the old men of industrial or electronic music! I think we see ourselves moving more and more into visual productions, or soundtrack music. That's where we come into our own, if you like: working with film, and providing soundtrack music for other people's films. If someone would give us the opportunity to do a soundtrack for a fairly high-budget film, we'd be quite pleased! I think we could do a good job.

R/S: You could have done a good job on *The Blade Runner-* . . . .For some time we've been interested primarily in soundtrack music, rather than the "latest" by any of these fucking new wave groups—

MAL: I know what you mean. You have to now search *outside* those areas (which were once a showground for creativity) to find something interesting, because the whole thing's become so predictable.

RICHARD: There's so many groups in England at the moment with the scratchy films and the slides—it automatically goes that if you do anything that's vaguely "experimental"—well that's what we're trying to move away from! We're bringing in the use of video as an alternative to what's going on, not just for the sake of it, but because it's new to explore and experiment with . . . .

R/S: I must say I like the New Guinea images that you modified in your video. You were always using music as propaganda anyway, to try and provoke people's minds—and bodies—

RICHARD: At the moment we're trying to do it through the body as a sidestep to the mind—that's the new tactic.

MAL: We're very interested in rhythms now. The basic inspiration or philosophy is that we're primitive, but primitive in an *urban* way—also primitive in our fascination with the ethnic primitive as well. I'm not saying we're an ethnic group, but we're aware (like in the Jajouka musicians) of that primitive force that goes through all of us. Instead of emulating ethnic primitivism we're modern primitives. I don't think we *contrive* ourselves to be that way, I think that's basically what we are—I think that's in us. We *don't* have a propaganda, we don't say *this* is what we're trying to interpret, *this* is what we are. To us, the way we work is very natural and the way we feel music is instinctive. Whether we try and make it commercial or whether we try and make it weird, the whole point is that it's instinctive, and in that sense I think we're primitive.

R/S: Trust yourself! I think it's admirable to remain in Sheffield, away from the supposedly advantageous distractions that London offers.

MAL: It's still close, but people aren't going to be dropping in on us. It allows us our identity. One disadvantage of London is that it can get very incestuous, full of wheelings and dealings, and that's what we don't want. Much as we feel a great affinity with a lot of people in London, our greatest affinity is with ourselves! For a group in our position it would be slightly easy to get engrossed in the superficial side—

RICHARD: We're bullshit fighters!

R/S: —and the fashion side—

MAL: I think we're getting a bit too old to be fashionable now!

R/S: How do you think the videotapes you've collected reflect you? What are some of the titles?

RICHARD: We don't want to get prosecuted for having too many bootlegs! Everything from *Clockwork Orange* to *Taxi Driver* to *Midnight Express*. Also real trash sci-fi and trash horror.

MAL: And European films like *Aguirre* and *Fitzcarraldo* which are still fascinating. You've got your kitsch American films for the trash element, and European ones for the subtlety. I mean, you need a bit of everything!

People's approach to video is so hampered in a lot of ways—the whole idea of the music business promo video we find annoying. We haven't produced a perfect video, but we've given some idea (just a sketch) of an alternative. And now we've started *Double Vision* which is not just an outlet for *Cabaret Voltaire* videos; we want it to be a *total alternative video label* which will bring out films and performances which might not be mass-marketable (but that doesn't mean they shouldn't be available). Where if *we* don't do it, there's a fair chance *no one* will. But the label has to be self-supporting. We want to make sure it's quite flexible—some videos we might get an order for 100 straight off, and other videos might only sell a total of 12.

Mal, Richard and Chris in front of Rough Trade, San Francisco 1980. (Photo: Clay Holden)

R/S: What have you read lately? Besides the new *William Burroughs Reader?*

RICHARD: I just read Andy Warhol's *From A to B and Back Again.* Before then I was reading Philip K. Dick's *A Scanner Darkly.* Before that I read *Cities of the Red Night* when I was in the hospital. I had my appendix taken out 2 weeks after I came back from Japan.

MAL: I just read a really good book, *Through a Black Sun,* by a Japanese journalist who was in Vietnam from '64-65. Before that I read *Auto-da-Fe* by Canetti.

RICHARD: I have a lot of books on military psychology which I pick up from time to time and read. I go through phases where I don't read anything at all, and then I'll have a total fit of reading for a few weeks.

MAL: I think reading should be a natural process. I think there's a certain elitist attitude where you feel *obliged* to have a certain amount of intellectual intake, which is very *bourgeois.* But reading should be something you do which you *enjoy*—you shouldn't feel obliged to take in this written data just for the sake of it, just to store up the knowledge. It takes me 2 weeks to read a book—I'm permanently reading, but I don't read 4 books a week and constantly feel, "Oh, I must get *that,*" because then you become just like a *record collector.* I think reading should be enjoyable and natural and something that you *use*—if you read 1 book and you use it for the rest of your life, that's greater than reading a book a week that's just *there,* of no use whatsoever to you.

RICHARD: I keep loads of books around for reference, so I can pick up a book and read maybe 2 chapters out of it. . . and go back to certain books every now and then and pick out certain things that crop up in a conversation or film or anything. I prefer to do it on that basis a lot of the time.

R/S: It makes sense to have information potentially accessible, so that if you *do* get curious about a topic, you can quickly look it up. Most people who don't read are forced to read—advertisements! And people who do read usually read what the reviewers select for them—they never bother to search out what might truly appeal to their *own* desires. If you're rebellious enough, you usually do find those weird books that do change your life and are off the beaten path; that really *become* influences.

> **Paranoia. . .the only healthy state in which to exist. There is a huge plot, but what is it?**

Anyway, you don't follow or focus on the philosophy of any particular person—

RICHARD: I prefer to take a little from everyone, to take the best bits out of what's available, mixed in with a lot of my own personal observations.

R/S: Reading philosophy involves a recognition process—it's not that you're learning something brand-new so much as you're *recognizing* something you already knew but hadn't formulated or verbalized.

RICHARD: Someone told us after watching us work in the studio that it was like the "street" amplified through some strange tribal process—

MAL: He said the studio was like all of the outside microscoped into one room, because we're working, we've got the TV on, the sounds are there—he thought it was just extremely tribal.

R/S: What do you think you've gained from traveling to other countries?

RICHARD: The thing that affected me like nothing else was the first time we went to America. And maybe going to Japan was next. Europe's not so far removed from Britain, really.

MAL: Whatever country you're in, everybody's sort of stifled by the jingoism of the country they're in—sort of an out-and-out imperialism that is totally subconscious in people (with us even, it's still there). It's only when you go outside your own environment that you can get rid of it, a little bit at least. It's good to travel and *exorcise* those things that are inside you, because you get too embroiled in your surroundings and your "way of life." It's nice to be jarred!

R/S: How did America "jar" you?

MAL: It's strange seeing America, because it's the way England is going but an extra step further—like walking 10 years into the future in England. I mean Britain's a consumer country, but not to the extent as America. You become aware of the way the society's geared—to the waste-and-design product theme, to the consumer. I don't mean just the products that are available, more the general attitude.

RICHARD: Just the spatial thing was pretty much of a shock—England's so small and a lot of it is built-up areas. But in America there's so much more room for everything and the roads are so much bigger. And the fact that (I don't know about all of the US, but) New York is a 24-hour place, whereas in England everything, during the week at least, finishes at 10:30. Maybe in London a few places will stay open later, but that's only fairly recently. A lot of places in Europe are more 24-hour, where you can exist at times that *you* choose, at times that suit *you.*

MAL: England is still geared to the 1870s, the Industrial Revolution, which is completely based on the work ethic. For over 100 years they've socialized and educated people to the notion that their moral right is to work. All the licensing laws are geared toward people working from morning 'til night, and to make sure they get up on time there's less distraction. They still live in that 19th-century dream; they've built into people's heads the ideology that if you're not working, then morally you are of no use to yourself or the community. *Now* they've got an entire generation of people who don't work, who've been taught that if they don't work they're lepers. And that's why this country's totally screwed up.

RICHARD: They're going to have to go through a process of de-control!

MAL: They've got this whole screwed-up generation of kids who've been taught at school that their only role in life is to work, and therefore justify themselves through work. Then when they finish school, they realize they're never going to work for the rest of their lives. A totally psychotic generation—which oddly enough we're detached from, yet because we've grown up through the same processes, we're aware of.

I suppose they'll bring back the poorhouses, and it'll be really Dickensian again. . . .

R/S: . . . Have any movies been shot near Sheffield?

RICHARD: They made one about the Black Panther, a guy who was a bit crazy—always used to wear a black hood. He'd got all the military gear and was obsessed with that—he'd been in the army. He robbed a few post offices and blew a few people away. And kidnapped this heiress and hid her in a drainage shed. The SAS got him.

R/S: How would you describe the SAS?

MAL: Seventy percent of them are volunteers from the army—

RICHARD: They're really well trained—

MAL: Almost like the SS. They're also very narcissist as well—they wear black silk flying suits which they ceremonially destroy after each mission.

RICHARD: They've got laser-sighted guns so they shoot along a beam of light, things like that—

MAL: During the Iranian embassy siege, all the TV channels stopped and showed the siege going ahead like it was a *film*—the end of the siege, the raid on the embassy, in real time.

RICHARD: And that's been made into a film now, *Who Dares Wins*. And real footage of the Falklands is going to be available on a 2-hour videocassette. I suppose the money's going to go to benefit families of men that were killed.

R/S: How many people were killed?

RICHARD: I think the final score was Argentinians about 1,000 dead, Britain 200 or 300. They used to show it regularly like football scores on the TV!

R/S: The news proves you don't have to develop virtuosity for years and years to produce interesting video—

MAL: Yes. But we don't like the attitude of *non-professional chic*. It was good when we first started—it was the *anti-*man stance—but that in itself has become a fashion, it's the unfashionable fashion. And we find that as people have caught up with us on that level, it's time for us to (instead of going against the techniques) use the techniques to *our* advantage—

RICHARD: Sort of tidy up the loose edges in what we do to make it more acceptable to more people, yet not really selling anything out. Opening a few more doors. Making a few tiny compromises so we don't have to make the big compromise in anything.

R/S: At this time it seems that formlessness and anti-form have been explored almost enough. You and a few others were in revolt against all the established forms at a time when no one else was; now you do the opposite—take the forms themselves and subvert them. Lyric content hasn't been compromised—you've used moral majority tapes, brain operation narratives—"this woman's brain has been split in two." What happened there?

MAL: The original tape said that, but on the tape we played back to you, a voice in the background was whispering "I know. . . ."

RICHARD: The woman's right hand and left hand were not coordinated in any way. It was like having your body cut in two—

LYNN: Her brain was saying *I want to wear the green dress* but her hand went for the pink dress. So, she might have wanted to eat the cheese in the fridge but her hand went for the ham. . . .

RICHARD: One side of your brain is "artistic," and the other side is more technical.

Richard in a sporting mood. (Photo: Vale)

R/S: Personal obsessions and interests?

RICHARD: Pornography, kitsch and firearms. We have to find some new ones!

MAL: I think there's a danger that if you're aware of them becoming obsessions, it can get very contrived. There's a certain amount of chic in getting an obsession with things that other people find repulsive. It's one thing to ignore bourgeois morality in being fascinated with something, but to go to the other extreme— then your attitude becomes just as bourgeois, but in a different area. *Inquisitive fascination* is about as far as I would call my obsessions—I wouldn't call them obsessive as such.

R/S: When you visit other countries, don't you look for specific things that appeal to you? For example, didn't you get some switchblades in Italy?

RICHARD: Yeah! I brought back a really big one. . . .

R/S: Also, didn't you buy some military clothing?

RICHARD: Yes, it's very functional. Good for traveling around in. The pockets are really useful.

MAL: *Functional* is one of the main things about them.

RICHARD: I used to wear military gear since I was about 14—it was part of the skinhead thing: army dungarees and military-type boots.

MAL: We were skinheads at a time when it didn't have the overt violence, the right-wing association. It was just a working-class youth culture, more fashion-oriented. The point is, they've just been *used*. They didn't set out to be a political movement, a right-wing spearhead—they were manipulated either through their own stupidity, or they were misinformed. They're very pliable as a mass. A lot of them are young and slightly gullible. The way people picture skinheads as a youth culture now is totally different from when we were skinheads.

R/S: Do you buy many records?

RICHARD: There's so many wankers. I don't go and see many groups and I don't buy many records by contemporary bands. There's nothing. . . .

REFERENCE

DISCOGRAPHY

7'' SINGLES:
EXTENDED PLAY (4-song EP): Talkover-Here She Comes Now-Do The Mussolini (Headkick!)-The Set Up. Rough Trade RT 003.
NAG NAG NAG/Is That Me (Finding Someone At The Door Again). RT 018.
SILENT COMMAND/Extract from soundtrack for 'Chance versus Causality.' RT 035.
SECONDS TOO LATE/Control Addict. RT 060.
JAZZ THE GLASS/Burnt To The Ground. RT 095.

12'' SINGLES:
THREE MANTRAS. RT 038.
EDDIE'S OUT/WALLS OF JERICHO. RT 096-12.
SLUGGIN' FER JESUS/Your Agent Man. Crepescule TW1 081.
THE PRESSURE COMPANY: Live in Sheffield 19 Jan 1982. Solid No. 1. (Cabaret Voltaire performed under pseudonym The Pressure Company to benefit Solidarity in Poland.)

LP's:
MIX-UP. Rough 4.
YMCA LIVE. Rough 7.
THE VOICE OF AMERICA. Rough 11.
RED MECCA. Rough 27.
2x45. Rough 42.
HAI! Rough Trade RTL 23.

TAPES:
LIVE AT THE LYCEUM. Rough Tapes COPY 001
CABARET VOLTAIRE 1974-76. Industrial IRC 35.
RICHARD H. KIRK: Disposable Half Truths. Industrial IRC 34.

MISCELLANEOUS:
RAISING THE COUNT. NME/Rough Trade C81 Cassette.
SEX IN SECRET/BAADER MEINHOF. Factory Sampler EP, Fac 4.
INVOCATION. Ghosts of Christmas Past LP, Crepuscule TW1 058.
OVER AND OVER. Flexi-disc for Vinyl magazine #13.
JOHNNY YES NO. Soundtrack for film by Peter Kerr, unreleased.

DOUBLE VISION VIDEOTAPES:
Send £20 for 90-minute videocassette to Double Vision c/o 267 Ellesmere Rd, Sheffield S4 7DP, Yorkshire England or write Michael Shamberg, 1050 6th Av, NYC NY 10018 (212) 840-0659. Or contact Rough Trade.

SOME BOOKS

Unlimited Dream Company/J.G. Ballard
From A to B & Back Again/Warhol
Stargazer (about Warhol's Films)
Popism/Warhol
Hospital Ship/Martin Bax
Fads/Skolnik
Diary of a Nazi Lady/Gillian Freeman
The Necronomicon/ed. Hay
A Scanner Darkly/Philip K Dick
The Big Beat Scene

Poésies/Lautréamont
SS Regalia
Beautiful Losers/Leonard Cohen
Last Exit to Brooklyn/Hubert Selby
Capone/John Kobler
Carlos: Terror International
George Jackson: Soledad Brother
CIA & the Cult of Intelligence/Marchetti
Confessions of Aleister Crowley
  (& other selected Crowley writings)
The Dark Side of History/Michael Edwardes
  (occult; "this ties up a few loose ends")
Mysteries of Life & Death/Prof Keith Simpson
Marquis de Sade/Iwan Bloch
The Voodoo Gods/Maya Deren
Prehistoric Germ Warfare/Robin Collyns
New Soviet Psychic Discoveries/Gris & Dick
The Living & The Dead/Patrick White
The Real Howard Hughes Story/Madden
Justine/Marquis de Sade
It's Smart to Use a Dummy/Hilton
Selling the War/Jacques Sternberg
Vietnam Inc./Griffiths
Crimes & Punishment/vol. III
The Third Mind/Burroughs & Gysin
  ("a good reference book")
OMNI Magazine
POLICE CHIEF Magazine

SOME VIDEOTAPES

Anything by Luis Bunuel
Anything by Warhol/Morrisey
Satyricon/Fellini
Roma/Fellini
Performance/Nicholas Roeg
The War Game/Peter Watkins
Dreams That Money Can Buy/Richter
The Rebel/Tony Hancock
The Criminal
The Man With The Golden Arm
Years of Lightning 1963/1967
  (British TV Cut-up Style Program)
I Spit On Your Grave/Meir Zarchi
Plan 9 From Outer Space/Edw D Wood Jr
The Exorcist/William Friedkin
Shivers/David Cronenberg
Scum/Alan Clarke
Bad/Warhol
Taxi Driver/Martin Scorcese
A Touch of Evil/Orson Welles
The Crazies/George Romero
Death Wish/Michael Winner
Empire of the Senses/Oshima
Blade Runner/Ridley Scott
Outer Limits (TV)/Joseph Stefano
Texas Chainsaw Massacre/Tobe Hooper
Enter The Dragon/Robert Clouse
Living Dead at the Manchester Morgue
Island of Mutations/Sergio Martino
Cannibals
The Third Mind
Psycho/Alfred Hitchcock
Clockwork Orange/Stanley Kubrick
Phantasm/Don Coscarelli
Fistful of Dollars/Sergio Leone
Apocalypse Now/F F Coppola
SS Program

Vanishing Point/Richard Sarafian
SS Experiment Camp
East 103rd Street
King Creole (best Elvis movie)
Headhunters (early 20's footage)
Brain (brain surgery series)
A Limited Nuclear War
Swedish Erotica
Seven Samurai/Akira Kurosawa
The Long Knives (S.A.)
Hells Angels on Wheels/Rich Rush
History of Riots
Rise & Fall of Idi Amin
King Kong
Johnny Yes No (CV did soundtrack)
Fists of Fury/Lo Wei
Shogun Assassin/Kenji Misumi
Doctor Who
The Hills Have Eyes/Wes Craven
Repulsion/Roman Polanski
Venus Flytrap (documentary)
War Footage
Auschwitz & the Allies
News From 1981
World's Most Dangerous Man
  (about Frank Terpel)
Beast from 20,000 Fathoms
Iran Torture Footage
Images of War
Papua, New Guinea
Panic in Needle Park/J Schatzberg
Waffen
Will Hays, Convict
Kagemusha/Akira Kurosawa
Kenneth Anger Films
Nightmares in a Damaged Brain
The Mad Foxes
Escape From New York/J Carpenter
Namid Desert Creatures
Zombie/Lucio Fulci
Don't Look Now/Nicholas Roeg
James Brown Story
The Frightened City
Leiber & Stoller
Mad Max 1 & 2/George Miller

Non

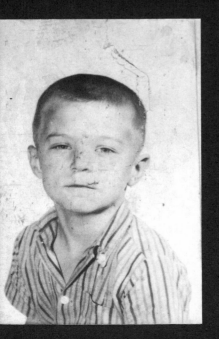  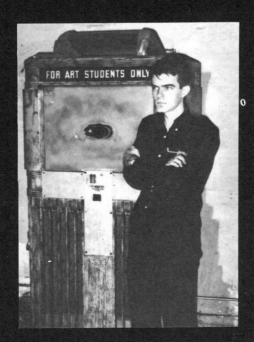 

I never understood alienation.
Alienation from *what?* You have to
want to be part of something
in order to feel alienated from it.

**Above photo: Ed Colver. Previous pages: Boyd as boy; Boyd in shooting gallery and next to 50's porno booth by Steve Hitchcock;
Boyd with Laurie O'Connell at Peoples Temple; large portrait by Ed Colver.**

Since 1977 *Non* (Boyd Rice) has systematically set out to destroy every assumption held sacred in the recording or performance of music. His first album, with a label showing pieces of records spread out on a floor, was more than a critique — the recording actually was a compilation of excerpts from many records, *treated.* (For example, Boyd assembled one track out of every time Lesley Gore sang the word "cry.") The next 45 was the first to offer extended possibilities for listener-modified playback, with 2-4 (he would have liked more) holes in the center for multi-axial rotation. The history of *Non*-musical innovation is documented and still available on Mute Records. Two new albums will soon be released.

Non's live performances offer sheer (but varied) noise at the pain threshold — the objective being to offer the listener *personal freedom* to impose shape, rhythms and organization on the offered input. He's used a shoe polisher, a guitar with a fan on it, as well as processed tapes of sounds generated by his own inventions. Cut in are various subliminals taken from sources like the last 45 minutes at Jonestown, quotations from newspaper headlines ("Water Balloon Prank Fatal To Pedestrian"), and excerpts from tapes made at Disneyland, Playland, Winchell's Donuts, and other fun spots.

Non considers his performances "de-indoctrination rites"—as he once said, "I think that most music is dangerous because it tends to systematize thought— you think in patterns—you *know* what's coming before you even hear it." After two European tours and numerous American dates, *Non* still succeeds in outraging audiences anywhere, *especially* music lovers....

Currently Boyd Rice is writing a guide to *Incredibly Strange Films,* co-written with Jim Morton of *Trashola,* to be published by Re/Search....

R/S: Which performances have made people the angriest?
NON: In New York I was one of the first people in years to actually get catcalls! People were screaming, *I want my $7.50 back!* And in Den Haag, Holland, they were *real angry.* Because in Den Haag everybody who likes music goes to every concert, especially if it's by someone from America or England. I guess they go to everything because there's nothing to do there.

They *really* disliked me. At the show I had these bright lights shining in their eyes so they could barely see me—they were trying to reach up and smash the lights, but the lights were just out of their reach. One guy in front who was a real hard-core punk was rolling around with his hands over his ears and actually crying—he had tears in his eyes. Somebody threw a beer glass that hit me on the forehead. And it broke, and I could feel this throbbing pain—it had a little bit of beer in it, and the beer ran down my face and I thought it was blood. I continued to be real friendly to the audience, which made them even madder, because they were so mad and I didn't care! They were shaking their fists at me, and I thought that at any minute there'd be a riot. So I took it as far as I thought I could, and then thanked them and left.
R/S: This was at an overwhelming volume?
NON: Yes, I always tell them I want maximum volume, but *they're afraid.* You need to have somebody right there to push it up a little louder when they turn it down. Like when Daniel Miller (head of *Mute Records*) does the sound, he does it real loud. One time I got the best vocal effect ever—my voice was completely *Arrrh-aggrrh-arrh.* And at the time I thought, *God what's he doing to those vocals?* I thought that because I was mad about something, he had turned it up extra loud that night just to be nice. A couple days later I asked him, "Hey Daniel, what'd you do to those vocals a couple nights ago?" And he said, "Oh, that must have been the night you blew the speakers."
R/S: Do you know of any actual physical reactions to your noise?
NON: One girl told me it had induced an acid flashback in her—she'd never had one before, and didn't

Boyd with broken records; photo taken for *NON* Black Album label.

believe they existed. Another girl reported it jarred one of her fillings loose, giving her a toothache. Some people find it torturous...some people find it extremely soothing and relaxing. Some people find it painful but like it anyway—at the end of one Deaf Club show some girls spontaneously started yelling in unison, "More pain! More pain!" I've always liked the idea of one stimulus being able to cause completely different reactions in people.

R/S: When did *Non* begin performances?

NON: Well, I did performances before I did *Non*—although they weren't really performances. *Z'ev* did them too—me and him did them at La Mamelle long ago when there really wasn't any other place. I just happened to be in San Francisco, and a guy called me up and said, "Hey Boyd, there's going to be a sound poetry event at La Mamelle—you can do sound poetry, can't you?"

I'd always known that words structured thought, and thought structured reality, so I was already interested in that area although I wasn't the least bit interested in "sound poetry." So, I did these things where I'd have about 8 people, and I'd give them a word and tell them to repeat the word until it became completely incomprehensible, until it was just syllables repeated.... If you repeat a word enough it becomes something else, like a blanket of sound, a big blur of sound. But that was just something I had an opportunity to do so I did it.

When I first started doing *Non,* I'd been making noise music for myself for a long time.

R/S: How did you get the idea?

Non with roto-guitar at the Deaf Club, San Francisco 1979; Laurie O'Connell from *Monitor* on background vocals. (Photo: Vale)

NON: I started doing my own music so I could have something to listen to. I liked music, but there wasn't any music out there that fulfilled what I thought music should be. I'd think, Well if I had invented the idea of music, having never heard music before, what I would I want it to be *for me?* What elements would it have?

I thought, Well it should be repetitive, and sort of catchy, but vague enough so you wouldn't really remember it or be humming it when you weren't listening to it. So you'd have to *experience* it *at the time,* and when the record was off—forget it! I started making musical tapes, and at the same time I started making a number of noise tapes that I played just for myself. I made my first record of the more musical tapes. And then I decided to explore the noise more.

When punk rock first came out, my friend Steve Hitchcock wanted to form a band, because he liked the ideas behind punk—he liked *anarchy,* but he didn't really like the music—he didn't think the *music* was an expression of the *ideas.* So he wanted to form a band that would take those ideas and give them form. Me and him got together with Robert Turman, who seemed to want to get involved—he had equipment and amps and we made this band for awhile, but it didn't work out. It was one of these *democratic* situations where nobody really got anything expressed—nobody ever pushed their ideas out there—everybody sort of just held back. Eventually Steve left, and I just sort of took over and made *Non* what it turned out to be.

While starting *Non,* I did a performance that was just a *Boyd Rice* performance. It was just a big long screech of noise with a lot of subtle stuff underneath that you could just barely hear. It lasted a long time. My idea was that I'd set it up and everything would just be going by itself and I'd leave. But every time I left, the audience would leave too, and when I came back to make adjustments so it would change and be different for awhile, everybody would come back in too. They had to have somebody to look at while they were listening to that....

Incidentally, Javier of the *Zeros* was in the *Boyd Rice* performance. He and I did some music together. It was just experimental, but it was interesting how he could be given this premise and he could just perfectly do something that was real experimental.

The first actual *Non* performance was in 1978, even

though I'd been making noise for years before that. It's not like I started doing something and then progressed, because I started doing exactly what I wanted to do, and it's changed here or there, but it's been more or less the same because *how can just noise progress?* It's hard to get it more noisier if it's just noise!—you can only get less noisier, and more musical or more structured.

R/S: In your earlier performances you used a shoe polishing machine and other devices—

NON: **Actually we used real devices so that people could see more real sound being made right before their eyes. We could use a shoe polisher as an instrument, playing it through a guitar, changing the settings, and get amazing frequencies. We had a roto-guitar too—a guitar with a fan on it.**

R/S: Who made that?

NON: **I did—it was an obvious idea to produce more noise with less effort—it sounded like a squadron of bombers taking off. But eventually it was just too much trouble to bring a shoe polisher and all this stuff. I was always interested in the idea of *doing less and getting more*.**

Actually when I first thought of the idea of making music, I thought of a whole orchestra of instruments that you'd be able to just turn on and they'd be working at the same time, producing repetitive music. But eventually I figured out a way to do it much easier, so I thought, Why build this whole orchestra of instruments (and drag them around) when I can do something extremely simple and get the same effects?

R/S: Give me just one example of these instruments.

NON: **I thought of inventing an organ made out of cows' lungs, windpipes and larynxes—8 or 10 sets of them in a series, hooked up to air compressors.**

R/S: That might be a little difficult to haul around. Now your act is extremely portable?

NON: **Extremely. I can put all my instruments in a lunch pail. I use tape recorders as musical instruments. I don't use them just as playback machines, I use them as instruments to get sounds out of that I wouldn't be able to get out of anything else. It's a very simple way. I have other things I've made to play them through, to structure and organize sounds into different rhythms—change them. . . .**

R/S: At one performance you cut in a tape from the last hours of Jonestown. Have you mixed in spoken tapes right from the start?

NON: **At one performance we used an indoctrination tape before we went on. It started out with kind of conventional material that people would like, then it got less conventional—sort of a subtle blend of these songs, getting more and more away from what people are used to, so that by the time we came on maybe they'd be. . . . It was a hokey thing to do—obviously it wasn't going to work, but I liked the idea of it.**

I also had taped quotes from the Manson girls saying things like "Rich people better watch out!" that were funny but would get people in a certain mood.

R/S: Your performances are quite short—

NON: **They started out being 20 minutes or a half hour but they've gotten shorter—the last one I did at the Whisky-a-Go-Go I think was 5 minutes long!**

R/S: You weren't on stage at all for that one?

NON: **No. I was sitting in the dressing room over the stage.**

R/S: Well, what happened? What was the performance?

NON: **It was a scarecrow. I had everything pre-arranged so that all I had to do was set it in motion. And people liked it—they clapped to a scarecrow with a plaster head.**

R/S: Your performances are intentionally not very visual?

NON: **Sometimes there were lights behind me, and you couldn't see me, but when I'd move, the lights would throw off different shadows. One time I had two huge horrifying, screaming clown faces behind me. But I usually make it as visually *bland* as possible. However, I don't have any firm commitment to look-**

Non stand-in onstage at the Whisky, Los Angeles 1982.
(Photo: Peggy Photo)

ing bland—I could go exactly the opposite at any time.

R/S: Once at the Deaf Club, you had Laurie from *Monitor* behind you. Why?

NON: **I had her come on and sing one song. She'd sing it so you could almost hear it, but not quite; ever once in a while you'd hear a couple words and start listening harder. . . then the mike would go away from her mouth. And it would be something innocuous, like a line from an Annette Funicello song: *All the chicks are bikini-clad* which would then fade back into noise. . .**

R/S: What effect would you want, ideally, in an audience?

NON: **I don't want specific responses. Like when people react really favorably or don't, I'm not moved by it one way or the other. If I had the audience in mind while thinking about what I wanted to do, it wouldn't be what I wanted to do. I'm trying to do just what I'd like to hear, with the minimum of intent, almost.**

R/S: Well, when I've heard the intense noise you've generated, after a while I start to impose patterns and structures on what I'm hearing, but at the same time they don't seem to really be there.

NON: **Yes, I think a lot of the noise suggests structures** in people's heads that aren't really there. Which is what I think it should do. I've made a lot of tapes of pure noise and I know there are no voices on them, yet you listen back to them and you'd swear there are voices. And on *Pagan Muzak,* even though that's just loops of noise, you can hear definite little melodies coming out...the most subtle elements can become very pronounced.

For a long time I've wanted to get ahold of these records that are made for mental patients, saying things like *wuhnyahuhwhuh*—sort of mumbled voices that are saying nothing really. And they'll play them for the patients and ask, "What's this man saying?" And the patient will say, "He's saying . . . ."

R/S: Obviously the patient says something relating to *his* problems. That sounds good—like a *sound* Rorschach test.

NON: **On the *Black* Album, there are a lot of voices. I don't know where they came from—they *sound* like voices and you can listen to them say certain phrases over and over again. And then at an abrupt point they'll start saying something else—you can tell they've altered the phrase and are saying something different. And I know all that's not there, but it's there for the listener.**

R/S: Describe the *Black* Album.

NON: **Okay. It's my first record and my earliest recordings, from '75 on. I put it out in 1977, I think. It's the first record you can play at any different speed, so you get 4 times as much for your. . . .! I followed that**

NON: **I did. Some of them have 3 or 4 holes.**

R/S: Ah, rare collectors' items. I only have a two-hole one.

NON: **Oh, sorry. Ideally I'd leave a big hole in the middle and people could put it anywhere they wanted to, but people won't do that. You've got to force them to—if that extra hole's there and it's real for them, they'll do it, but if it's not, they'll (pathetic tone of voice) "Oh, I don't know, I'm not going to play it off center." But if they see it's in the record, *Well*. . . .**

In the first record I even wanted loop grooves—I wanted *overlapping* loop grooves.

R/S: What are overlapping loop groves?

NON: **Theoretically there would be about three of them, and they'd overlap at certain points, and they might do random things—the needle might go in a pattern for awhile, then change. But over the phone, long distance, I couldn't even get the pressing plant to do a loop groove. On the second record, I persevered, and finally got it.**

R/S: How many copies were made of the first record?

NON: **Eighty-six. I ordered 75 but they accidentally made 11 extra.**

R/S: Was that all you could afford?

NON: **Well at the time I thought, How many people in the world are going to want to listen to this kind of music? I wasn't aware that there might be a market for it. You're sitting alone in your room doing this and you think, Gee. . . . Like I thought I invented tape loops—I thought I'd found the perfect way to make repetitive**

with the multi-axial single, which can not only be played at all 4 speeds but off-center too, so you get *way* more for your money.

R/S: Didn't you have some difficulty getting the single made with more than one hole?

NON: **The record company wouldn't do that—I had to drill all the extra holes myself.**

R/S: Didn't you want even 3 or 4 holes?

music. I was real—I hate to say *bummed out*—to find out there were other people doing this. . . .

R/S: After the multi-axial single, didn't you do the world's first 7" album in a 12-inch sleeve?

NON: ***Pagan Muzak,* all loop grooves. Then a 12" single: one live song, one studio song I did in London, and another real old thing I did in 1978—more poppy, repetitive, really dense material. I did the *Frank and***

Boyd album (don't know when that's coming out; hate to think it's lost in the vaults. That was done with Frank of *Fad Gadget.*) Now there's a live album that should be out any time, a *real* album, of performances all over, in different styles.

R/S: Sort of like *The Best Of?*

NON: Well, I've tried to present noise as simplistically as possible, but I've found a whole bunch of different ways to go about it—different styles, different approaches. So it's kind of like a spectrum of those different possibilities.

R/S: You work principally with noise. So why do you like a lot of blatantly pop music, usually by female vocalists?

NON: I've always liked female vocalists because of the quality of their voice—it's so high-pitched. Those high frequencies have always really appealed to me! The music sung by girls seems to be poppier, more lively. What I like about all those different types of music by *Peggy March, Annette, Manuela and the Five Dops, Lesley Gore* (I always liked *Johnny Crawford;* even though he's a boy, he has a high voice and sings kind of the same sort of songs that these girls do), *Abba*—all these types of music seemed like they had a different mentality behind it. I didn't even look upon it or consider it as music—I was looking for a certain *underlying feeling,* a feeling that's in a lot of things like certain weird movies. But when that element's there, that indefinable element—

R/S: Does that "element" involve a random psychotic

elements blending together to form something that's much more than just the sum of the parts.

R/S: Can you give me an example of this?

NON: *Sandie Shaw* did a song about being obsessed with this guy, following him around everywhere, until finally she caught him. And he was everything she dreamed of, and this and that. But then, after awhile, all of a sudden she was with him one day and realized that she didn't want him anymore. So she tried to leave him, but he wouldn't go for that, and then he just followed her everywhere she goes, and says he doesn't want anyone new!

A lot of the songs deal with paranoia—hers are a lot more cold and paranoid than some. There's a line in a *Johnny Crawford* song which says, "Everyone in town/wants to put me down/with their rumours." Everyone in town—jeez! There's always this fear of persecution and delusion of grandeur in these songs, all these overblown fears. He's got another one where he just sits looking at this chair; his friends tell him it's empty but he can see her sitting there. He knows he's crazy, that he's living in the past; but he says, "People say I'm just playing a game/but to me it's all the same."

And Annette's songs are always about these weird abnormal characters that are somehow endowed with real positive connotations. Like *Jo-Jo the Dog-faced Boy* is a guy so ugly that his face is covered with wool and he looks like a dog; he wears weird clothes and drives an ugly old car. But everybody likes him

paradox?

NON: Yeah! (laughs) That, and it seems like a lot of the music was written by adults for children, so there's this whole weird, twisted perspective of what an adult thinks a child will like. Like, they'll make the production overly childish...or certain things that would ordinarily be subtle they'll make overly obvious, and so on down the line. And you'll get all these different

because he's such a *wild guy.* See, the very characteristics that people would ordinarily find repulsive are what make him interesting and exciting. That's great input for kids, you know!

A record like that more truly communicates; the structure, her voice, the content, is like wilder than Captain Beefheart could ever hope to be! That's what I like about a lot of this music—it forces a certain hebephrenic mental state on you. You can be a serious adult and listen to some of this music and it sort of cuts through all the nonsense, all the false barriers you

Bottom to Top: Martin Denny (next to tiki), Harvey Ragsdale, Julius Wechter, and Augie Colon. (Photo from *Exotica III*, Liberty Records)

erected as you've "grown up." So-called intelligence and sophistication which people attach so much importance to, and *think* give them clear perceptions, are the very barriers which keep them from ever having any clear perceptions.

R/S: What do you like about *Abba?*

NON: They're getting a lot more paranoid and stranger, saying a lot of vague—I wonder if *they* know what they're getting at. There's a certain *Abba* mentality—I don't know what it is; a certain lack of intelligence and sophistication?—that seems to permit them to come up with songs that are really haywire, like that heavy-metal women's lib song they wrote. And I like their music, too—it has that lack of sophistication that's really childish and pure and basic. But at the same time they're extremely sophisticated in their whole way of operating—their production qualities, the way they run their business, etc. They've managed to be cold and calculating on a lot of levels, while somehow preserving a naive and childish quality.

I think Americans have really lost that, because even when I was a kid—I remember being on a bus going to summer camp in the fifth grade, and "Sugar Sugar" came on the radio. And all my friends—they were just little kids, fifth-graders—they hated it. And "Dizzy" came on and they hated that too. Because here were songs that were just direct, catchy, and happy, and even fifth-grade kids were too sophisticated to like something that was bubble-gum. And I think that gets in the way of people's experience of life on so many different levels.

R/S: Didn't you meet Martin Denny?

NON: Yeah, he's still playing at this hotel on Maui. He's been there the past 4 years, throughout the week. After he played his set I went over and introduced myself. We just started talking.

I asked him how he got interested in exotic sounds, and he said that when he was a lot younger he traveled in Peru and became interested in ethnic and exotic sounds there. Later on, in 1956 at The Shell Bar in

Boyd Rice with identical tiki 25 years later, Maui, Hawaii. The tiki has since been removed.

Waikiki, he and his band would play outside and these birds would make bird sounds and more or less interfere. Since it was such a prevalent sound, they decided to incorporate it into their act. They started having members of the band do birdcalls.

R/S: Vocally?

NON: Yeah; different members of the band were talented in that direction. And then they made the *Quiet Village* album which became a Number One hit. He said it was in the charts for 13 weeks.

Anyway, I asked him how he got these strange instruments he uses. He said they knew people who worked for the airlines who would bring them back unusual instruments. They'd try them out and build a number around different odd instruments. He said he was always interested in sounds and always interested in experimentation.

R/S: Did he have any theories of sound?

BOYD: He said that when a writer writes a book, he introduces all these characters and elaborates on them. And that's what he was trying to do with music—every theme represented a character. He said *all* sounds represented colors as well. When they played the Tiki Bar in the International Marketplace, they had colors rhythmically blinking, and the rhythm of the percussion interacted with this big fan that swung back and forth in front of the stage. Sort of hypnotic.

He said they were always trying something out—weird instruments from Bali, anything. Sometimes it worked and sometimes it didn't, but they always kept doing it because they never knew what they might find. Back then there was *nobody* doing anything similar—nobody was using any primitive or ethnic instruments except the cultures that created them.

On one song they used brass pans—they'd hit them and gotten a really good sound, so they got them in 4 or 5 different sizes and used them just as an instrument, basing a whole song around them. You know, that's like Z'ev....

R/S: Can you describe any other instruments?

NON: One was made specifically for the soundtrack of *The King And I*. It was made out of cut-off pipes of different lengths fastened to a huge log, and it sounded like a gamelan. It was played with mallets or hammers. It weighed a ton, and was impossible to take around, unless they were playing one place for long periods of time. They designed one song around this instrument, but since it was only used for the one song, it was kind of impractical. Then this guy who had the largest collection of instruments on the East Coast bought it. It was shipped to him the cheapest way possible—on a slow boat through the Panama Canal—and now this guy in New York rents it out, and it's named after Martin Denny.

R/S: Did he say anything specifically about harmony?

NON: He said that harmony isn't what makes music interesting, that *dissonance* is. He said that when things grate against each other the sound seems to have a *bite* that appeals to the ear.

R/S: Did he modify existing instruments?

NON: They took apart a xylophone and reconstructed it so they could do a perfect glissando on it. Ordinarily all the notes on a xylophone are like all the white keys on a piano, but they took it apart and put the black keys in with the white keys so they could be able to run up and down the notes.

> The degree to which I like something is directly proportionate to the extent it bypasses existing standards,

R/S: What do you think makes Martin Denny so noteworthy?

NON: Once in a while somebody does something so personal, so much *them,* that it seems just completely separate from everything else. What Martin Denny did back then was completely different from anything people were doing. Later, after he became popular, a million people put out "exotic" albums, but he was using all these strange instruments and these *unclichéd* sounds and I think it had a more direct appeal, was more genuine—at least to me.

It was such a strange idea to combine primitive instrumentation with relaxing, easy-listening arrangements—can you imagine the mind that would combine those two?

He was really interested in the idea of things being *incongruent.* In the old days, when they were playing the International Marketplace, they'd be playing some exotic number and then go directly into "Frankie and Johnnie." He did weird arrangements that only he would think of, like playing "Tiny Bubbles" in a classical style like Tchaikovsky or Bach. The most normal songs, in completely improbable arrangements.

R/S: Did he do any film soundtracks?

NON: He did the music for a film called *Forbidden Island,* by the same guy who made *Crab Men From Outer Space.* They did a song based around a drum made out of a log.

R/S: Does Martin Denny ever tour?

NON: The band owned so many different instruments that it was impossible to travel—all these delicate, weird, primitive instruments. He said they didn't like to travel anyway, because all the guys were in love with Hawaii—the beach and everything. You know, playing in Detroit when it was snowing?!

R/S: What instruments does he use now?

NON: He just does solo piano, but interestingly enough he uses tapes of bird sounds. Sometimes he uses a rhythm generator but mostly he does solo piano. What he does is extremely intricate—it's hard to believe that there's just one person playing it....

R/S: Lately you've been paying a lot more attention to films that have some inexplicable mentality...to the extent that you're writing a book about them: *Incredibly Strange Movies* (co-written with Jim Morton of *Trashola* fame). Can you state what ties them all together?

NON: It's something *extremely* elusive—that's what gives them the quality of being exceptional. You can tell that films which on the surface appear to be complete opposites share a special vitality that transcends the elements of the film.

When I was young I wanted to like horror films, and went to see tons of them. But I felt they were always the same movie—they always had the monster get killed in the end, etc. Eventually I got tired of them because they weren't fulfilling the promise that I thought they'd made to me!

Then one day I saw *Moonlighting Wives*—it was on a triple feature with a couple of horror films in a cruddy theater—an early low-budget sexploitation film. And right from the start I thought, *What's this? This is different—I haven't seen anything like this before. How'd this film get into this theater?* I think it starts out with a policeman talking about lust circles that were forming around the country, where bored housewives would go into prostitution because they were bored and wanted something to do, and they wanted money to buy pretty things. So, they were trying to crack down on these: "This could be any town, this could be the town *you're* living in."

It started out with amazing weird sets and weird actors and everything about it was *off,* somehow. The whole film follows their story: the housewives getting together and making the arrangements, the police sending guys out into the field undercover, gathering information, etc. Then at the end, the police arrive and arrest everybody just as they'd all converged at this house and were dressed up only in their underwear and black halloween masks. (That film was by Joe Sarno.)

Then a short time later I saw Herschell Gordon Lewis's *The Gruesome Twosome.* I saw that with a couple normal horror films in a cruddy theater; I wasn't expecting anything. It starts off with a couple of wig-heads talking to each other-wig-heads with faces drawn on them like with a ball-point pen, in front of this backdrop, and holes cut in the backdrop with people's hands coming through moving these heads while they were talking to each other, saying these jokes that weren't really funny.

I couldn't believe what I was seeing; I kept looking around the theater—I felt like I was in a dream. The whole film, one scene after another, was just incredible.

This lady runs a combination wig shop and dormitory for girls, young co-eds, and her son lives in the back room. He's mentally deficient or psychotic, and he takes the co-ed girls that live there and kills them and cuts off their scalps, and then their scalps are sold as wigs in the wig store. And I thought, This is just a one-in-a-million film; it's just some strange accident that this happened out into the world.

But right after that I saw *The Incredibly Strange Creatures Who Stopped Living and Became Mixed-up Zombies.* And I couldn't believe how great it was. Actually when I first saw it it was playing under the title *Teenage Psycho Vs. Bloody Mary,* at Halloween. The ad said something like "See living monsters rip from the screen and carry off members of the audience." It also said, "1001 of the weirdest scenes ever." And it showed a woman and said, "She keeps monsters in cages for pets." And it showed a man, and said, "He kidnaps wild go-go girls."

R/S: What are some other films you've selected?

NON: *Terrified* (with Rod Lauren) is about a young man obsessed with the idea of fear, who's writing a term paper on the subject of fear. His friend's been turned into a "slobbering oyster" by this horrifying accident that happened to him out in the cemetery at the old ghost town—somebody poured cement on him, up to his neck until his mind snapped. This guy Rod Lauren thinks he'll be able to go out there and come to terms with terror which has plagued him all his life. So he goes out there and...it's an amazing film.

R/S: What about *Equinox?*

NON: Apparently the guy who made this film saw some special effects footage Jim Danforth did, and he said, "Hey, this is great footage! We oughta somehow film a whole story around it and work it in." So

The King of Noise Music meets The King of Surf Music, Dick Dale.

Cash Flag AKA Ray Dennis Steckler, the creator of *The Incredibly Strange Creatures Who Stopped Living And Became Mixed-up Zombies, The Thrill Killers* and other classic films.

they came up with this wild incoherent story. The original footage was shot a long time before the movie was shot, so when they integrated it together you see things like, when they cut back and forth, the length of the girl's hair will change; she's wearing tons of makeup in one scene and absolutely none in the next. It was real rich with that sort of detail.

> I think "intelligence" imposes order and clarity where none exists. I'm definitely against that, just like I'm against rationality and determinacy and seriousness and so on....

The plot is that they go out to have a picnic and visit some old professor, but when they get out there the house has been smashed in. Then they run into some old kook living in a cave who croaks, "You want the *book!* You want the *book*, don't you?" "We don't want the book." But he gives it to them anyway, and it's an old Black Magic book. They read it and accidentally call up these monsters, these big gumby-ish monsters....

Decoy for Terror is about a demented artist who kills his models because they won't stay still. He's trying to paint a painting of a dream that torments him, and he thinks that if he paints the dream it will stop tormenting him. But he can't find a girl who can stay still long enough for him to....

R/S: What else will your book have in it?

NON: It's got whole sections on sexploitation, LSD films, beach party films, drivers' ed films.... There's interviews with major figures like *Ray Dennis Steckler* who made *The Incredibly Strange Creatures.*

R/S: Are there any LSD-sexploitation films in there?

NON: Yes, several. There's a drug-Little Red Riding Hood sexploitation film. Little Red Riding Hood is this hippie girl who goes to take some grass to grandmoth-er's house. The wolf sees her, follows her there and gobbles up grandmother, and is dressed as grandmother when Red gets there with the grass. Then I guess they smoke some dope and have sex. The wolf is wearing a great wolf mask that looks absolutely crazy....

All these films compose a definite genre but not in any traditional sense. All these films are tied together by something *exceptional* which can definitely be perceived yet not easily defined. It's usually a combination of different factors in each film. Sometimes it's using sets that are real places and actors that are real people; sometimes it's the actual plot and dialogue, sometimes it's *because* a film is low-budget—there are an almost limitless combination of reasons why a film will be exceptional. Many of these films are overlooked *because* they can't be readily categorized in any genre. Some films succeed in spite of huge budgets (*The Ten Commandments*). Other films remain sleepers for years until some accidental discovery by some famous "critic" brings them widespread public attention (*Peeping Tom*).

Most films, you go see them and right from the beginning you know how they're going to turn out—the characters aren't believable and even if they were convincing, they're so uninteresting you wouldn't care what happened to them anyway. No amount of technique or style in a film can help such a basic situation.

A lot of the films in this book are considered to be bad, and yet in a strange way they succeed where all the others fail. It's a shame most of these films are obscure, because they're far "better" than what people consider to be "great films"—they're more entertaining, more unusual, yet more genuine and more truly effective. For one reason or another, all the films I discuss seem to transcend all the cinematic criteria that are usually applied. That is why they're all *Incredibly Strange Movies!*

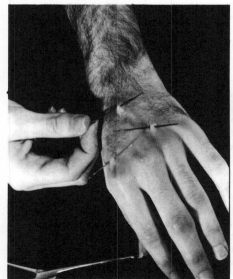

Boyd administering personal variation of acupuncture therapy. (Photo: Bobby Adams)

Javier Escovedo (of the *Zeros*) and Boyd Rice in Tijuana, 1977, having purchased switchblades and pointed shoes.

R/S: Have you ever played any practical jokes?

NON: When I was younger my friend Barry Alfonso and I used the phone to test out people's credulity— just to see how far you could go. We'd pretend to be delivery persons—people would get really scared that we would deliver something they didn't want or hadn't ordered.

We had a double-talk phrase that was incomprehensible—just below the threshold of understanding. They'd ask, "What are you going to deliver?" and we'd say, "Well, we have a ga-shack-gonna-have-a-hear, and we have to bring it by some time today—it's been on the loading dock for awhile and we *have* to get rid of it." They'd say, "You have a *what?*" and we'd

Boyd Rice at the Main Street Station, Disneyland, 1964.

say, "Yeah, is there going to be somebody there to sign for it?" and they'd say, "But what do you have?" and we'd just keep skirting the issue and they'd be afraid that we were going to deliver something they'd have to pay for.

Every once in a while we'd call up and the person would ask, "Oh, are you from Sears? Is it about the couch?" And we'd say, "Yeah, we've got the couch . . . . Did anybody call you about that smoke damage?" And they'd say, *"What* smoke damage?" We'd say, "Well, it wasn't really *burnt* in the warehouse, but it's mostly on the back—you won't even see it. But the discount will probably be on the bill." They'd say, *"Hey,* wait a minute—what are you talking about?" We'd say, "Is somebody going to be there around 2:30?" And they'd say, "Hey, wait a minute!" and we'd say, "Well, we'll see you at 2:30—have someone home to sign for it!" and hang up as they were saying, *"Wait* a minute—"

We got a woman to cry over the phone.

R/S: How?

NON: We called up a woman and told her we were *the police* and that we had her daughter—her daughter had been down in this main part of town indecently exposing herself and setting fires. And the woman goes, "Omigod! I've been *expecting* something like this." And we said, "She was with a bunch of Hare Krishnas at the time." And the woman goes, "Oh, my god. I knew my daughter knew some Hare Krishnas—I knew something like this was going to happen. Oh, my god." And it got worse—everything we'd say, the woman would go, "Oh, *no no no."*

Then she started crying, "I'm sorry—excuse me, I'm sorry to act this way." And I said (deep voice), "I understand, ma'am, I have a daughter of my own . . . . Ordinarily we'd just release her into your custody, but arson's a pretty serious charge—you better come down to the Sheriff's sub-station right away." She sobbed, "I'll call my husband at work and we'll be right down."

R/S: You're tapping into a set of verbal and behavioral conventions, ferreting out people's vulnerability. By sounding "official" and evoking their obedience-to-authority conditioning, you can manipulate them into all kinds of seemingly correct but ludicrous behavior.

NON: You can do it in person sometimes, but over the phone you can do it to *anybody.* One time, at about 2 in the morning, Barry and I picked one guy out of the phone book and woke him out of a sound sleep. Barry said, *"Hi!* I'm sorry to call you up this late at night, but my friend and I just got into town, and you said if I ever came to town to give you a call. So here I am." Meanwhile, you could hear the wife in the background real groggy, coming in and saying, "Who is it? Who is that?" And Barry says, "Well, we're going to look for a motel tomorrow, but it's kind of late tonight—do you think maybe we could come over and stay with you?" And the guy says, "Uh, well, *sure*—I don't see why not!" So Barry says, "I'm sorry to inconvenience you—I know it's late, but I'm not familiar with this town at all; can you give me directions on how to get to your place?" And the guy starts giving him really clear instructions, but Barry keeps getting confused and asking him more and more directions, finally saying, "Well *here*—talk to my friend—he's more familiar with the town." And he handed the phone over to me.

Boyd Rice at "The Happiest Place In The World."

I said, "How do we get over to your house?" and the guy was explaining. And I said, "Oh, I hope these bags of cement we have won't be a problem." And the guy says, "Huh?" I say, "We've got quite a bit of cement, and we kinda need some place to put it for a week or so. How are you fixed for space?" And the guy says, "Well, my wife and I are in a mobile home, and we don't have much room." I said, "Well, there aren't many of these—maybe you could move the couch out and put them between the couch and the wall. It wouldn't take up much room. Or, you could put 'em on the grass, and I'm sure a week of cement on that grass wouldn't kill it." And the guy was saying, "Cement?" and I said, "Oh, you know—these *bags.*"

The guy's wife was getting real pissed off in the background, saying: *"Who is it? WHO'S coming to stay here?"* and you could hear him arguing with his wife. Then the wife grabs the phone away from the guy and says, "Listen, I don't know who you are, but this is kinda late at night. Can't you find a motel room?" And I said, "Well. . .we're strangers in town, and we'd really feel uncomfortable staying in a motel room." Then I said, "Hey! But how's this? We could pay for *you* to go to a motel room and then we could sleep in your trailer. I think we'd like that a lot more!" Then the lady says, real mad, *"We aren't going to go stay in any motel room— YOU stay in a motel room! WHOEVER you are!"*

It's amazing how people are willing to go along with *anything,* no matter how outrageous it is. I've had

people almost ready to get on a plane and fly across the ocean.
R/S: Come on!
NON: I really did one time. This was in England. I called up this British guy who worked as a session musician doing back-up vocals and said, "Hi. I'm calling from the 'States." I sounded American, so he bought it. I said, "We need you for some sessions in New York—we're going to be laying down some heavy tracks" and all this double-talk. And the guy completely bought it. I could have said, "Hey, how would it be if you get a ticket on a plane and come right over and we'll pay you as soon as you get here?" but we didn't take it that far. We just didn't call him back; we let him fantasize for awhile. He'd really screwed over a friend of ours—that's why we'd called him.
R/S: Why do you think people are still interested in Manson?
NON: There's a human instinct that wants or needs that kind of focus—like, why are people so fascinated with Hitler 40 years after his death? I think we're talking about people not having anything in *themselves.* In Manson's case he probably represents a kind of self-actualization that people unconsciously would like to have but can't.
Most people, when you ask them who they are— their personalities seem to be defined by what they like—
R/S: And what they buy—
NON: The rock stars they listen to, the TV shows they

63

Boyd beneath a crossroads of the world. (Photo: Bobby Adams)

watch.... You ask a Star Trekkie, you know—*that* defines their whole personality and shapes their whole lives. Take away that input and they'll be nothing. And almost everybody's like that to an extreme degree. People have forgotten what it's like to be living and walking around, having direct experience or real feelings.

In a field of vision your mind sees everything. Like whenever I'm with people I'll always be the first one to see cats—I really like cats. And other people'll go, "I don't see any cats"—*then* they'll notice them.

R/S: Your knowledge and desires influence your vision—

NON: That was obviously the case with Adolf Hitler. From the time he was a child he knew *exactly* what he wanted to do, what he was *going* to do, and he felt it so deeply and his fantasies about it were so vivid that he didn't even know where fantasy stopped and reality started, and consequently they just blended. He always acted like everything he thought was going to be an actuality, and in fact it happened!

When he was a youngster, he drew these complex plans for completely redesigning the city he grew up in. His friends thought he was just a nut because—how's a kid ever going to be able to do *that?* Yet he never doubted that he could do it. Eventually he got to the position where he carried out these plans, down to the most minute detail.

R/S: That's what surprised me about this book on Nazi insignia I was reading. There were hundreds of awards, like a certain gold one for women with over 15 children, a silver one for women with over 10—rewards for every conceivable achievement. But despite this diversity of design, Hitler had to *personally* approve each one before they could be manufactured. And he must have had a million other things to do as well.

NON: Well, when you're in a position like that you want to make sure that everything's done right! If I was leader of a country, I wouldn't want some kind of award to go out that I didn't know about. Like—who the hell put *that* out? It's like making records—you don't want to leave important things like the design up to record companies.

R/S: Hitler and Manson are amazing—their power came from other people believing in their words.

NON: People always believe that there's a *right* thing to believe, or that eventually they're going to hit upon it, someday. Or they'll think they're pretty right but that eventually they'll run into some person who's more right than them—

R/S: That's the guru pathology—

NON: Basically people don't want to give up what they believe in, and even worse—*give up belief altogether.* 'Cause people can see inserting another belief, and saying, "Well, I won't believe in *this* anymore but I'll believe in *that.*" That's easy, but people can't just remove *all* belief. Because they've always had "standards" to judge things by, and if they removed all beliefs, they just wouldn't know how to exist!

People think they *know:* "Oh, look at that ugly person!" Or, "look at this tacky painting!" But somebody, somewhere, has told them what's what. And then they wonder why they can't enjoy themselves more! Why there isn't more to life than *this?*

I kind of *always* never put any value in what everybody told me. At the same time, I thought that things

Boyd Rice and Laurie O'Connell at the Spahn Ranch just before it burned down in 1982.

that seemed *superficially* to go against these values didn't really have any value either. I'd be in church looking around at people and thinking, "Now these people can't *really* be believing all this. They can't believe a word this guy's saying." So I got interested in witchcraft and Satanism, then I thought, "Well that's a crock of shit too—all Satan is, is just the *opposite* of all that other crap I don't believe."

So there was a whole spectrum of other values—not just religion, that I didn't believe in or think was important. When people rebel against religion, they just give it credence. If they really *didn't* believe, they wouldn't do a thing about it. They'd just go on with their lives.

R/S: Don't you think rebellion is important?

NON: People prefer to have a *symbol* of rebellion that they can buy, or pay homage to. To fuel their conversations. Something that in reality isn't the least bit rebellious at all.

Take James "Rebel Without A Cause" Dean. Well—he didn't rebel against *anything!* The things he believed in were "common decency" and "doing the right thing." He was supposed to be the only decent guy in a corrupt and twisted world—where values had become corrupt. But all he ever was, was a "decent guy" who just had the same ideas that everybody else has. What a rebellion!

At the scene of a serious accident in Los Angeles, 1981. (Photo: Andrea Juno)

SOME SONGS

March/Lulu
Run/Sandie Shaw
Kusse Unterm Regenbogen/Manuela
Love & Kisses/ ''
Horch, Was Kommt Von Draussen Rein/ ''
Es Ist Zum Weinen/ ''
ABC/ ''
Wenn Du Leibst/ ''
Helicopter US Navy 66/ ''
Hundert Jahre Und Noch Mehr/Peggy March
Spar Die Deine Dollar/ ''
Wedding In My Dreams/ ''
Puppe Mit Dem Goldnen Haar/ ''
Male Nicht Den Teufel An Wand/ ''
Die Maschen Der Männer/ ''
Einmal Verleibt, Immer Verleibt/ ''
Ein Boy Wie Du/ ''
Little John/ ''
Ich Hab Ein Herz Zu Vershenken/ ''
Goodbye Goodbye Goodbye/ ''
Hello Heartache, Goodbye Love/ ''
It's Easier To Cry/Shangri-La's
Indian Giver/Annette
Party Girl/Bernadette Carol
The Big Hurt/Susan Rafey
Popsicles & Icesicles/Murmaids
Mal Nein Sagen Könn'n/Gitte

Hei, Hei, Hei, Mein Herz Ist Nicht/ ''
Mehr Frei/Ric Gerty
Cease To Resist/Beach Boys (rip-off of Manson song ''Cease To Exist'')
Sick City/Manson
Cease to Exist/Manson
Big Iron Door/Manson
People Say I'm No Good/Manson
Home Is Where You're Happy/Manson
Look At Your Game, Girl/Manson
I Once Knew A Man/Manson
Eyes Of A Dreamer/Manson
I'll Never Say Never To Always/ Manson Girls

SOME SONGS (WITH COMMENTARY)

1) Dumbhead/Ginny Arnel (A tale of stupidity and self-hatred)
2) I Wish I Knew What Dress To Wear/Ginny Arnel (Decisions, decisions)
3) Rebel Rider/Annette (Death Before Dishonor)
4) Roses On The Sea/Peggy March ('')
5) Endless Sleep/The Poppy Family (Love & Death & Water)
6) Bermuda/Linda Scott (Further Love, Death & Water. Recorded in pre-Triangle days)
7) There's No Blood In Bone/Poppy Family (A love song)

8) The Sun Goes Down/DD, D, B, M&T (A man about to die)
9) Seasons In The Sun/Terry Jacks ('')
10) Nightmare/Lori Burton (Fake Shangri-Las' song by 60's singer-songwriter)
11) Leader Of The Pack/The Compacts (Fake group from a 60's compilation LP. Listen closely)
12) Motor Beine/Benny Quick (No comment)
13) Feelin' Groovy/The Specialists (Hip rendition of the 60's standard)
14) Help Yourself/The Now Sound of Sandi & Salli (Wild version of the Tom Jones classic)
15) California Nights/The King Cousins (Blissfully bland version of Lesley Gore's hit)
16) Cherry Hill Park/The Specialists (Extended version; a pulsating freak-out)
17) On The Trail/The Charles Randolph Green Sounde (A personal favorite for over 10 years)
18) No Matter What Shape Your Stomach's In/The New Classic Singers (Vocal orgy)
19) Spinning Wheel/The Specialists
20) The Age of Aquarius/The Specialists (Insightful astrological excursion)
21) Everybody's Talkin' At Me/ ''
22) Aries/The Zodiac (''A Real Trip'')
23) Tiger/Krista (A salute to Abba by the well-known trio, Krista)

REFERENCE

SOME BOOKS

Killer/about Carl Panzram
Six Years With God (Jonestown)
Impressions of Africa/by Raymond Roussel
The Encyclopedia of Barbie Dolls
Will You Die For Me?/Tex Watson
The Psychopathic God (Hitler)
The Complete Books of Charles Fort
Your Children/by Charles Manson
My Life With Charles Manson/Paul Watkins

SOME MAGAZINES

Alarma (Mexican)
Alerta (Mexican)
Homicidio (Mexican)
Weekly World News
California Highway Patrol

SOME FILMS

All Films: Ray Dennis Steckler (The Incredibly Strange Creatures That Stopped Living and Became Mixed-Up Zombies, Thrill Killers, Wild Guitar, etc)
All Films: Ted V. Mikal (Astro Zombies, Corpse Grinders, Worm-Eaters, etc)
All films: Joe Sarno (Young Playthings, Moonlighting Wives, etc)
All Films: Herschell Gordon Lewis (Gruesome Twosome, 2000 Maniacs, etc)
Decoy For Terror/Enrick Santamaran
Dementia (Daughter of Horror)/John Parker
Equinox/David Allen & Jim Danforth
Mondo Cane/Gualtiero Jacopetti
Mondo Bizarro/Cresse & Frost
Love Camp 7/   ''

Mondo Bolordo
The Cool and The Crazy/Wm Whitney
Reform School Girl/Edward Bernds
The 17 Floodgates
Death Smiles on a Murderer/Massaccesi
Day The Earth Froze/Julius Strandberg
House of Dark Shadows/Dan Curtis
In the Land of the Headhunters
Badlands/Terrence Malick
Pretty Poison/Noel Black
-30-/Jack Webb

SOME RECORDS

The Incomparables
  (every record recommended):
Peggy March
Lesley Gore
Annette Funicello: The Story
  of My Teens, etc.
Martin Denny
Abba

Plus:
The Paris Sisters Sing From The
  Glass House
Johnny Crawford/His Greatest Hits
Johnny Crawford/I Wanna Be A Good Guy
The Poppy Family Featuring Susan Jacks
LIE by Charles Manson
The Things We Did Last Summer/
  Shelly Fabares
Manuela: Die Grosse Erfolge
Sandie Shaw: Pye file series
Space Escapade/Les Baxter

Choo Ja Kim: Golden Hits
Filipinki: It's Us!
Meet Ginny Arnel
Dark Shadows
Susan Rafey: Hurt So Bad
Diane Renay: Navy Blue
The Legendary Stardust Cowboy:
  Who's Knockin' On My Door (45)

DISCOGRAPHY

THE BLACK ALBUM. First *Boyd Rice* LP. Released with solid black cover and no title. Later re-released on Mute with glossier cover embossed with *Boyd Rice* in lower right corner. Playable at any speed.

KNIVE LADDER/MODE OF INFECTION. First *Non* single. Besides the songs it came with 3 loop grooves. Extra hole allows record to play off center. Re-released on Mute records. Live recording of "Knive Ladder" was the first song of the first *Non* concert.

DARKER SKRATCHER (compilation LP). Contains "Cleanliness & Order" by Boyd Rice and Daniel Miller. Also contains version of *Non-Watusi* that somehow changed completely between the time the tape was mailed and the record was pressed. Exactly what happened still remains a mystery to all those involved.

PAGAN MUZAK. First *Non* album. Contains 17 loop grooves, playable at any speed. Also has second hole for off axis playback. First pressing contained one side with grooves, the other blank. Second pressing contained the same grooves on both sides. 7'' disc in 12'' cover. Second pressing had serial #3301 etched in record.

RISE. 12'' *Non* single. Also contains "Out Out Out," a live recording from SO36 in Berlin, and "Romance Fatal Dentro De Un Auto" recorded in 1978. Mute Records #015.

FRANK & BOYD. An album done in collaboration with Frank Tovey (of *Fad Gadget*). Recorded in London the week before *Rise*. As yet unreleased by Mute Records.

PHYSICAL EVIDENCE. An album of live *Non* performances recorded over a period of years in Los Angeles, London, Dusseldorf, Paris, Berlin. Mute Records.

MISCELLANEOUS

A bit from the BLACK ALBUM was used on an album released by United Dairy records in England. No further information available.

A track from PAGAN MUZAK was used by German group *Der Plan* as background for a piece they contributed to a German compilation album. Again, no further information available.

Horrible bootleg tape LIVE AT THE PRESS CLUB features the worst *Non* set ever, but also contains a version of Charles Manson's "Sick City," sung by Boyd with Laurie O'Connell and backed up musically by the *Meat Puppets*.

Watch for Boyd Rice's forthcoming book, *Incredibly Strange Films*, co-written with Jim Morton of *Trashola*, the monthly newsletter for fans of the grotesque, which is available free (send $3.50 to cover postage) from Jim Morton, Suite 583, 109 Minna St, San Francisco CA 94105.

At Alfred Jarry's old residence on Rue Cassette, Paris, 1979

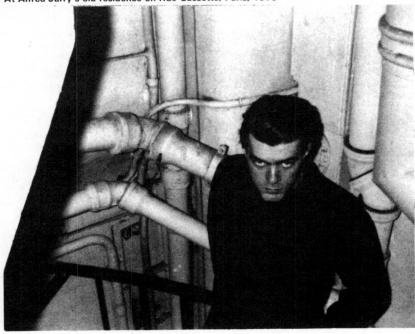

MONTE CAZAZZA

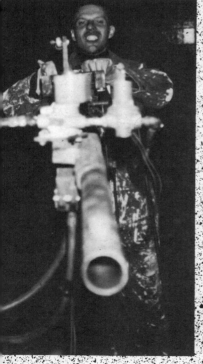

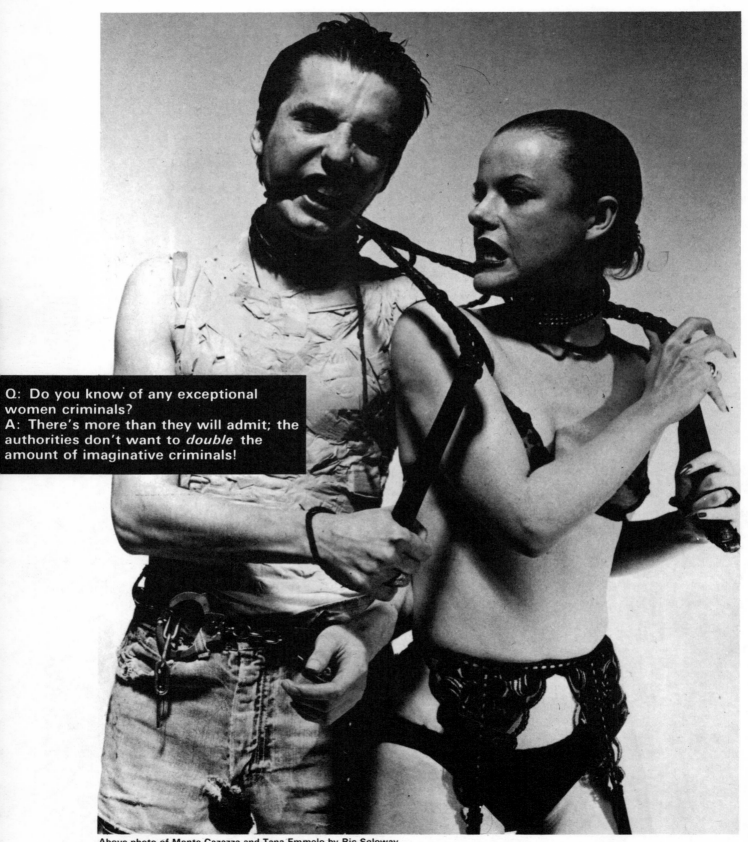

Q: Do you know of any exceptional women criminals?
A: There's more than they will admit; the authorities don't want to *double* the amount of imaginative criminals!

Above photo of Monte Cazazza and Tana Emmolo by Ric Soloway.
Preceding pages: serial photos of Monte & Cosey by G. P-Orridge; Dart Gun photo by Vale; large photo by Mark Berlin.

The most underground artist in this handbook is *Monte Cazazza* from San Francisco. His notoriety stems from an erratic history of insanity-outbreaks thinly disguised as art events, beginning in the early 1970's through the present future. Along with disrupting the Bay Area 'Dadaist scene' and ridiculing the 'Correspondence Art' network, he was the first to make an *artists'* film featuring fist-fucking and child pornography. His territory was all and everything forbidden, taboo, repulsive, sexually, politically and morbidly explicit—transmuted into shock graphics, collages, performances, sacrileges, photographs, films, videos, records, interviews, writings and inventions.

Mr. Cazazza's work has given a new and deeper forensic significance to the term 'hardcore.' The 'worst' human impulses, desires and behavior as documented by history and science are examined with an optically precise scrutiny. . . .

Very few artists can *prove* by their history to have pursued their life's aims with genuine disdain for society's opinions and rewards. It can safely be said that by his work, which is mostly unprintable, Monte Cazazza has *demonstrated* a focused, perverse *commitment* undiluted by compromise for the sake of ambition or the mere desire to please. A commitment that is the only one justifiable: to the purity of one's inner vision, fed from an endless resource in today's world: *black humor*. And for today's world, laughter is the only medicine left. . . .

R/S: Tell us your earliest acts of mayhem?

MONTE: There were lots of acts of mayhem. When I first had to go to school, I didn't like it. So I sat there for about a week and just screamed. Unbeknownst to me, if I had sat there about another week I probably never would have had to go to school, because they would have ended up giving me a tutor, or something. But I didn't know that, and my voice gave out before they relented.

This was in Catholic school in Philadelphia. I had this nun who really hated me—she used to hit me all the time. See, I was like the example—*God's retribution*.

R/S: I thought that was illegal—

MONTE: Not in those schools—in those schools you *kneel to the boss*, as *Cabaret Voltaire* would say. So what happened was—one time she was smacking me and finally I said *I've had enough of this!* and ripped her habit off. Of course, her hair was cropped about half an inch—all the kids thought she was totally bald—and she flipped out. Then they sent me to see

the priest because they thought I was possessed. . . The look on her face was priceless. And she never hit me again either after that.

R/S: When did you leave home?

MONTE: The first time I started running away was when I was about 9 years old. I would hide in museums. I would hide in libraries. I even slept in a very expensive hotel once. But then I would get caught— about 3 days would be tops before someone, *somehow,* figured out that I wasn't supposed to be where I was, and get ahold of me, and start demanding who I was and where I lived, and why wasn't I in school etc. etc.

R/S: Tell us about your High School experiences?

MONTE: My parents had moved to the suburbs, which I detested immediately. I hated everyone that lived there. So in high school, literally, for one year I didn't talk to anyone. Just went to school, sat in the very last seat in the first row, and didn't talk to anyone because I didn't like anyone there. No one knew anything about me, I was just this person, and mostly they left me alone. I didn't have any friends in high school and I didn't want any.

The police, though, came to arrest me once. I had this *business* going where I would shoplift cartons of cigarettes—my whole locker was filled with cigarettes. And I was selling them to everyone very cheap. Teachers, everyone. I used to go into these 2 big supermarkets with my gym bag and I would just fill it up with cartons of cigarettes and go home. And one time I got caught shoplifting. The store people called the police and they showed up. Somehow they figured out that I must have been doing this for a long time, because of their inventory or something. I don't know how they added 2 and 2 together, but. . .first they talked to me, and then let me go home. Later on they got a warrant to search my locker. So I'm sitting in history class and these police come in and tell me I have to go with them. I wouldn't tell them the combination of my locker, so they smashed it open and found the whole thing just totally filled with cigarettes. And I thought I really was in a lot of trouble

On top of old smokey
All covered with blood
I shot my poor teacher
With a forty-five slug.

With a forty-five slug
I blew out her brains
They then had me committed
For the criminally insane.

They said to plant flowers
On the grave of that old maid
They said to plant flowers
Instead I threw a grenade

—Monte Cazazza, 1975

then, but actually nothing else happened beyond that point. They just confiscated them all and told me I better not get caught shoplifting again. . .and I better not sell any more cigarettes. . . .

I think that because all the teachers were buying cigarettes, they were all kind of implicated. They asked me what I was doing, and I said I was just trying

71

to make money and better myself, in the American way. The best thing was that I didn't smoke!

R/S: Do you remember some books more important to you?

MONTE: *Thief's Journal* by Jean Genet, which I gave a very explicit unappreciated book report on. I used to go to this porno store and they would let me buy all of the Olympia Press books in the green covers published by Maurice Girodias because they didn't have any pictures in them. I had a deal with this guy because I sold him cigarettes really cheap. I had a whole collection of them: *Tropic of Cancer, Naked Lunch, Stradella, Whip Angels,* etc. etc. Someone I would like to interview very much is Maurice Girodias—I think he's a *very* important person who's never really gotten the credit he deserves. He took a lot of chances, publishing those books at that time in the early Sixties—most of those books would have never seen the light of day—or the black of night—if it wasn't for him.

Another of my favorite authors was Daniel P. Mannix, who wrote a book on the Roman games called *Those About To Die;* a book on a nineteenth-century English cult called *The Hellfire Club; Memoirs of a Sword-Swallower;* and a book on Aleister Crowley, *The Beast.* Mr. Mannix caused me to search out other books in these veins. I found a good book called *The Bad Popes*—definitely not approved by the Catholic church! Also, Ballantine Books published a number of books in a series—one was titled *Rumor, Fear, and The*

broadcasting on this special frequency. You need an extra large aerial to pick it up, but you can get it on a regular TV with a special converter box. That's how they get a lot of what they show on newsreels—they just chop out bits to use for a story in the evening. . . .

They've been trying to train people for newscasting so when they're telling a lie, there's *no stress* in their voice. So even if you were monitoring with a stress analyzer, you wouldn't catch it. I want to get one of those really bad: you can watch TV, and if someone's giving a speech, you can tell immediately whether or not they're lying.

A lot of big businesses have voice stress analyzers hooked up to their phones, so when someone's quoting their "lowest price" or whatever, they can go, "Hmmm, I think he's probably *lying.* . . ."

R/S: How can you beat that, or lie detectors in general?

MONTE: A good little trick that I read in a crime book is: if you ever have to take a lie detector test, what you do is, you keep *wiggling your toes,* right? For some reason it wrecks the test. If you just keep on doing that they can't tell what the hell's going on. These 2 murderers discovered it accidentally. So simple—that's what you have to do.

R/S: That kind of information used to be unavailable. Since the Freedom of Information Act, the CIA must be doing *something* to maintain their secrecy—they're not going to give that up without a whimper—

MONTE: The CIA's transferring all their information

MARY BELL

Mary Bell
Mary Bell
Child of Hell
Child of Hell
One half wicked.
One half good.
Small strong fingers
Go round his tiny neck

Child of Satan
Child of God
Two opposing forces
In one body.
No side wins.
They both remain.
"I only murder, so that
I may return."

Mary Bell
Mary Bell
Child of Hell
Child of Hell
One half wicked.
One half good.
Small strong fingers
Go round his tiny neck

Portrait of Mary Bell by Val Denham/Lyrics: M. Cazazza.

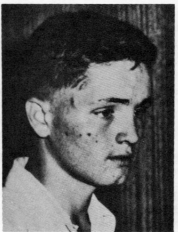

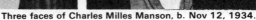

Three faces of Charles Milles Manson, b. Nov 12, 1934.

Madness of Crowds (by J.P. Chaplin)—which from a historical viewpoint are quite good, because they really give you a trashy, but concrete view of what went on, and humanity in general.

You get to see how the world really works from books like that. They're not the kind of books that your high school history teacher is going to recommend you read, but *I* recommend you read them!

R/S: Most people don't get their information from books, but from the news—

MONTE: There's a secret broadcasting station in Europe, the European Broadcasting Union. They're broadcasting film 24 hours a day, from all the hotspots like Iran or Ireland. It's on all the time, unedited,

onto videodiscs. They've developed something like a *Need To Know* code—unless you have the code, you can't find any bit of information. There's something like 30,000 bits on each disc—you could spend your whole life looking for it and never find it. The Freedom of Information Act got them into so much trouble that now they want to get rid of all printed material: *"You* find it—*we* don't know where it is. But we can't let you look through all these discs, because all the information's stored randomly, and a lot of it's *sensitive."*

R/S: . . . How did you happen to write a song on Mary Bell?

MONTE: I've always been interested in criminals and criminology. The first time I was in England Mary Bell escaped. The second time I was there she was coming up for parole. Every time I was there she was in the news. So it just coincided—I read the book on her, *The Case of Mary Bell,* and thought it was interesting…and sat down and wrote the little nursery rhyme. That's how it got on record.

R/S: Wasn't that record a nod in the direction of the Manson girls (who recorded a nursery rhyme)?

MONTE: Well, it has other references. My perception on it, whether it would actually occur, historically speaking, was: after I'd be dead, little girls would be jumping rope to that, and no one would remember where it came from—it'd just end up being this jump rope song, which I hope, after I'm dead, happens.

R/S: What attracted you to Manson?

MONTE: What attracted all these thousands of other people to him? What attracted CBS, ABC, NBC, all these newspapers? I'm not the *only* person attracted to him. When you start looking at all the aspects involved, it's a really interesting case. He didn't get a fair trial—he didn't have a snowball's chance in hell!—the president declaring him guilty—it's a very complicated case. Technically, I don't think he should be in prison. I don't think anyone really knows what went on in that case except the people directly involved. The trial was a shambles, the whole case very interesting: where it occurred, who the victims were, and how everything kind of tied it together. It was almost like fate that a lot of that was going to happen. A real interesting reflection of this culture and society.

R/S: At the London Wax Museum you can see Manson and three of the girls. You can also see Gary Gilmore executed before your very eyes, staged every 60 seconds.

MONTE: I'll have to go there and shoot my own Super-8 film of that! Gary Gilmore's another person I'm definitely interested in. What was interesting to me was not the crimes he committed. Here was this person who was sentenced to be executed, and he decided, Since I'm sentenced to death, the state should carry out its responsibility and execute me. What was interesting was—the whole time this was going on there were thousands of people trying to stop him—the ACLU, his family, other prisoners who didn't want to be executed

(because if *he* got executed, they might be next, and it would set this precedent for other executions), and he was under so much pressure to break down. What was interesting was how he was able to maintain his persistence of vision, or just persistence, through all of that. Everything, including all the TV coverage, was just fascinating. And he looked great on television—he looked like a saint, he looked like Joan of Arc going off to be burnt. When he went on his hunger strike, he really looked *beatific* in his white prison coveralls, when he told everyone to go to hell and not interfere in his execution and *let's get on with it!* What he was saying was, My life is a total mess, it's totally fucked up, and I don't want to rot in prison for the rest of my life, so it's preferable for me to be executed, and at least go out with some semblance of dignity and style, rather than be cut down inch by inch.

R/S: Isn't Jonestown also one of your main interests?

MONTE: Yes, and I hope to be doing a film about that soon. I have a lot of material that hasn't really been seen yet; material from the Peoples Temple auction. The Government Report *(The Assassination of Representative Leo J. Ryan and the Jonestown, Guyana, Tragedy Report)* is a very good book. You can't get it anymore; since Ronald Reagan came in they took it off the shelves. And I would love to see the *classified* version, because the gaps that are in the version I have leave much to the imagination….

I mean, there were a lot of people involved in that

Gary Gilmore Memorial Society. (Photo: Coum Transmissions)

whole thing—Jim Jones did not do all that by himself. He had a lot of cooperation from a lot of people in the government. He knew almost every politician…. And I have a lot of tapes of different prayer meetings—one, I happened to be watching that Leonard Nimoy program on TV, *In Search Of,* and they had this program on psychic healing, and at the very end they had about a twenty-minute segment of a healing that Jim Jones had done in Los Angeles. I just happened to have my tape recorder on at the time.

And I got other tapes, including a tape of the last 40 minutes—on our record [*California Babylon*] all those people screaming is from a prayer meeting. The last 40 minutes where everyone is committing suicide is very much calmer—that makes it really scary, I think, because it's not all these people freaking out, it's people lining up and taking their last drink and—there are some children crying, but it's not total pandemonium. And, who made that tape—was it a CIA agent?

I even went to some meetings at the Peoples Temple in San Francisco about 2 years before Jonestown. Someone just told me I should go there, and I went about 3 or 4 times to meetings that were open to the public. Most of them that were public were only open to the public for a certain amount of time, then you'd have to leave and the meeting would continue on. Really scary and really interesting at the same time.

Jones was very charismatic, without a doubt—very charismatic and very knowledgeable in controlling crowds. Very determined and in some ways a very receptive person because he was able to receive all that energy and use it, like a circular relationship in a way. Any person, no matter who they are, can only handle so much—he could only handle so much energy, and they were giving him more and more and more. And it gets to be like Catch-22, and I think that's what happened.

R/S: How could he have avoided it?

MONTE: It's very hard, because it's very tempting—it's like drugs. Just from doing a few concerts, I know it's very tempting. If you don't know how to use the energy, or what you're doing—it just gets totally out of control.

share a lot of responsibility for what happened, who have never had any charges leveled against them—any at all. Except for Larry Layton, and it looks like his case is going to be dropped.

But he just happens to be the scapegoat, in some ways, for what actually happened. But people like Terry Buford might have their share of the guilt, and nothing's going to happen to them. And if I have some strange accident, like a truck hits me—you'll know why! Because if you step on people's toes, you can make dangerous enemies.... But if something happens—it *wasn't* an accident! Just like that CIA guy they found in the snow with his pants pulled down, in front of his cabin. He was the main prosecution witness for that CIA-Libya case with Frank Terpel. They said that he died from exposure—but all he had to do was break a window to get in. What a calling card—dead with your pants pulled down....

R/S: They don't even bother to cover up their crimes any more....

MONTE: They're just totally sloppy. But what can anyone do?

R/S: Most of these criminals are men; do you know of exceptional women criminals?

MONTE: There's the Manson girls; the Honeymoon Killers; Sara Jane Moore, who tried to shoot the President; the Baader-Meinhof gang, all the women involved in the SLA, etc. etc. There's more than they will admit; they don't want to *double* the amount of

Jim Jones the teenager.

Jones-aid: contains arsenic

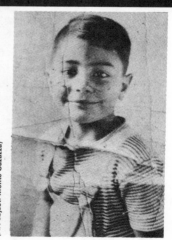

Jim Jones the boy.

At the same time, all these other maniac religious leaders—it's what *they* want, too. The thing that disturbed them about him was—Jonestown could have blown the whole ball game for everybody. But it didn't, because they squashed that fast. There were never any giant investigations into what went on—the government report should have been a *starter* report. But they realized there was too much at stake there—as far as I'm concerned they swept that under the rug fast, and nailed the rug down after they did.

There was too much at stake. There were a lot of government officials involved in that; a lot of integral relationships that were never talked about, that never came out. There are people running around now who

imaginative criminals. They're having *enough* trouble with all the lone male maniacs that are out there, without having lone females, and *couples* who are probably the most dangerous—they can watch each other's backs.

R/S: Male and female crime act—

MONTE: Myra Hindley and Ian Brady. None of this is very new—there have been ritualistic murders since Day One, and probably every other type also. There is a whole *industry* devoted to all that, so I'm not being all that macabre....

R/S: What about the vampire trial you attended?

MONTE: Jim Jocoy and I attended that. And we hope to be doing a more extensive article on that in the future. Believe me, he was a goner from the word go—the jury had made up their mind way before the trial was over to *hang him high!* They did. At the same time the Dan White trial was going on, and from my viewpoint this guy, Richard Chase—if *he* wasn't insane, nobody was. And Dan White gets to be found not guilty and insane and Richard Chase, who definitely was insane, was found guilty and sane and sentenced to the gas chamber. So it was pretty interesting watching these 2 cases occur at the same time.

R/S: I've read that the majority of criminals don't get caught.

MONTE: Some people don't get caught. But it's not a life I would recommend to anyone. If you're going to do that, you better have a *mental set* that you're not going to get caught. A lot of people do these things and they are sorry for them—they *want* to be punished, which is why they get caught. These days there seem to ·be a lot fewer criminals with integrity.

R/S: What do you mean by *integrity?*

MONTE: Well, it doesn't take much guts to snatch an old woman's purse. And any of these so-called bad dudes that are out there that think it does, are full of shit. And I've met many of them in my brief stays in jail, and they don't impress me one bit. I think there's a difference between doing that and appropriating something you may really need and use. Taking it from a store or larger institution than yourself is a lot more difficult, and requires a lot more intestinal fortitude than just victimizing someone who's weaker or

cation for getting it that way. I don't advocate *any* type of illegal activity, I think it's far better to not get involved in the legal process—as far as I'm concerned, jail is no place I want to be, nor do I want to see any of my friends in there. Etc. etc. etc. *You don't want to get involved in that process*—believe me, it is not worth it.

You have to know what your limitations are and work within those, and if fate happens to present you with a golden opportunity, well then you can make the most of it!

But it can also get to be a form of *addictive behavior*—which I think is very bad. That's what happened to me when I had my little business dealing cigarettes—it got to be so easy I was going totally mad. Walking out with ten cartons at once—*could I make it eleven?* That's probably why I got caught. When it starts becoming a form of addictive behavior, you should get out of that immediately. Because people can't control themselves. The trick is to not reach that point with whatever you're involved in.

It's really hard to maintain that balance, because you're not taught how to—you only learn from experience and from what other people can pass on to you. I mean, I think there should be informative booklets like, *What Is Stealing For? What Is Sex For? What Are Drugs For?* I think there should be more research into areas like that....

R/S: What *are* drugs for?

MONTE: I don't think chemicals should be used for

Sandy, Ouisch, Cathy, and Mary.

Myra Hindley

Ian Brady

more defenseless than you are. I don't recommend that people break the law. Then again, I don't *not* recommend that people break the law. It depends on the situation, what you're capable of and what you think you can get away with, and what you're going to do with what you appropriate. Sometimes you're just taking something that no one wants anyhow. If you're going to put it to much better use, I can see a certain type of logic to that. But I don't think you just take things to supply yourself with various thrills...biochemical entertainment.

If you need a certain tool in order to accomplish a certain project and the only way you can possibly get it is by appropriating it, then there might be some justifi-

entertainment purposes; I don't think that's their function.

R/S: Do you still do casualty simulation?

MONTE: Yes. Sleazy taught me things, and I keep practicing. You look at pictures in different books, and then try and make it look even better! Maybe more or less extreme depending on the situation. I'd like to be doing a lot more of that, but materials are expensive. If someone doing a film could really *pay me,* I could do a lot more....

R/S: What were you holding out on that poster?

MONTE: A cow's heart. I tried to procure a human one but I was under a deadline. Mine came from one of those UFO experiments...

R/S: What's your interest in dream images?

MONTE: A lot of my work comes from dream images, from dreams that I have, and a lot of my future work is going to come from that. Because it's an area that I'm interested in and pursue actively.

R/S: Do you keep notes?

MONTE: Yes, I keep journals, and I like to read other peoples' dreams. If people want to send in dreams and dream images.... A lot of my favorite filmmakers' films deal with that aspect of things—that's what I'm interested in.

R/S: Which filmmakers?

MONTE: Bunuel, Roman Polanski, Fellini, David Lynch, Kenneth Anger.... The people that I prefer—that's where their imagery comes from. A lot of it is based on reality, too, but it's also intermixed with all these things, just like your life is! When you're awake you're awake, and when you're sleeping you're having these *experiences* which in some cultures are considered more real than the ones you have when you're awake.

R/S: Like the Senoi of Malayasia.... When Boyd Rice was staying here, some of the most fun moments were getting up in the morning—he'd say, "Oh! I had this amazing dream...." How do you keep up the discipline of keeping a journal?

MONTE: I used to have a really big one, but one day in a fit of despair and anger I burnt it, which was a very bad loss for me.... You just have to try and force yourself. It's best to do it as soon as you wake up or shortly after—the most efficient way is to have it near where you sleep. You have to kind of *train yourself.* In the morning, if you remember it, write it down right away! Or at least turn on your tape recorder. Because what will happen later is you will totally forget it—*you will not be able to recall it.* I've forgotten about a lot of them; that's the way it works—you have to train yourself to record them, and it *is* hard. But you can increase the percentage of the ones you remember by writing them down.

There's one book called *Creative Dreaming* by Patricia Garfield—it's a little wishy-washy in some aspects, but it can give you a few pointers.

I believe that you *can* use dreams to solve some of your problems, and to try and manifest more of your *destiny.* It is not easy, and does not work 100% of the time, but *nothing* does. Nothing that is worth anything is easy—it doesn't always work, and is not the total answer—you can look at *anything* that way.

R/S: You mentioned an interesting word—*destiny.* How do you think people can have that manifested to them, and work toward fulfilling it?

MONTE: I think that you can, but you have to make very difficult decisions about whether you want to do

People's Temple Children's Black Light Discipline Room. (Photo: Jim Jocoy)

that or not! And you're going to have to pay a heavy price. And it is not pleasurable—it's *painful*. There's resistance—there's always resistance to anyone trying to manifest their destiny, even if they're trying to do it in the correct manner, because society is not structured to have people do that, and they don't want people to. That's my perception.

I'm just speaking for myself, *as always*. I'm not speaking for anyone else, or any philosophy, nor do I want any followers or adherents. Because collaboration is great, but I don't need any *fans!* I'm only interested in dealing with people on a collaborative or equal level. At any point in time, some people know more from experience than others, but you can still deal with people on an equal level, because *who knows?* Later on they may surpass what you're doing—which is always the goal. Then one is doing one's job. And it works out for everyone's benefit. It's like evolution—one long big chain, you have to keep it going.

R/S: That's the only aspect of mail art that appeared valuable—

MONTE: Yes, but I do not believe that it did, because a lot of those people had *no* conception of what they were doing—it became a fad. Genesis and I had a conversation about that—someone had said, "Well, do you have examples of your mail art?" Some of them I

Monte next to his Los Angeles environmental artwork forcibly exacted from convenient building wall. (Photo: Lynda Burdick)

have taken pictures of, but they were like *personal letters* that I made for specific people. I don't have them anymore—I didn't do them to print one thousand copies of them! They were *letters* that I did for specific people, on specific topics, for *that* person. They were not *art* to be put on some gallery wall or in some magazine. And I think all these people got confused with doing that, and having these big shows with just *anything* in it. Just because it was sent through the mail made it mail art, but it didn't necessarily make it of any value! I guess my viewpoint is more elitist than other people's, but that's the way I am.

R/S: I don't think it's *elitist,* I just think none of us have all the time in the world. We have our work that we really want to *do,* and we just want to get rid of every distraction—

MONTE: You do, and especially when people don't want to put any effort into it. I get a fair amount of mail from people, and I answer a lot of it, I'm not impossible to get ahold of. I make it a little bit difficult, but that's to separate people, because I don't have the constant amount of time necessary. There are certain people I have been writing to for a long time, but that's because they put *effort* into what they write to me. They don't just write to ask for things—they send things to me also. They enter into a *dialogue.*

R/S: Is it possible to state a reason for performing—or, your next live performance?

MONTE: Okay. I don't know. One, I could just be an egomaniac. Two, I'm just so disturbed that the only way I can not totally lose my mind is by *doing something.* I don't know. I try and structure events so that no 2 performances are ever exactly alike. It's just something I fell into and started doing, and I didn't have any ulterior motive.

R/S: Do you have any thoughts on developing the will?

MONTE: Yes, I think that psychology is half the battle. And probably anyone can do almost anything. It's just their lack of self-confidence, and derogatory training, that stops them. And it's a really sad fact that makes the world a much less interesting place. It's humanity's loss that this is still continuing to happen.

In some ways I've been lucky, just because of certain chances. But I also capitalized on those chances when they occurred, and tried to *recognize* them—but actually I've decided that I didn't capitalize on them enough!

You should be doing work because you *want* to do it. You think it's valuable and worth doing. And maybe it's just part of your personality. That's a really involved and very complicated question, and I don't really think there is one total answer; there's all these different types of answers that enter into it. And as Mark Pauline would say, "All work is dirty." It's all dirty work no matter what it is, and that's the way it is. If people don't realize that, and they are going to get into these forms of activity, they should stay out of them if they don't expect that. And they should not interfere in our work—because it's hard enough to do already. No one is writing you big checks—all along, what you've done is because *you* wanted to do it.

R/S: Well, isn't this a masochistic society?

MONTE: I want to take my rightful sadistic place! From my viewpoint of the people I know, whose work I appreciate, their reasons for working are not just money or status, but reasons that spring from their basic emotions. Reasons that money cannot buy! Because if it *doesn't* come from that, then all of this is for naught. . . .

(Brief Conversation Between Monte Cazazza, Henry Morgenthau Jr, Andrea Juno & Vale)

MONTE: Did you see NASA's projection for colonies in space, with golf courses and shopping centers?! That's the *last* thing I need....Do you read *Aviation Week and Space Technology?*

HENRY: Yes, they were the first to break the news about Russian particle beam weapons. The diagrams showed massive cylinders of metal surrounded by the beam projectors. If anything could start a war, it could be a breakthrough in anti-missile technology. Once a nation has a 99% kill rate on incoming missiles, it can get aggressive with impunity.

MONTE: Well if *you* built it first, you might decide, "We can have the first strike!"

HENRY: Everybody calls America imperialist, but at the end of WWII just about every other industrial nation was decimated and we were the ones with the atomic bomb. If we had really wanted world control, we could have taken it right then. We are the only country in the entire history of earth that had a wide-open chance at world domination—it was just sitting in our laps, but we let it go.

MONTE: If America had listened to General Patton, all the Russians would be speaking English now!

VALE: It's the propaganda war now. How do *you* think mind control works?

HENRY: Persuasion, subliminal advertising. It's impossible to inspect all the TV commercials frame by frame. They could be intersplicing pictures from porno films into ads for wonder bread and rice crispies. They did this in *The Exorcist,* so I heard. In the first edition of the film, they spliced in scenes of gruesome, bloody auto accidents from *Red Asphalt* and *Wheels of Tragedy.* People were getting physically sick because they were seeing these single frames spliced in. Supposedly the producer of the film admitted to the deed, and he took the frames out for the second release.

MONTE: In *Thief,* if you listen carefully you can hear very low frequencies that are used subliminally to create tension—just like you're right there stealing something. If you've ever stolen anything you'll *know* what I mean. It's a natural feeling you get in that adrenalin-high state. Those low cycles are quite dangerous, physically dangerous. They can affect your heart rate—if I had a computer and the time and the money I could probably give you a heart attack with sound.

Monte Cazazza and Cosey Fanni Tutti. (Photo: Genesis P-Orridge)

HENRY: You know resonant frequencies affect you. A troop of soldiers marching across a bridge can set up frequencies that shake the bridge apart. *Nikola Tesla* understood this completely. He said that given a low horsepower motorized pendulum swinging this little weight back and forth, he could shake down the tallest skyscraper in New York by putting it at the top and slowly building up the vibrations. Each body structure has its own resonant frequency which can be turned against it. Strobe lights tuned to the right frequency can make you nauseous. As a weapon you could aim ultrasound at people with a point transmitter and a parabolic reflector, and—

VALE: I thought strobes only affected epileptics—

HENRY: Strobes can synchronize with *anybody's* brainwaves. Epileptics are just *super-sensitive.*

VALE: Are you saying that epilepsy is a matter of degree?

HENRY: Right. There's grand mal epilepsy and petit mal. They can be induced in anyone. Epilepsy is hyperactive neural firing. That's why they cut the corpus callosum—to stop this uncontrolled firing from spreading. Television can do something like that too. The electron gun scans at a certain frequency that gets your brain into the alpha wave state. That's the relaxed state where you don't do too much thinking about what's coming in, you just integrate it.

VALE: Why aren't people who absorb lots of TV data smarter?

MONTE: Because of what they're programmed with.

HENRY: You're in that state being imprinted with bullshit—anti-perspirants and soaps. I'd like to think that the massive rush of data is helping people, but I read a study that correlated low intelligence with amount of TV watched.

MONTE: You've got to develop a hypercritical mind—

HENRY: That's like dodging arrows. I guess that if you can scan a tube and take the bullshit they throw at you and see how it's bullshit a million different ways (cause they're always trying to fool you)—that's good experience for living in the real world.

Bill Moyers went around to a lot of kindergarten kids and posed the question, "If you had to chose between never talking to your daddy again and never watching TV, which would you choose?" More than half of them would rather watch TV!

VALE: Can a computer read your mind yet?

HENRY: It's a question of receptor technology. They've found that when people think words, they actually move the muscles in their lips and tongue as though they were pronouncing the words out loud—it's just the *amplitude* is lower. Knowing that, you can infer neural firing in the motor cortex, and special electrical waveforms associated with each word thoughts.

I saw a demonstration with Rebecca Mahoney, a hot-shot computer programmer, sitting in front of a *CRT* wearing a hood which has a large number of disc electrodes on the inside. She can think simple words: *near far left right up down* and *stop* and the computer can analyze the *EEG* waveform and move a dot around on the screen in accordance with her wishes. Multiple electrode recordings allowed the computer to classify the waveforms with a high degree of success. It is actually the thought that produces the waveform which the computer can recognize. This is technological mental telepathy—even though it's limited, it's a beginning.

MONTE: Don't you think that some people are just extra-sensitive, and that's what mental telepathy really is?

HENRY: Definitely. Schizophrenics feel they are receiving radio transmissions from other people's brains, and that they are transmitting their own brain waves to others. They could be people with very good "neural hearing" who can hear sounds the rest of us don't hear.

ANDREA: Isn't there an invention which electronically monitors the eyes so that paraplegics can push buttons just by

A whole nation could be held hostage by their own genetic codes.

looking at them?

HENRY: I've seen the actual state-of-the-art devices at SRI. Dr. Hewitt Crane showed me his invention which is not only for wheelchair invalids but also for fighter plane pilots who look at their targets, then push a button to fire the missiles. That's probably the main reason it's being developed. How does it work? Your eyeball isn't a completely round sphere. The colored part of your eye sticks out a bit; that's why your contact lenses don't slip into the white part of the eye.

They can bounce infrared beams off that part of your eye, and by gathering and analyzing the patterns of reflected light, tell where you're looking in 3 dimensions. Since the shape of the lens changes to focus on near or far objects, the light reflected off the front and the light reflected off the back of the lens will form different patterns depending on the focal length.

They're making new discoveries in pupillometry; when you see something you like, your pupils will get dilated. They have pairs of pictures of girls, one unretouched and the other altered so as to have large pupils. Guys will always pick the girl with the dilated pupils. More attractive. If they want to find out if somebody's gay, show them a homo porn flick, and watch their pupils!

MONTE: Professional gamblers usually wear sunglasses so people can't check their pupils to see whether they have a good hand.

HENRY: These kind of technologies with military applications are usually kept quiet. They have satellites with optical technology capable of reading license plates and recognizing faces from orbit. If it's the best it's probably top secret.

VALE: What do you know about control by drugs, like hormones?

HENRY: Hormones by definition are the natural drugs of the body. They can't really make new hormones, but they can make new chemicals that mimic natural hormones, like birth control pills.

MONTE: The receptors in your brain are shaped to fit certain types of chemicals. Heroin works because it's similar to the brain's natural opiates—endorphins and enkephalins.

HENRY: Tranquilizers generally suppress neural activity. Any agent which is going to make it harder for a cell to fire, anything which raises the threshold at which firing occurs will depress central nervous system (CNS) activity. Shoot up speed, and there's a lot of firing. People on downers—a lot calmer. Too much speed can produce amphetamine psychosis.

VALE: How does genetic warfare work?

HENRY: It's possible to alter the genetic code with a virus, which works parasitically by inserting *its* genetic code into the nucleus of the cell, so that the cell starts using that code to make more viruses. Sometimes, instead of immediately making more viruses, the cell just incorporates the viral DNA code into its own, going into hibernation, and then 5 or 10 years later it can express itself. A cell which appears perfectly healthy can be a host for dormant infectious viruses. That's a basis for a delayed action genetic warfare agent.

If you're going to set up a country for destruction, you don't want to do it all at once, with people falling dead in the streets. You want something that's going to make them feel a little queasy, make their thought a little hazy, and do it continuously over a time period of months. A whole nation could be held hostage by their own genetic codes. Put it in the water supply....

MONTE: You never know about fluorides—

HENRY: That's something the right-wingers were right about. They didn't want fluorides perverting their precious bodily fluids. Involuntary medical treatment—I don't think that's right.

VALE: How does pain function neurologically?

MONTE: A lot of pain is a psychological interpretation of what under other conditions may not really be painful. Like exercising—there's a certain amount of pain associated with that, but it's not really pain.

VALE: The pleasure-pain equation.

HENRY: It was found that in the male monkey there were separate systems for erection, for ejaculation, and for orgasm. With an electrode in the separate orgasm system the monkey would stimulate this region and go through a total orgasm without erection and without ejaculation. Given the apparatus with which it could stimulate itself once every 3 minutes for 24 hours a day, the monkey stimulated this site and had orgasms once every 3 minutes for 16 hours, then slept 8 hours and started again the next day.

MONTE: Full time job.

HENRY: Sixteen hours—he's working a double shift. There's reports where the monkeys self-stimulated to total starvation. At the end they looked like concentration camp survivors.

MONTE: I have material telling how they tested the effects of the neutron bomb on monkeys. They built a big treadmill, had the monkeys wired up, and subjected them to neutron radiation. They put them on the treadmill and with electroshock kept them walking until they fell over dead. The idea was to find out how long soldiers could keep moving after they were exposed to neutron radiation. I'd like to see those films! See the flash, see them drop....

(For a report on relevant psychological experiments (recently published in a small edition by Monte, Henry, and Jim Jocoy) send $7 ($10 air foreign) to "Report" c/o Re/Search)

ADDITIONAL BIOGRAPHY

Monte is a necrophiliac in action. Rather than stifling his nightmares, he throws them in the face of the world. At the College of Arts and Crafts in Oakland, his first sculpture consisted of a cascade of cement that blocked the entrance of the school. He was dismissed the next day.

Passing from hospital into prison, he surfaced with pornographic collages in San Francisco. In 1971, invited to a weekend of conferences on art in the woods, he brought along an armed bodyguard and garnished the food with arsenic. At breakfast he dropped bricks painted with the word 'Dada' on the feet of people convened to eat. And at the dinner table he burned the partially decomposed, worm-infested body of a cat. His bodyguard blocked the exit and several guests fell sick from the stench.

In 1974, Genesis P-Orridge and Cosey Fanni Tutti were fascinated by a photo showing Monte covered with blood on the cover of *Vile Magazine*, vol. 1, no. 1, February 14 1985. Together, they fabricated the famous Gary Gilmore Memorial card, posing blindfolded on electric chairs. It was reproduced on T-shirts. Six thousand copies were sold in Britain; it was on the cover of the *Hong Kong Daily News*.

In 1977 Monte entered the studios of Industrial Records to record 'Plastic Surgery,' 'Busted Kneecaps,' 'Fistfuckers of America,' 'Hate,' and 'To Mom on Mother's Day.' His first 45 is out of print. A film was made with *Throbbing Gristle* where Monte and a 14-year-old boy were electrocuted. He plays also in the film *Deccadance* of Kerry Colonna with razor blades.

Monte seldom goes out, except on Halloween when he goes out with a cheap plastic mask, a green army bag filled with livers and hearts (like Hermann Nitsch) and the head of a bloody mannequin used by medical students to learn mouth-to-mouth resuscitation.

(Translated by Dalia Judowitz from New Wave *#13, available from Aline Richard, P.R. Bureau No. 93, 75010 Paris for 30 French Francs)*

DISCOGRAPHY:

TO MOM ON MOTHER'S DAY (45, Industrial Records, IR 005, 1979)
SOMETHING FOR NOBODY (EP, Industrial Records, IR 0010, 1980)
MONTE CAZAZZA LIVE (C60 cassette, Industrial Records, IRC 28, 1980)
CALIFORNIA BABYLON (LP, in collaboration with *Factrix;* $8 from Subterranean Records, 577 Valencia, San Francisco CA 94110; Sub 26, 1982)
STAIRWAY TO HELL (SS 45-007, special package with 45, $12 from Sordide Sentimental, B.P. 534, 76005 Rouen Cedex, France; 1982)

MONTE'S FILMOGRAPHY

REVOLT 2000. 1974 (stolen from Monte).
DIARY OF A RUBBER SLAVE. 1974 (stolen).
MONDO-HOMO. 1974 (stolen).
MYSTERY MOVIE (in collaboration with Cosey Fanni Tutti and Genesis P-Orridge, 1976)
DEATH WISH (in collaboration with Genesis P-Orridge and Peter Christopherson, 1977)
SXXX-80 (in collaboration with Tana Emmolo Smith, 1980)
BEHIND THE IRON CURTAIN (1980)

MONTE'S VIDEOTAPES

Videotape of performances at the SCALA CINEMA and Live at OUNDLE SCHOOL (write Industrial Records, 10 Martello St, London E.8, England)
NIGHT OF THE SUCCUBUS (write Box 977, Berkeley CA 94701; produced in collaboration with *Factrix*, 1981)

EXHIBITS/GROUP SHOWS

1) "New York Correspondance School Exhibition under the auspices of Ray Johnson." Whitney Museum. 1970. New York City, USA.
2) "Marcel Duchamp Club West," organized with Barry McCallion. San Bernardino Valley College. Oct-Nov 1971. San Bernardino, CA, USA.
3) Mostly Flowers Gallery. Mar-Apr 1973. San Francisco, CA, USA.
4) "International Encyclopedia." Anderson Gallery. May-June 1973. Richmond, VA, USA.
5) Wall Mural. National Research Library. 1973. Ottawa, Canada.
6) "Exhibition of Degenerate Art." Done in collaboration with Stuart Horn at the South Street Gallery. Pornography, violence, sex posters plastered all over; reconstructions of crime scenes left on streets. Apr-May 1974. Philadelphia, PA, USA.
7) Hayward Annual Show. Curated by Genesis P-Orridge at the Hayward Art Museum (Arts Council of Great Britain). Room with 3 reading tables, each displaying a large book filled with correspondence from Skot Armst, Monte Cazazza, Al Ackerman (The Blasters). Collages, photos, news clippings, personal writing, small objects, assemblages—some letters 3'x4' in size. Lines of people waited to read the correspondence (which only proves that people love gossip). July-Aug 1979. London, England.

from the desk of MONTE CAZAZZA

REQUEST LIST

If you have any personal experience with or know of sources of: audio tapes, films, video, photos, slides, documents, manuals or artifacts, on or about:
★ Self-Defense ★ Magic ★ Psychic Phenomena ★ Dream Imagery ★ Pornography ★ Survivalism ★ Weapons ★ Hypnosis ★ Murder and Death Rites ★ Religious & Other Cults ★ Terrorism ★ Electronic Devices ★ Animal & Human Experimentation ★ Ecological & Corporate Disasters & Accidents ★ Medical Mutations ★ Subliminal & Psychological Methods of Control ★ Chem-Germ Warfare ★ etc. etc. ★ Particularly desired is tape or LP of *Language of the Wolves* in very good condition.

I would be interested in receiving them and will put this information to good use. If used for a public event, appropriate credit will be acknowledged. For forthcoming concerts I especially need tapes of children, wild animals, environmental events and sexually explicit behavior.

Send to: PO Box 977
             Berkeley, CA 94701 USA

PERFORMANCE ART EVENTS

GUERRILLA ART. Street activities and events. For example, molotov cocktails left on street. Large display titled "Defend Yourself!" featured board with knives stuck in it (free for the taking). Mannikins dressed as winos and bag people left in alleys, with hidden cheap cassette recorders playing tape loops of screams and ranting and raving. Spring 1972. Oakland, CA, USA.
ONE THOUSAND DOLLAR PROPOSITION. June 1973. Censored.
FUTURIST SINTESI. Galeria 591. Sex-religious show; giant statue of Jesus got chainsawed and gang-raped into oblivion. Dec 21, 1975. San Francisco, CA, USA.
OUR FRIENDS THE SIAMESE TWINS. Shattuck Ave. Studios. Lecture with medical slides featuring live demonstration of quick separation of Siamese twins. May 16, 1976. Berkeley, CA, USA.
RADIO AND TV ASSEMBLAGE AND DANCE. Shattuck Ave. Studios. Giant wall construction of televisions and radios playing for 3 days (& nights) straight. June 25, 1976. Berkeley, CA, USA.
MANIC MOVEMENT. Collaboration with Kimberly Rae. Berkeley Square. Kim tied up on spring-mounted platform; Monte appears squirming on floor in black body bag, cuts self out, cuts Kim loose, then destroys toys and props with hatchet to loud Romper Room record. Ended in fire. Jan 30, 1981. Berkeley, CA, USA.

CONCERTS/MUSIC

F. CLUB, with *Throbbing Gristle* and *Clock DVA*. Tapes, synthesizer, processed voices including recording of the Leeds Ripper. Tana Emmolo on guitar. First music performance. Feb 24, 1980. Leeds, England.
SCALA CINEMA, with *Throbbing Gristle* and the *Leather Nun*. All night *Industrial Records* concert, with films of William S. Burroughs, Brion Gysin, Kenneth Anger, Otto Muhl and Herman Nitsch. Tana Emmolo in collaboration. Feb 29, 1980. London, England.
OUNDLE SCHOOL, with *Throbbing Gristle*. Performance in main lecture hall of all-boys school. Special subliminal sex tapes; a near riot; documented by video. March 16, 1980. Oundle, England.
KEZAR PAVILION. Performance spectacular with *Mark Pauline* and *Factrix*. First time working with *Mark*. War machines; spinning swastika with Monte inside; Scott & Beth B films; also showing of "Behind The Iron Curtain" by Monte. Dec 6, 1980. San Francisco, CA USA.
BERKELEY SQUARE. Guest appearance with *Factrix*. All music, more sedate show. Dec 12, 1980. Berkeley, CA.
ED MOCK DANCE STUDIO. "Night of the Succubus" in collaboration with *Factrix*. Films, slides, organic robots, dance by Kimberly Rae, dart gun used for first time by Monte, electro-shock, dental surgery on dead animal-machine. Member of audience angrily attacked 'rabot' with chair, shouting that it wasn't 'erotic.' Video available. June 6, 1981. San Francisco, CA USA.
L.A. PRESS CLUB, in collaboration with *Factrix*. Show featured medical and Hiroshima slides, projections and slides by Ruby Ray, and a new electronic torture device, *The Tingler*. Two people fainted from viewing "SXXX-80." Sept 4, 1981. Los Angeles, CA USA.

REFERENCE

SOME BOOKS

(This booklist represents only a small section of my library)

by William S. Burroughs:
Naked Lunch
Soft Machine
Ticket That Exploded
The Job
etc. etc.

by Brion Gysin:
Brion Gysin Let The Mice In
Here To Go
The Third Mind

by Daniel Mannix:
The Hellfire Club
The History of Torture
Those About To Die
Memoirs of a Sword Swallower
The Beast (on Crowley)

by Lord Russell of Liverpool:
Scourge of the Swastika
Knights of Bushido

by Colin Wilson:
The Occult
The Outsider
Order of Assassins

by Peter Beard:
Eyelids of Morning
End of the Game

by Yukio Mishima:
Forbidden Colors
Sun and Steel

Six Years With God/E.Mills
The Strongest Poison/Mark Lane
Suicide Cult/Kilduff & Javers
The Assassination of Leo J. Ryan
   and the Jonestown, Guyana, Tragedy
Executioner's Song/N.Mailer
The Case of Mary Bell/Gitta Sereny
Theory & Practice of Hell/Eugene Kogon
House of Dolls/Ka Tzetnik
Diaries of Joseph Goebbels
The Loves of Adolph Hitler/
   Gerald McKnight
Inside the Third Reich/Albert Speer
Spear of Destiny/Trevor Ravenscroft
Our Lady of the Flowers &
Thief's Journal/Jean Genet
Music for Chameleons/Truman Capote
The Exorcist/William Blatty
Samuel Fuller/Nicholas Garnham
Velvet Underground/Michael Leigh
Farouk/Michael Stern
Satyricon/Petronius
Extremism U.S.A./John Carpenter
Helter Skelter/Vincent Bugliosi
The Family/Ed Sanders
Killing of Sharon Tate
Child of Satan/Child of God by
   Susan Atkins
My Life With Charles Manson/
   Paul Watkins
Assassin's Diary/Arthur Bremer
Mass Murder in Houston/John Gurwell
Man with The Candy/Jack Olsen
Colour Atlas of Forensic Pathology
Colour Atlas of Human Anatomy

Transvestism/David O. Caudwell
Sexual Secrets/Douglass & Slinger
Novo Vision/Yves Adrien
Andy Warhol's Index Book
Andy Warhol: Stockholm Exhibition
Pornographia/Staeck

SHOTGUN NEWS $15 subscription from Box 669, Hastings NE 68901.

CAZAZZA IN PRINT

-Schmuck #1, 12/72. Beau Geste Press, Great Britain.
-File, vol 1 #2-3, 1972. Toronto, Canada.
-8x10 Art Portfolio, 6/72. NY, NY.
-Fluxshoe, 9/72. Beau Geste Press, Arts Council, Great Britain.
-N.Y.C.S. Weekly Breeder, Vol 3 #3, 1972.
-International Image Exchange Directory, 1972. Talon Books, Canada.
-N.Y.C.S. Weekly Breeder, Vol 3 #6, 1973. San Francisco, CA.
-One Thousand Dollar Proposition, 1973.
-All Star Correspondants Calendar, 1974. Pub by Stuart Horn.
-Vile #1 (Cover), 2/74. San Francisco, CA.
-Nitrous Oxide #1 (Editor). 1974.
-Ovum, 6/74. Uruguay.
-Strange Faeces #15, 1975. U.S.A.
-Wet Tip Reports (Co-author with Judith Bell), 1975.

-Vile, Vol 3 #1, 12/75. San Francisco, CA.
-''White House Cancer'' (Author). 1976.
-''Thirteen Tragic Tales'' (Author). 3/76.
-Hong Kong Standard (front page), 3/8/77.
-Vile, vol 3 #2, 1977. San Francisco, CA.
-Time, 1977.
-Nitrous Oxide #2 (Editor). 11/77.
-File, vol 3 #4, 1977. Toronto, Canada.
-Virus, Winter 1977. Montreal, Canada.
-Sordide Sentimental, 12/77. Rouen, France.
-Widows and Orphans #5, Winter-Spring 77-78. Pub by Jim Jocoy.
-Widows and Orphans Calendar, 1978. Pub by Jim Jocoy, Sunnyvale CA.
-A Salute To Jacqueline Kennedy, 1978.
-Industrial News, 6/78. Pub by Industrial Records, London, England.
-Entropy-Intermedia, Vol 2 #1, 1978. San Francisco, CA.
-Widows and Orphans #6 (with Tana Emmolo & Jim Jocoy), 1978.
-Mr. Prolong, 1/79.
-Primary Sources #3, 1979. London, Eng.
-Industrial News (Special edition prepared for Hayward Annual). London, England.
-Industrial News, 9/3/79. Pub by Industrial Records, London, Eng.
-Blue Booklet, 1979.
-Slash, vol 3 #5, 1980. World Update (Intv with Mark Pauline & intv with Factrix). Los Angeles, CA.
-Industrial News, 11/4/80. Pub by Industrial Records, London, England.
-Isolation Intellectuelle #0, 1980. Rouen, France.
-Re/Search #2, 1981. San Francisco, CA.
-Re/Search #3, 1981. San Francisco, CA.

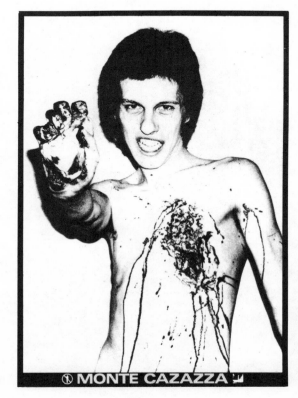

⊗ MONTE CAZAZZA ⏻

ACKNOWLEDGEMENT

"I want to express my appreciation to the following people. Without their support I would have not been able to continue: Throbbing Gristle esp. Genesis P-Orridge, Factrix, Tana Emmolo, Ric & Cheryl Soloway, Subterranean Records, Sordide Sentimental, Marzy Quayzar, Deviation Social, and Mark Pauline.

"Basically I think the idea of putting out this issue of and on Industrial Culture is beating a dead horse. While all of the various people involved were doing their initial work, they were paid very little attention—just met with dishonest animosity. However, resistance does make one stronger and keeps one on the right track....

"It is really only after the fact that bandwagon jumpers have decided to hitch a ride on our little virus. Well, if people think it is for fun or entertainment, they are in for a bad surprise....

I'm not here to publicly educate people, especially when they are too lazy to go out and educate themselves or make any attempt to do so. When all they want to do is sit home and watch TV and play video games, and elect second-rate actors for president....

I did this article mainly because of Vale's persuasion and involvement and for my own mercenary interests, in order to continue work which stems from rebellion. At this point in time I personally consider the sum total of my work to equal only failure. I am not interested in other people's opinions on this subject, nor do I need their approval for my continued existence; time shall vindicate me."
—Monte Cazazza

SORDIDE SENTIMENTAL

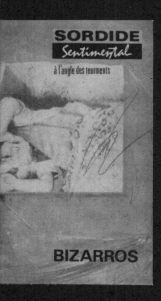

Jean-Pierre Turmel

The mind is greedy for information, its morbid hunger is gargantuan. Our eyes, ears and all our senses are like so many maelstroms sucking reality into these inner chasms whose depths we cannot plumb.

Preceding pages: Artwork and Photo by *Sordide Sentimental.*

Sordide Sentimental (literally sentimental sordidness) is more than a small avant-garde record company—their personal creativity saturates everything they have released. Beginning in 1976 they premiered graphics by the subsequently famous/influential *Bazooka* group, issued the first records by *Throbbing Gristle* and *Joy Division,* all the while maintaining a perversely high standard of philosophic content in their unusual, limited edition packages. Subsequent records reflected an almost incongruous variety of musical choices—from extremely primitive rock to sophisticated synthesizer productions.

Each record was accompanied by a strikingly designed folder, a warning, a thought-provoking text, graphics, sometimes a color print—all enclosed in an 8½x11" plastic pouch. To date the series cumulatively represents a most individual achievement—destined for appreciation by individuals . . . .

Disdaining Paris as needlessly bustling and vapid, Jean-Pierre Turmel and Yves Von Bontee prefer the late medieval splendor of Rouen, a town of 100 cathedrals, several preserved alchemists' homes, and the L'Aitre Saint-Maclou, a rectangular courtyard carved with a vast frieze of macabre objects—hundreds of skulls, bones and similarly sinister symbols commemorating the Black Plague of 1348. It's difficult to fault their decision—there are enough old bookstores, record stores, cheese, wine and food shops to supply a demanding connoisseur. Jean-Pierre is a gourmet cook and wine expert—if anything, *Sordide Sentimental* reflects the sensibility of a post-rock'n'roll Huysmans . . . .

In this interview, Jean-Pierre and Yves reveal some motives and insights to Andrea Juno and Vale . . . .

JPT: It is difficult to think of history as progress. Maybe it is, maybe it is not—who can decide?
R/S: Maybe some progress is made, in the sense that penicillin can save a lot of lives . . . but then new viruses develop that are resistant to penicillin. Syphilis may be gone but herpes is here.
JPT: We have new technology but man himself is always the same—a sort of ape completely controlled by something inside him he can't understand, something more animal.
YVES: But the man now on earth is not the same as the one who was there 2000 years ago. There is an interrelation between the technology created by man and the man—through that you can have a kind of evolution.
JPT: Perhaps. I always say perhaps— *no certitude!*
YVES: Whether it's good or it's bad, it's an evolution. You can't stop it.
JPT: We could also ask the question: who needs the sense of history? Because our life is very short. So, do you feel really human? Do you feel yourself part of humanity? For myself, I feel completely outside. So in that sense, a sense of history means nothing.
YVES: I don't know what "humanity" means.

JPT: I know—humanity means *the rest!* I am a completely egocentric person.

R/S: That ought to be made a first condition of education—training to feel apart from humanity.

YVES: Everything people talk about is perhaps true and perhaps wrong. You have to take in the world and not just consider the words in themselves. When you use words, you use them with "meaning" but also you use them with your own experience, your own symbols, your complex imagination, dreams, everything. People will receive that. . .but they also don't receive that at all.

When I am writing, most of the time I try to stop in the middle of a sentence, just to try to oblige people to continue the sentence with their own imagination, and to work with the meaning. I hate people only wanting to receive, who don't want to give anything, who don't want to participate. You stop, and that is all.

When I write for myself (in my journal), I'm writing in French and I stop writing in French and write in German, and then I stop writing in German and put an English word into a German sentence, and I mix it up. I put my own experience into words and if it sounds better in German, I do that.

R/S: It might be funny to compile a list of half-sentences that anyone could finish as soon as they read the first few words—a lot of our communication could be reduced to those.

JPT: Yes. It's an interesting game to play with a group of people. They may be discussing one subject, and at one moment everything seems to be okay. Suddenly you ask them, "You talk about this [concept] — what does it mean?" And one by one, what you see is that each person has a different definition of the concept. Finally, it seems that they understood each other, but in fact it was complete illusion.

Often people use words as slogans, but they don't really *know* the exact sense of the terms, the words. For instance, if you ask people, Tell me, what is a fascist? you will have one hundred definitions (or more). And if you tell them, A fascist is one who wants to destroy capitalism, they will say, Oh, you are crazy! But it's true—that's found in texts—fascists wanted to destroy capitalism. So, where is reality?

YVES: Yesterday I was in Germany and an 80-year-old man told me, "Yes, there is a great difference between fascism which was Mussolini's, and Hitler's which was National Socialist. Hitler's wasn't fascism."

JPT: In a way he was right, because "fascism" came from the word *fascio* which is an Italian word. Always the same problem: words are the basis of all illusions.

R/S: I think one of the big problems today, which J.G. Ballard has illuminated, is that the myths that really matter, that affect people the most powerfully, are not the ones held up that we ordinarily think of as myths. For example, the space program, the car crash death, the great collective myth of the coming nuclear destruction—one doesn't necessarily regard these as *myths*.

JPT: I like very much Ballard—he really sees the world like a forest of symbols, myths and so on. He describes worlds which are mythological worlds. The new gods are not very different from the gods of antiquity—for instance, the movie stars, monsters, everything like that.

R/S: He's brought precise medical and scientific terms into the vocabulary—

JPT: I like the fact that behind the man you always see the animal. And the difference is very thin.

I think a good question would be to ask: What is the difference between man, and the new man—

R/S: If there can be one—

JPT: Because we can't ask now what is the difference between animal and human. Everybody is trying to answer those questions, but there is no real answer.

R/S: Ancient Egyptians had an interesting model to explain the diverse abilities humans display; each animal represented a principle of nature, or *neter,* and humans embodied different neters—not necessarily just one, although usually one predominated.

JPT: Some humans are very intelligent with a little brain, and some humans with big brains are complete idiots. What is the conclusion? An elephant has a very big brain—

YVES: But it doesn't have any cortex.

JPT: I like very much theories. Theory is a pleasure in itself. I like theories not because they reflect the truth—

R/S: Oh, *theories*—I thought you said fairies!

JPT: Most of the time theories are fairies! That's excellent—you have a very good unconscious.

R/S: That's part of the big game—to gain more and more access to the unconscious, where creativity comes out of—

JPT: Yes.

YVES: I like theory too, because it's used to destroy the meat—

JPT: —of reality, of the truth.

YVES: We use it in a simple way. We are always building lots of theories with which we can destroy reality, to make a splash.

JPT: When somebody asked Epicurus a question, he used to give 10 or more answers, saying to the person, *Choose.* It is astonishing to me that this simple evidence was known in the past, thousands of years ago, but it's not still understood by people. It's more than a problem of culture—the problem is they refuse. Something which is very constant is imbecility, and you can do nothing against that.

YVES: People don't want to find themselves.

R/S: Because people are taught to be lazy and to be satisfied too easily?

JPT: Yes, and also, they are afraid of everything, by the facts of life. If you tell them there are many answers to one question, they are afraid—there is no stability, they are walking on quicksand. Even the ecologists who seem to be very intelligent, positive and so on—finally, what is their vision of the world? It's a vision of an ecology which is completely *fixed,* without any evolution. So it's crazy, it's not an ecology, it's only conservatism. Use the right words!

And it seems that each time you are trying to open a door, there are one thousand people who shut it. And in fact they are very intelligent; all these people know they can't destroy these new ideas, but they know that the best way to attack the ideas themselves is to change the orientation of the idea in a negative way, always. The only conclusion is always to escape from the masses—always.

It's always the same game of hide-and-seek from them. One of the other conclusions we find in *Sordide*

Sentimental is that you can't really use logical argumentation, logical arguments. The only way to try to change things is to attack on the very subliminal level, the level that they can't understand. If they understand, it's finished!

For instance, the punk movement. First, most people reject that because they don't understand. Little by little they understand, so it was not very dangerous. They can take it and change it, because they knew it.

There is something interesting in the *I Ching* which says if you want to convince your enemy, be your

> I personally think that *theory* is the most important aspect of our civilization—everything, every moment in our life, is only *theory*. People don't really live, they first need a reason, an explanation, to hate or to like. For most people, a thing without theory does not even exist.

enemy first. Be inside your enemy, inside his logic. After, you can change him like you want. And it's the same for any concept. And it's what the masses are doing: first they reject—that's the good moment of any revolution. It's the moment when they don't understand. But after, once they understand, it's finished!

YVES: They take what they want from it, change it, and project back, feed it back, diluted.

JPT: I like very much the ideas of *SPK* about subliminal influences. To use very important words—you choose a word and put it in place very carefully in a special place in the text, so all the influence is on this word, but people read it and notice nothing. But that word is in their heads. You can do it also with images. Finally, that is what we are trying to do more and more. Often it works.

R/S: Is that your theory of music too?

YVES: We have many theories of music.

JPT: I should want to play music; it's a question of time and room.

YVES: It would be interesting to only play *fou* music—music for brain-damaged people. Most of these brain-damaged people are put away from society; people don't want to hear from them, or see them; they think they are sick and dangerous.

R/S: There have been shows of paintings that have traveled around—*art of the insane, art brut*. But *music* of the insane—that's hardly been publicized.

JPT: The question we could ask is, what do we mean by music? Because for people music is first to go on stage and play in front of a mass of people. But it could be something else. You could do, for instance, only records. You could do, of course, only music for yourself without any records. There are different questions. If it is only music for myself—like I was saying, I

have a lot of things I would like to express. And I would like to compose, but finally, for myself. The problem of the stage is completely different, because you are confronting, literally, the problem of the masses. They are in front of you, and what will you do?

My position now is to use a new weapon: *deception*. And it's also a new weapon that Genesis uses. I'm interested in the final results. The interest in deception is: when people are deceived, suddenly they don't protect themselves. Their defenses are dropped—

R/S: Because you distracted them and slipped in another way.

JPT: So, it's the ideal moment to send some disturbing concept in. It's a new way I'm trying to explore.

R/S: How can you use deception?

JPT: For instance, you are saying something which seems not very extraordinary—people are awaiting something brilliant, and you give them something grey. They don't understand, and their reaction is to think, Oh, they are really boring. But at the end you put something short but really disturbing—an idea. This is dangerous for them.

R/S: The confusion principle.

JPT: Look, for instance, at the people in front of *Throbbing Gristle*. Little by little they are accustomed to provocation, to aggressivity, things like that. At the end, people are proud. So it's finished! You have to do something else. Most bands, what are they doing? They are trying to do more and more, but it's failure. Apart from the fact that most bands are boring now, finally, they are not boring enough!

YVES: Most of the time they are on a stage to promote a record, nothing else—

R/S: A most boring motive.

JPT: The problem is to give an interesting deception. It's not easy, it's very difficult. The only way is to develop the concept of evidences. There is a deception in the audience when they say, It's evident! By that they mean banal, obvious. But often most evident things are not banal. On the contrary they are very important, but it is these important things that people reject. So maybe one way is to write again, say again, all these evidences. For instance to say, There is no perfect theory. If you say that to people, they say, Yes, it's evident.

R/S: While they're buying imperfect theories all the time in the form of books and records!

JPT: People always expect you to do one thing; if you do something else . . . .

YVES: But it takes a lot of time and energy to do something else—

JPT: Yes, there is the risk of saturation. Personally I like very much playing this game of hide-and-seek. It's very fun.

R/S: What do you think of the theory that there's a sort of bell curve to almost every creative project—everything has its beginning, ascendancy, peak and decline? That you can't keep doing *anything* very long?

JPT: That's true. Most people are very afraid of decline; they are afraid to be without a new fashion. If they don't have a new fashion, it's horrible—life stops suddenly. For us, it's not important. There is no new movement—it's not important; we continue.

YVES: We have enough energy to do something for

ourselves. Most people need food—either music food or image food or TV food—they just want to be fed! But there is no food anymore. What can they do? Go to church and pray?

JPT: Take the rock critics in the newspapers. When there is a new very clear movement like the punk movement, it is fantastic for them because they have no anxiety, it's perfect. Life has a sense—there is a fashion. Suddenly the punk movement goes down.

YVES: What can they say? What can they do?

JPT: They are completely obsessed with what is new now. What is it, and where is it? And the anxiety is so strong that they create, themselves, anything.

R/S: New Romanticism this month, Rap Music next—

JPT: Anything only for one week. Like a junkie, if you have not your normal drug, you take anything. Most people, they are junkies. And from time to time they don't have their drug, so they take anything.

We used to accuse the record companies of doing uninteresting fashions. But everybody is accomplices—the audience, the record company, the rock critics, all have the same interest—they need a new fashion, all of them. This is the major obsession of the rock market: what will be the future? Horrible....

YVES: And they always say how nice the past was.

JPT: The rock movement is interesting because it's a micro-society. It's easier to analyze, but in fact it's the same. About the stage, the fact to play on stage—I think that's very important, because there is a religious dimension to the fact of going on stage. God is dead, but we still need a religion, and rock is a religion. It needs its martyrs—

R/S: And rituals. When you say we need a religion, do you think there are more creative substitutes for rock as a religion?

JPT: What is the need of any religion? To communicate with the gods. What are the gods? The gods are inside us. It's always the same problem.

When the human speaks, he often says the contrary of reality. Often. So when he speaks about the heaven, in fact he is speaking about inside. I can say the contrary of the same sentence I said just a few minutes ago, and suddenly it seems true—it's often like that.

It's often interesting to play this joke: you take any affirmation, and completely say the opposite. Often you are very surprised by the result—often it seems more appropriate. This is not far from the Zen system of absurd communication. Somebody says a word, another person says something completely different, and suddenly something springs into view—

R/S: A psychic leap.

YVES: We are so conditioned to avoid the real problems that often it's very simple—if you take the contrary you find what is true.

JPT: Yes, it's alchemical. I think it's the *Zohar* which said what is up-side is like what is down-side.

R/S: "As above, so below"—by the legendary Hermes Trismegistus. How *do* you think people can evolve faster?

JPT: I'm just trying to make evolve a very small number of persons, no more. Because I think for the rest it's finished! If I try I shall destroy myself, it's too much. Some people say that *Sordide Sentimental* is elitist. Yes, in a way it's elitist, because we are not trying to give a solution to everybody.

YVES: We just want to be ourselves.

JPT: We are sending some words here and there, and from time to time there is a good reply. That's all. And I think it's fantastic. For the rest—give me a reason to do something for these people. What are they doing for me—nothing but trying to make me a slave.

R/S: But once in a while you meet someone like my friend who's very young, 15 and—

JPT: Very young? You need to start much earlier—the most important years are the first 3 years! The difference between the old and the young is that the young have more energy. That's the only difference—the old ones are tired, so they stop to agitate. The young ones are not doing anything, they are just agitated, so they follow the first one who makes movement in pure imitation—no real expression.

We have a very interesting man in France called Henri Laborit (author of *Decoding the Human Message,* about biochemical processes of the brain). He helped the filmmaker Alain Resnais with the film *Mon Oncle d'Amerique.* The writer's a biologist who found an anti-anxiety drug, among other things. One time I saw an interview with him on TV. They projected some films about new youth, young people who are "doing things," and the man who did the interview asked him: "They're more interesting, aren't they?" Suddenly Laborit laughed: "Oh—they're completely idiots, like the others!" Little by little he destroyed completely everything the young people were doing—that they were only imitators doing bullshit, and so on. It was

Monte Cazazza Record Package Art (ptg on glass): Mark Beyer

MONTE CAZAZZA

art: loulou picasso-bazooka.

completely depressing for the interviewer, but for me it was really exciting!

There was another interview in Cannes in which Laborit explained everything about Resnais' film. At the end, his conclusion was again to smile and say, "Anyway, that film will have absolutely no consequence about the evolution of humanity."

You can say to people what are the problems. But nothing works. I'm not sure—maybe the solution is subliminal influences. Maybe it's the only way—to work with the symbols.

R/S: The advertisers spend millions and seem to think it works—why not turn it toward a more ideological reorientation?

JPT: The last election in France 2 years ago was proof of the strength of subliminal influence. In fact the elections were completely absurd; people don't vote for anything reasonable, they vote for a dream. The person who wins is the person who gives the strongest dream. But you need to be intelligent—if you tell them, "I will give you twice as much money," they will go, "Oh...." You have to be more subtle, for instance: "We give you an image of a France that is very quiet. This is our dream: a quiet, peaceful France." And it

works. The late President gave them numbers; technical, logical things, and people looking at the TV said: "Oh, it's boring." (He lost.)

In fact, the only work for a politician is to find new dreams. In politics, like everywhere, there is a fashion. From time to time the fashion is to give technological information. And after, it will be to give a dream. It's only a question of fashion.

We have been very influenced by the *Internationale Situationniste.* We try to continue in this vein.

R/S: When you were talking about deception—that seemed to be originated in practice by the situationists. In San Francisco, 1973, they plastered the city with official-looking posters with the mayor's seal and phone number, entitled DID YOU EVER FEEL LIKE STEALING EVERYTHING? and offering a free "I Like To Shop" button and a free $50 coupon toward the purchase of anything if you came down to the mayor's office. The mayor's phone was jammed by calls.

JPT: The situationists saw we are living in a society of consumers. Consuming is more than consuming objects; we are also consuming more abstract things, and fashion is one of the most important.

R/S: Fashionable attitudes, likes and dislikes—

JPT: We could say also that we are living in a world of theory. People need theory for anything—a theory for the weekend, a theory for what to drink, what to wear, what to eat. Suddenly you see everybody in the street jogging—I think that will change as they begin to have some problem with their legs, heart, and so on. Everything is like that.

I have no particular theory about food, except we need good food without many additives. But what to eat—I have no theory. I am trying to listen to my own body. Suddenly if you like to eat something you have not eaten for many years—like one month ago I had the desire to put vinegar with potatoes; suddenly it was very attractive to me. A few months before it was with a very special cheese, *gruyere,* which I don't like very much—it seems tasteless. The problem, again, is to fight conditioning.

The human is very flexible; he can eat nearly everything. Of course, some things are more or less interesting.

R/S: Diet for an Industrial Culture—

JPT: It's not an industrial culture, it's an industrial *life!*

R/S: That's right, you work in industry as a worker in a gas refinery.

JPT: Many years, for Shell Oil. Now I'm behind a desk, with buttons, alarms, and so on—we are living in a science-fiction novel! In my life, my industrial life is not far from a certain asceticism, because physically it's very hard for the nervous system. And you can compare it with the asceticism of the saints who for instance stopped eating, stopped drinking, stopped sleeping, to try to find a very special level of consciousness—or unconsciousness. That's the problem—what is the definition of this very special level? Is it still consciousness, or *unconsciousness?* We are between them, like a robber....

When you are very tired, suddenly images come from the inside to your conscious spontaneously. And I notice that after holidays, I was completely unable & incapable to write the texts—I needed to go back to the factory and be very tired. So I can say that for me, industry is something very close to mysticism!

The separation between creative life and the other is not so clear. It was clear at the beginning—my reasons were rational: I prefer to separate my creative life from my job only for the money. But after a few years, I noticed it was not separated. I noticed this industrial life was necessary for my production. So now I can't stop, because I have the feeling that if I stop, my ideas will stop.

R/S: Didn't you refuse the offer of being fully paid for editing a science-fiction magazine?

JPT: My reason was: it would be necessary for me to meet persons I don't really need to meet. Or *want*. It's not a need and it's not a desire, so—I think it's horrible, and very limiting for yourself. And very destructive—you oblige yourself to do something you don't want. I think that's the worst alienation, because *you have still the illusion of doing something you like!*

If you are going to the factory, you know that's something painful. You are not going to the factory telling yourself you are doing something fantastic. You know exactly what you are doing—you know it's for the money. It's a very evident form of prostitution, but very clear. Finally, I want to be clear with myself, I'm trying to be clear. What I saw in the professional fields (for instance science fiction, rock magazines, and so on) are some people who finally were not very happy to be doing what they were doing. And at the same time they were proclaiming they were doing what they wanted. I say they are lying! They can lie to other persons, but the worst thing is they lie to themselves.

R/S: Their vision is clouded by notions of glamor—they think they're doing their creative work, *writing,* and getting paid as well. Of course, they never question the *content* of what they write.

JPT: There is also the specific fact of their own vision of what is a critic—a critic of science fiction or a critic of rock. For them, finally, it's a failure. Because most of them wanted to be a science-fiction writer or a musician in a band. So in their mind, to write a text about somebody else is horrible.

In fact, it's very interesting—to write articles is a real way of expression, like doing a novel. For instance, when Huysmans wrote some critical articles about art, he was really creative·in his texts—not a simple critic with a small c, but *text.* It was something important, it must be important. But what we see is—all these critics are only doing *paraphrase*—

YVES: "The slide guitar is good, and the synthesizer works okay, and the first song has this kind of tempo and...."

JPT: That's all. it's bullshit.

YVES: No new information.

JPT: The best critics give information; the others are only trying to—I don't know. I think the only way is to use what you critique as a stepping-stone for yourself to go elsewhere. You need to do more, not only describe. Most critics are only vampires—they take but do not give.

YVES: Quick writing—

R/S: Like fast food. They stay away from real ideas.

JPT: Where is the information? You can't give a definition of information—information *about what?* They can't avoid the subjective, but they pretend to be objective. And it's untrue. So, confronted with this problem, we decided to be completely subjective.

YVES: Anytime you use words, you *are* subjective. You use words in your own way; you can't be objective.

JPT: We don't give people direct information. For instance, we don't say "they began there"..."at that moment"....and so on. Often we talk about something else. And finally, everything goes to the same point, because things are not separated.

R/S: What is the theory of transparency?

JPT: Why that's transparent!

YVES: To say what you want to say, what you mean exactly. For example, we could say we are doing *Sordide Sentimental* to bring people more information, to show off more art. In fact it's not true—we say it's for ourselves. Most people don't say that. We do that for ourselves.

JPT: For instance, transparency for *Throbbing Gristle* is to say, We are also people who drink tea. Because that's not obvious for most people.

But it's something else, the theory of transparency. In my mind, it's also a way to control people.

YVES: You say what you want to do so people know what you want to do.

JPT: For two reasons. We notice that for instance you can say to somebody, I am a crook. Finally you do it, and the fact that you tell him that you are a crook doesn't stop anything. But another consequence of the theory of transparency is that we pretend to say the truth. But what is truth? There is no truth. So finally, we are obliged to say that we are still trying to control people. So perhaps the ultimate consequence is that there is nothing transparent!

I said to Genesis: "You have been too much influenced by this theory." Because he doesn't notice all the consequences of the theory. Yes, in *appearance* he seems to be transparent; for instance, in his problem with Cosey he was very "transparent"; he said things are like *that,* and like *that.* But was it really the

> In this world we make everything a sign: the network of correspondences is infinite and it's that which feeds the major illusion of the real and·its definitions.

truth? We can't be sure. The only true thing behind what he was saying was that he wanted to control Cosey again. That was the only *sure* thing. So I talked to him: *"Stop to use this theory."* That was last year.

But it's also very interesting to use as a joke to play. It's good training for yourself, but you need to be very careful, because the *illusion* is so easy.

R/S: You can take the theory of transparency to a point of self-justifying godhood, where you think you're so pure, so transparent, that you can't even recognize your own most devious power motives.

JPT: You said the word, *pure.* There is in Genesis, behind the fact he pretends to be the devil, the fact that he wants to be pure. That's why I talked with him about the concept of the scapegoat, because he wants to be the innocent victim; he wants to be pure.

R/S: When reading books about Jonestown, I noticed how often Jim Jones would predict repression was going to fall upon the church—how he would even have members fire guns outside the meetings and then announce, "They're here; they're going to kill us all now! But I can save us!" I'm sure you've read about all those control tricks.

JPT: There are many aspects to this theory. For instance, if you pretend to be something which you are not—if you pretend to be a "rocker" yet you come from a very bourgeois society—if you tell people you come from a high society it's okay. Not as a provocation, very simply. Suddenly you are transparent; people will not notice you. But people always notice people who don't accept what they are. So this is a good aspect of the theory; the conclusion is you need to know exactly what it is you are trying to know. Of course, that's not completely possible, but....

Genesis accepted being a different person. He used part of my letter in a magazine [*Vox #12*]:

> "An individual has many personalities or characters at the same time or alternatively (recent cognitive brain theory supports this). Most people little by little eliminate the personalities considered to be dangerous by their peer group or societal unit and finally keep only one: the social personality...one dimensional, 'flat' people. But other people, called paradoxically 'individuals,' are always trying to develop all their personalities, even if there's an internal conflict between them. So we can clearly see that the individualist person logically must use 'we' to name himself whilst the person who belongs to the masses must use the 'I'. The first is multi-dimensional, the second is uni-dimensional."

I use a sort of paradox—it's a joke with words.

The conclusion of Genesis: "One of the Temple functions is to encourage and support the development of multi-dimensional individuals. Hence our use of the 'we' in our texts. Our enemies are flat."

R/S: *Enemies*—hardly anyone knows they exist!

JPT: Yes. I am obsessed by what is the nature of this limit of separation between the conscious and the unconscious. Because we have not a precise idea. How can you imagine this limit—is it a wall, a no man's land?

R/S: I visualize it as a chain-link fence; a net of repressions—

JPT: Yes; I am trying to find a symbol for this.

R/S: Sometime there are big holes in the net; mostly there are small holes.

JPT: Is it like the surface of the separation between air and water, or is it something like glass? And why at some moments does this limit seem to be permanent? I'm obsessed by this problem; for me the door is the symbol of passage from the conscious to the unconscious. How to open the door? Maybe with drugs, maybe with fatigue. The true thing is that the separation is not so absolute.

R/S: You can get a glimpse of a vision or an idea at the oddest time—walking down the street, some little detail can trigger it. You get an idea and then you catch that idea and work on it.

JPT: That's why the situationists said it was good to walk down the street. They said it was the first political thing to do....

Yves von Bontee in J-P Turmel's living room. (Photo: Andrea Juno)

THE ILLUSION OF OBJECTIVITY

"The first difficulty that man encounters...is to look things straight in the face: HIS BELIEF IN WORDS MUST BE TORN TO PIECES." (Korzybski)

Among the things which plague the "suffering" human species, it seems to us that his attitude towards *language* is one of the most heretic: while he seems to continue to pose himself certain questions on his existential belief or beliefs, he accepts as an axiom the innate and immovable quality of this language which he considers to be unique, and even as a tool, or rather a semblance of a tool of communication. Not that we argue about its necessity in the expression of individuality, of intercommunication, or the manipulation of abstractions and cultural transmission, but rather the restriction of its use to a farce of communication embedded in the iron-clad rites of "good" thinking, of egalitarianism, of pseudo-civism, of monotheism, making it a rigid structure, the servant of some pretense of a unique "truth."

The structure of this language, too often considered to be self-evident, reflects that of the world as it is—or was perceived by those who have developed it; projected into the world, it is unavoidably retroactive, although unconscious or voluntarily hidden. It is responsible for that monolithic system of double-values which supports, and imprisons words which are then *fixed* in a binary system, thus excluding them from any further influence. It ends up in the monopoly of that pretense of a unique "truth," notably upheld by monotheistic religions which are responsible for a real cultural, intellectual, and spiritual imperialism; furthermore it creates a childish mentality through identification, normalization and sense of security with it...and finally ends up by restricting our perceptions.

The absence of any analysis concerning the mechanisms which finish in the elaboration of the language partly explains this blind belief in the word; it is enough to note the concurrent phenomena in the structuralization of the word to show its necessary *subjectivity*. In fact, whatever may be the element or primary event which wishes to be ex-pressed (note the idea of pressure) is situated at infinitely varied levels of "reality": be it external or internal, microscopic or macroscopic...this event is first of all *perceived*, then transformed into a secondary message which is transported to the nerve centers which *integrate* it before the final stage occurs: the production of vocalization. The intervention of perception, bringing into play the various senses which are hence difficult to isolate with any rigor, that of the brain which in the same way works on the primary event, giving it color according to its feelings, passions, anguish and education... up until the eventual metamorphosis, which is dependent on the *individual*, the unique, in whom intervenes a certain determinism, partly influenced by education; a genetic, cultural, socioeconomic determinism which furthermore undergoes an evolution in time.

On the basis of this evidence, any belief in a unique, timeless, objective language, supporting a state of double values, is precarious. It thus becomes necessary to *beware* words, to permanently—but "intelligently"—*unlearn* Education, to protect the *individual* by a selective *isolation*, based on a perpetual re-creation; to have a progressive graduation (thus working against the knife of the double-value system), to be un-safe, to hold a multitude of truths (thus working against The One Truth) with a temporal projection which is no longer linear, having an evolution towards the infinite, but one which is in spiral form.

"We, Sordide Sentimental, are projecting through the medium of our publications, our vision, our doubts and incertitudes, our internal and external conflicts, our loves and our hates...we manipulate, in order to justify our expectations and pre-suppositions, our "realities."

—Yves von Bontee (tr by Malcolm Duff)
Hamburg-Rouen, Sept-Oct 1982

REFERENCE

DISCOGRAPHY

SORDIDE SENTIMENTAL SOMMAIRE (BOOK). 62p book, out of print.

THROBBING GRISTLE: We Hate You Little Girls/Five Knuckle Shuffle. 1977. Out of print.

JOY DIVISION: Atmosphere/Dead Souls. Out of print.

BILLY SYNTH: Hartzdale Drive Destruction/Indigestion.

ISOLATION INTELLECTUELLE No. 0. collages. Out of print.

ISOLATION INTELLECTUELLE No 1. Ptôse Production: Women In The Moon. For Danny Dupic.

BIZARROS: The Cube/Underground.

DURUTTI COLUMN: Enigma/Danny.

TUXEDO MOON: Une Nuit Au Fond De La Frayere/Egypt.

ISOLATION INTELLECTUELLE No 2. Blameless Act: Ado (Humain Trop Humain) Untermenschen/Blameless Act.

MONTE CAZAZZA: Stairway To Hell/Sex Is No Emergency.

(all limited edition packages 40 French Francs from: Sordide Sentimental, B.P. 534, 76005 Rouen Cedex, France. Do not inquire about out-of-print packages.)

SOME VIDEOTAPES
LIBRARY OF JEAN-PIERRE TURMEL

Some Call It Loving/John B Harris
The Shout/Jerzy Skolimowski
Heart of Glass/Werner Herzog
Apocalypse Now/Coppola
Night of the Hunter/Chas Laughton
Eraserhead/David Lynch
Glissement Progressif du Plaisir/
  Alain Robbe-Grillet
Dehors, Dedans/Alain Fleisher
Pandora/Albert Lewin
A Bigger Splash/Jack Hazan
Pirates and Warriors/Kung Hu
A Touch of Zen
Le Cri du Sorcerier
Teenage Sex
Femme ou Demon/Jonas Middleton
Shogun Assassin/Kenji Misumi & R Houston
Solaris/Andrei Tarkovsky
Stalker
2001/Kubrick
The Great Gatsby/Jack Clayton
Dernier le Porte Verte
Naked Prey/Cornel Wilde
The Mother & the Whore/Jean Eustache
Celine & Julie Go Boating/J Rivette
Children of Paradise/Marcel Carne
Je T'aime, moi non plus/Serge Gainsbourg
All films/Kenneth Anger

SOME RECORDS/PRE-1976

All Records by:
The Seeds
Tom Rapp & Pearls Before Swine
The Third Ear Band (UK)
Silver Apples
Mayo Thompson & Red Krayola
Mandrake Memorial
Neu (Germany)
Gene Vincent
The Trashmen
13th Floor Elevator
Comus (UK)
Beacon Street Union
Twice as Much (UK)
The Troggs
Them (UK)
Velvet Underground
Pink Floyd with Syd Barrett
Captain Beefheart
Egg (UK)
Chocolate Watch Band
The Head Shop

SOME RECORDS/AFTER 1976
ONLY OBSCURE BANDS

Bunny & The Lakers (Canada)
Raw War 45 (early Diodes, Canada)
Systematics (Australia)
The Maker of the Dead Travels Fast
  (Australia)
EST (Australia)
Son of Sam/Chain Gang
TC Matic (Belgium)
Coitus Int (Netherlands)
Aroma Plus (Berlin)
Debris/Static Disposal (USA)
Savage Republic (USA)
Home Comfort/Mark Glynne & Bart Zwier
  (Netherlands)
Circle X Internationale (USA)
Husker Du (USA)
Ballet Mecanique (Denmark)

SOME BOOKS
LIBRARY OF JEAN-PIERRE TURMEL

(Huge Science Fiction Collection)
Là-Bas/J K Huysmans
Against Nature/J K Huysmans
Ste Lydwine de Schiedam/J K Huysmans
Roberte Ce Soir/Pierre Klossowski
Le Souffleur/Pierre Klossowski
Sade Mon Prochain/Pierre Klossowski
Short Stories/Giovanni Papini
The Torture Garden/Octave Mirbeau
The Soft Machine/William S Burroughs
Ubik/Philip K Dick
3 Stigmata of Palmer Eldritch/P K Dick
La Jongleuse/Rachilde
Diary of a Seducer/Kierkegaard
Précis de Décomposition/Cioran
The Ego and His Own/Max Stirner
Mass Psychology of Fascism/Wilhelm Reich
The Crystal World/JG Ballard
Night Squad/David Goodis
City of the Dead/Herberth Lieberman
Story of the Eye/Georges Bataille
L'éroticism/Georges Bataille
Hollywood Babylon/Kenneth Anger
Kitsch/Gillo Dorfles et al
Encyclopedia of Symbolisme
Panorama of Science Fiction
History of Science Fiction
History of Nazi Cinema
Écran Démonaique
Les Tatouistes
Pictorial History of Sex in the Movies
Pictorial History of Strip-tease
Histoire de Science Fiction Moderne/Sadoul
100 Years of Science Fiction Illustration
Hier L'an 2000/Jacques Sadoul
Monstres et Vampires
Le Sexualité
L'homme et ses idoles
Mummies of Guanajuato
Fantastic Engravings of Wendell Dieterle
Barbarella
Histoire de L'Insolite
Amour, Érotisme et Cinéma/Ado Kyrou
Le Dossier Hitler
Hitler et Ses Femmes
L'enfer Nazi
Hans Bellmer
Pour Tuer les Temps
Le Musée des Supplices
Le Musée des Vampyres
Le Musée de la Bestialité
Le Musée du Fétichisme
L'art de Dessin Animé
Obliques/de Sade
Obliques/Bellmer
Masochisme au Cinema
Sex à L'Écran
Les Mathematiques
Juliette/de Sade

SPK

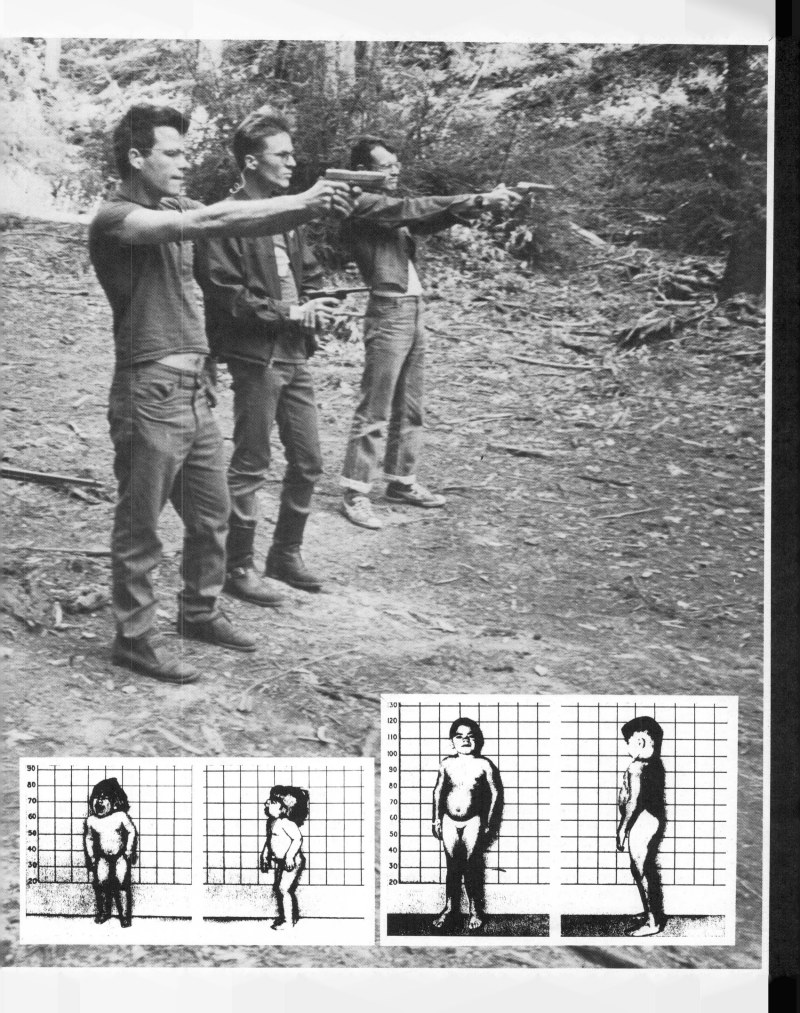

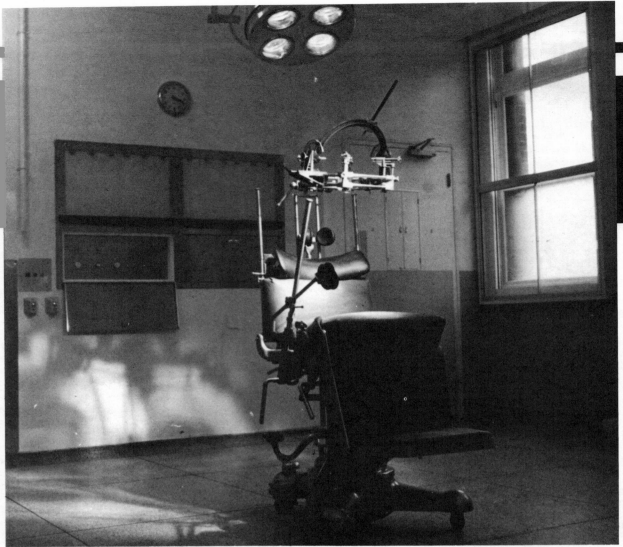

Above photo: Andrew Hickinbotham. Previous pages: artwork courtesy SPK; photo L to R: SPK member, Mark Pauline, Matt Heckert, SPK member, by Vale. All artwork throughout: courtesy SPK.

The name *SPK* derives from a group of mental patients in West Germany who, inspired by the Baader-Meinhof, set up their own terrorist unit with a slogan *Kill Kill Kill For Inner Peace And Mental Health.* This group, the *Socialist Patients Kollektiv,* blew themselves up while trying to make bombs in their mental hospital.

Since 1978, *SPK* has been the *nom-en-hommage* of an Australian entity revolving around one person now living in London. The "group" has released 2 LPs, 6 singles, 2 pamphlets, cassettes and a videocassette, and has made several tours of Europe and America. Their graphics are *graphic*—the front cover of the *Industrial Records* 45 was a photograph of a shish-kebabed male organ with the title *Meat Processing Section* by *Surgical Penis Klinik.* It was not generally displayed in record stores.

In San Francisco they distinguished themselves by eating brains from a sheep's head (1981), and by using a live flamethrower onstage (1982), inadvertently setting a member of the audience on fire. In concert, their relentless sonic assaults are complemented by vivid (as in blood red) color slides, video and film projections. Definitely sensational, but memorable.

In the near future *SPK* plans to release psycho-probes into the soundtrack medium, troublesome videos, as well as more research reports on the proliferating epidemiology of mental and emotional disturbances. What follows is an interview with Graeme Revell, plus Dominic Guerin, James Pinker and Karel van Bergen, an aggregate for *SPK's* 1982 U.S. tour . . . .

> "The Russians were reported to have used succinyl chlorine on Israeli prisoners in Syria, 1973. The victim feels himself dying for lack of oxygen, although the effect is transitory, but there is then the threat of a repeat experience.

R/S: Can you explain why in your work you present images from forensic pathology, venereal disease and hardcore sex?

SPK: I'm not so interested in sex images. Hardcore porn usually seems to follow certain *obvious* lines. Like there's always some kind of power relationship going on, even in sexual perversion—especially so here, because it's heightened. Probably the *a la mode* variant of the moment is SM—I guess that's been a la mode since the 1700s...

R/S: Now some major publisher is trying to launch a *middle-class* S&M magazine—

SPK: That's just a kind of mirror of an almost archaic society—porn is like a spectacle state society in microcosm, and that's why I don't find it very interesting, really. To come back to Freud, even though I don't agree much with all that Freud says, *death* is a great deal more powerful than sex, or at least as powerful. And there's a real fascination with images of yourself as dead, or images of others as dead. Today, even, when I was shooting guns with Mark Pauline I was quite terrified of what they can actually do: you're just holding this little lump of metal in your hand, and having seen forensic photos and things like that, you can all of a sudden imagine just one tiny slip-up in half a second and some guy's got a fucking red hole out the back and he's dead, you know. Somebody—it could even be a friend. That kind of image is really basic dream material, I think. And to actually see it, especially in a fairly clinical sense, not in one of these B-grade movies' violence-for-the-hell-of-it sense, is very striking. It is to me, anyway.

Plus a lot of what we're doing is dirt, is filth, and we live in a society that pretends to be exceptionally clean. It cleans up everything, it paints facades and makes things shiny and bright. I think the unifying theme is that we are very conscious that whenever there's a winner in a clean society, there's a filthy loser as well. But that tends to be just shoved away either in a back ward or a jail or a back street or a dirty little squatter, whatever you call it here.

We have got this childish, if you like, fascination with the genre—it may not be childish but I will always admit that I am fascinated at looking at it, for probably not very noble motives. A reasoning behind that fascination may be that we feel as though we are hitting at the soft underbelly of society...at an area where there's a great deal of vulnerability. And people often criticize us for being negative, but it's just a *focus of attention*.

There's another reason behind our medical interests specifically, and that is the pretentiousness of science. There are some things which science does:

testing procedures, all kinds of procedures which are not at all different from *rites*. And in several years' time they *will* be looked upon as bizarre rites, simply because of the techniques involved. We're just trying to put ourselves ahead, say 5 or 10 years depending on the acceleration-of-history factor, so we can look at them, thinking, My God, how stupid....Yet this pretends to be the state of the art; *this* is what humanity has achieved. We look back on old medical procedures now and we think bleeding, and the putting of typhus victims in hot baths—the old Tchaikovsky stove—

R/S: What's that?

SPK: They used to throw TB victims into boiling hot water and if they survived, it *might* get rid of the TB. They did that to Tchaikovsky's mother when he was very young, and that's why he deliberately drank infected water at one stage of his life and more or less committed suicide (and they threw him into the bath as well). We're trying to exhibit that kind of thing and show how close to magic it is. In a lot of ways we're not trying to say it's ridiculous, we're just trying to question the idea of *truth* associated with it, and isolate its mechanisms, its obsession with empirical verification of everything—that nothing can be true unless you can see it to be true. Because this acts to the detriment of the *imaginative faculties* which could come up with something in a surrealist sense (or whatever sense you like), but because it's only *art*, it's never accorded the value of other "truth" like sciences.

People think: Oh yes, that's interesting, but we would never actually form any belief in an *art*. But I think great art is the equivalent of science—you can believe in it equally as much as you can in science. It's very important to *believe* in the power of the imagination, and not just let the rationalistic function, the logical side of the brain, dominate.

R/S: Don't you think the roots of this comes from a convergence of scientific research and art? If you're reading *Maldoror* which was written over a hundred years ago, it's obvious that Lautreamont had completed a certain amount of scientific study, in biology at least, before he elaborated imaginatively...

SPK: All the way through 20th century art that's been very important. Our whole project is to independently get our sound production to a kind of a research stage where we *can* be totally precise about everything we do—do everything with a laboratory perspective. The same as *Mark Pauline* was talking about today: he says he's only just getting to the stage where he can almost challenge military-technological development using layman's technology—show that they're not the only ones that can do it. Obviously he can't get to nuclear technology, but he *can* build a helicopter, for example; he *can* build his own laser. And it's just to *de-institutionalize* the process of science, and to link it with art. I just hope the process can continue without requiring enormous sums of money.

R/S: Back to the problem of using medical images—some people think you're just trying to raise people's threshold of shockability—

SPK: That's really just a function of novelty...a strangeness index. We find that somebody who's been exposed to those sort of images for a few months doesn't really get shocked by anything at all. And none of that affects me like one particular guy in the mental hospital I used to have to wake up every morning. He had gangrene all through his body. He couldn't speak, and he had a leg and an arm on one side and nothing on the other side. He used to have pressure sores all over him because he sat all the time in a wheelchair, and he'd shit and piss himself in bed every night. So every day I'd pull back the covers and there'd be this pile of feces—a foul smell at 6 in the morning. I had to pick him up and get all this shit over my arms and chest—there was no other way to do it—and take him down to his bath and desperately try and—can you imagine how difficult it is to put somebody in a bath when they haven't got anything on one side of their body to hold them with? So each time he'd tend to twist and fall and go in headfirst. And if he heard a female voice he'd scream at the top of his lungs.

R/S: He didn't want any women to see him in that state—

SPK: That's right. That was the ultimate for me—there's nothing that's ever remotely bothered me since!

R/S: Another accusation made is—you're just engaged in criticizing society, but you have no positive suggestions, or *vision* to offer.

SPK: I think that's shortsighted to a very large extent. When we first started playing, I can't really think of many other bands who attempted to put out fairly uninterpretable noise walls like we do—probably only *TG*. So we were characterized as being *just like TG*. We thought we didn't sound very much like them at all; in fact we desperately tried *not* to sound like them.

Now, what happens when people first come across this sort of thing is: they can't differentiate between products like that, or between ideas. I think our sounds are an attempt to give an impression of a different world order. And we were being *critical,* but we were also trying to be *positive* in the sense of trying to put in a lot of energy, because one of the things we were criticizing was *apathy*. And, we were giving impressions of *different landscapes*.

Also, being positive is not just *our* problem—it's the listener's as well. And we can put in a lot of energy, we can create *our* landscape, but if they can't see any differentiation, if they just find that whole thing anti-music (which we don't think we are), then I guess we've failed to a certain extent. But then I think they've failed as well to understand what we're doing.

I think our visuals reflect a bizarre world view...a sense of beauty in the bizarre. We're not totally stoic, depressive types who forbid anyone to have an idea of beauty, but what we do reject is any aesthetic idea which is dictated to us either by a convention, or a social more or anything like that—most of that's just Tinsel Town stuff, or overly stylized...it's just all watered down—it doesn't bear *any* relationship to any *real unconscious processes*. That's why in a way we don't really tamper with any of the images, we don't bring that kind of conscious learned art into it. We *do* do collages, but more recently we haven't been—reality seems to be sufficient. And I think there's a beauty in everything—me personally, I'm trying to surround myself with a kind of a world I would like to live in (even though I couldn't live in it). A Fellini or Jodorowsky landscape or something rather more obscure, inhabited by freaks—just so everything wasn't so fucking *normalized* all the time!

R/S: How do you relate your work to Dada?

SPK: I think that in all great movements there is an immense process of ideas very early; they get watered down in such a hurry, and don't get developed either. What happens is: the ideas get swamped in the products. The thing that annoyed me about Dada was that even though they were attacking the bourgeoisie, they were entrenched—doing it with a kind of flippant looseness. It wasn't precise enough. I'd like to show how a line can be developed from then to now, probably visually more than any other way. *Man Ray's* photographic work is just brilliant—

R/S: As well as the result of accident—

SPK: The solarization was completely accidental.

R/S: But it was his recognition of its potential that mattered, not so much the accident.

SPK: So—there's a great deal still to be done, especially with film and video. That's what we really want to work on.

R/S: There's still so much potential, especially in film collage, *moving* collage. Max Ernst took the collage to an advanced development, yet he never used modern photographs, or modern scientific photographs.

SPK: I've always been very conscious that the most important thing about collage or Cut-ups is *what* you're cutting up. There is such an immense amount of material still to be cut up. After this bloody obsession with structuralism that we've had to go through in the 60s and early 70s, finally people are deciding that we've got to get *content* back into the thing, somehow.

And, most important, our work will be centered around the idea of an *inorganic unconscious*. I really enjoyed that short story by *J.G. Ballard* where he re-wrote the horoscope, saying, "We've got to get rid of these Chaldean farmyard animals." That's a really important realization: that the *modern* unconscious *must* be different from the blood-shit-piss-organic-womb-phobias Freudian-associated neurotic gamut unconscious of yesterday. We've still got a large organic hangover.

But, say if you were writing a prelude to a description of the insanity of a future society, you can easily imagine what all the psychos of tomorrow will have running around in their brains. You've got a lot now—radars controlling them, radioactivity, brainwaves being read, stuff like that, that hasn't really been *developed* yet! There's an immense scope there for future collage ideas, that also ties together dreams, the unconscious, madness. (But everyone's mad in a sense.)

So, I hope we can work towards a kind of formalizing the pluralistic possibilities; to open up the space for a much wider range of unconscious delusions and artis-tic/creative inter-possibilities....

Something you find all the way through philosophy is a basic idea of *primum moveos:* there is something in man that causes him to try to transcend himself. One of the big questions in philosophy seems to be why man alone seems to be like this. So, when you encounter the idea of man as, say, the desiring

> Hypnotism, brain implants, drugs, ultrasound etc do exist, but really think that control as direct physical imposition is nothing compared to *soft consent* problem. Fact is, 99% of the population don't *need* to be controlled....

machines in Deleuze, I think that was limiting the idea to one kind of description. I didn't think that desire need be couched in terms of machine imagery. Then again Duchamp had quite a machine idea; he designed senseless machines, bachelor machines. A sad sardonicism in that.

R/S: Which of your aims do you feel is most difficult?

SPK: Something that I would personally like to achieve is the ability *not* to be able to discriminate between quantities of beauty. For example, making love with what appears to be a very beautiful woman and making love with a pinhead or mongoloid: ques-tioning the differentiation in the sense of being able to overcome it. There might be an erotic fascination for making love with a "freak," but I think there's always that mental discrimination. I like to question *every* idea of beauty, but I think that seems to be one that's almost impossible to get around. *Fetus Productions* was showing pictures of deformed children and ques-tioning the idea of Miss Universe, but as far as their own personal experience went, they never did any-thing to prove they believed their theories. And I think it's important to show how you can live in the idea.

R/S: The world's still ruled by the idea of eugenics—

SPK: Even though it changes subtly. Over a very short period of time (about 10 years), the model of a female body changes. Twenties skinny, Thirties quite plump, Fifties large breasts—Marilyn Monroe, Sixties thin again, Seventies getting taller. And maybe the very erotic response is dominated by that kind of motiva-tion. It's disgusting really, but there's so much media overkill that even an intelligent person can't get around it. I guess we're just an extremely visually-oriented species at present in our development; our aural faculties are very, very poor. Certainly smell is almost ruled out—by pollution, body sprays and a mil-lion varieties of soap.... We can distinguish fuck-all as far as hearing goes—the minute you get any kind of noise signal coming in, the 20th century human being is still quite poor at translating that into any kind of meaning...

R/S: What do you think is the value of so-called primitive cultures?

SPK: Of course, to us the *Aboriginals* are very close. If you look at the Australian aborigine, they're almost decimated. I don't think another culture in the world's had their society destroyed like that—thousands were hunted down like animals. The Tasmanian aborigine didn't even know how to use fire, and *that's* primitive. I don't think there's another one being discovered any-where who didn't know how to use fire, and it gets *cold* there.

R/S: Mastery of fire required some kind of intuitive leap. Everyone's trying to develop their instincts—that faculty by which you make intuitive leaps....

SPK: I think that the area of archetypes is one of the most important ones to look into—Jungian, post-Jungian.... A French anthropologist called Durand (whom I'm very influenced by) has this idea of arche-types as types of movement, as dynamic processes, rather than static forms of information. If you apply that to the unconscious, you *could* do something by looking at primitive societies and seeing how they reason, or *un*-reason, and come up with something different. Yet to leave everything to spontaneity is inimical to me. I've never been a great fan of spontaneity—I think you get a lot of rubbish turning up.

R/S: Then again you can also have the trance state—

SPK: Sometimes, sometimes. But sometimes a lot of drivel comes out of it! It needs to be directed in some way. This is the problem: I never feel *anti-*rationality—I don't think we should go into *irrational-ity* pure and simple. That's just the back side of the mirror—you can't see much there. In a way, you have to be quite rational to be irrational, or to be consist-ently so, anyway. You've got to really look at logic—you get pre-rational consistency theorems, things that seem to have some claim to truth. I think logic's an important area of study—it claims to precede mathe-matics and be a complete science—there is nothing you can do with it, therefore it must be true. Hopefully someone will come along and disprove the whole thing!

R/S: The problem with logic is the often-present x factor; often there are not enough information bits to begin with.

SPK: Right. There're also the well-known *paradoxes,*

97

which are sort of unprovable, like Russell's paradox. And I read in an article on Artificial Intelligence about a problem which is basically this: whatever you think of, there's always something outside that which doesn't fit in with what you've just thought of, that can annihilate it.

I don't know; I would just hope that this whole "Industrial Counterculture" can have the ability to actually become a guerilla movement in some way, a propagandist guerilla movement, instead of just another little set of ideas.

R/S: Basically you look at the people actually involved: very individualistic yet—

SPK: All quite cooperative in a way, as long as they don't have to live on top of each other—have meetings, and shit like that.

R/S: And some are conspicuously able to defend the convolutions of their careers—

SPK: A lot of that is the ability to rationalize yourself out of awkward questions...there's a lot of *ex post* justification of things that really you do just for the hell of it. Most of the people are sort of smiling when they come up with some kind of justification—there's a lot of humor that goes on. It's just the ability to handle the required argument systems...while continuing to entertain.... *Entertainment*—now there's a loaded word!

R/S: I think true entertainment involves new information or new angles or new ideas. There are thousands of new patents taken out every year—somebody should start a weekly maga-zine dealing with the patents taken out *that week,* just taken as ideas. The context could be the pleasure of invention.... I'm sure Mark Pauline gets a certain satisfaction out of piecing together meat and metal parts and a motor to create an entity, a rabot or centipede that actually works, that's got a life of its own—its own biorhythm, or bio-mechanoid rhythm....

SPK: Robot terrorists, for technical mayhem! No, I don't think they'd make great terrorists. To be a terrorist you've got to have a good publicity organ—a public voice and public opinion. And that's where the Red Brigades succeeded where the Baader-Meinhof didn't. They're precise—they don't blow up anybody that they're not trying to blow up. They don't put bombs in rubbish bins on trains—they go up to a guy and they knock him off, like the Mafia does. And they've usually got some bloody good reason. And from what I've read, they've usually got all the symbolic implications— when they kidnapped Moro they took him from a certain place like the Fountain of Youth to the Place of Death in Italy. It was beautiful the way they organized it—

R/S: Poetry and revolution—in the best sense!

SPK Yes, it's a great shame they'll have to come to an end eventually. In fact it's a shame that they have to do it at all, but I guess they have a lot of fun doing it as well.

R/S: A short and exciting life.

SPK: *Mark Pauline* came up with the statement that he thought wars were fun! I said, Well what about Vietnam—isn't there a difference between that

Brickworks, Australia.

and . . .? He said he guessed so, but he still liked the *idea*—the gratuitous violence, out-and-out instinctual killing. That's something I find very, very questionable. I don't care if bloody America runs around killing itself, but to wander off into another country where it's got no fucking business and kill the natives for no apparent reason, is totally beyond. . . .

I'm definitely anti-violence. Even though we might *show* violence, I think it's in a *negative* sense. I'd rather there were no violence. Given that there is, Malcolm X said once: "Violence is neither right nor wrong, it's an aspect of the situation." Since there *is* violence, obviously there has to be more—in order to counter it. I think that's the way society gets away with a hell of a lot: it pretends to be passive with respect to violence when in fact it's committing atrocities all the time—but they're hidden. And that's a lot of what *SPK's* got to do with it. We're showing *their* atrocity exhibition, whereas they don't choose to show it, even though they perpetrate it all the time. Such as when they try to make juxtapositions with accepted things, like drugs to mental patients, while the same drugs with the same side effects, when administered to soldiers, is the ultimate horror.

Also, the idea of distinctions between hardcore pornography and soft-core pornography—if you do linguistic analyses you find just the same situation in both, men and women in the same situation, except the softcore stuff is a lot more subliminal—it's *more* dangerous in a way because of that. I find most of the *soft* things, the ordinary things that go on in a society, like advertising, quite atrocious—they're an atrocity on *my* brain, that's for sure. I feel as though I'm being needled all the time, from everything that comes in. It's possible to say I'm exaggerating, but really, if you have got a kind of self-respect for your own intelligence and your own ability to think, this sort of thing coming in at you *all* the time is insane.

Of course, any person who's *adjusted* can deal with it—that's what adjustment's called—filtering, really. Obviously you can't get away from it. I stay at home, I don't watch television, but it's always there, you know it's there. Every person wears it all over themself, and you can't get away from yourself. It's a paranoid unconscious space we live in.

Art brut painters like *Robert Gie* whose painting I love—I always think: God, what would it be like to be a psycho, and to actually be able to *hear* all this crap over the airwaves all the time, and to not be able to get away from it. Imaginary or real, it doesn't make any difference—if you could hear, say, KUSF 24 hours a day, rattling away at your brain. . . . I guess we must thank 'god' that we are *not* telepaths—what would we be hearing? If it was just drivel it wouldn't be worth it.

R/S: Why do you like *Art Brut?*

SPK: Because it's so original. A lot of the trends in art have been pointed to, often very much before they became popular. And very unself-unconsciously, very primevally in a way, usually from no knowledge position.

R/S: No *verbalized* theory—

SPK: Just a perfectly sort of naive artistic attitute in a way, but still in a weird way reflecting the times. But I think even more are the little landscapes that are painted so accurately. I suppose all art is about the unconscious, really.

I respect *Dubuffet* for what he did—giving up his career, just devoting himself to be a researcher, collecting all that stuff. He tours it around Europe all the time.

Art brut is not necessarily *mad* art, even though a lot of it is from institutions—jails and mental hospitals. It's also people who've died in their home and when they found them 6 weeks later sort of rotting away, their house was covered with murals or bits of writing. Some of it's quite ordinary art, but the people them-

> A lot of what we're doing is dirt, is filth, and we live in a society that pretends to be exceptionally clean.

selves were so obsessive about what they did. So it's just a collection of people that have no artistic training, not much knowledge of art, who just documented their mental processes. It suggests that there are millions more that do the same thing, except not quite so obsessively. . . who would never be heard of. In fact, people that never even documented what their capacities actually are. That's what it suggests. . . .

Obsession's not necessarily about quantity but about commitment. Or, there are people who've almost had no output—wrote half a poem, but that half a poem was fucking good (there are plenty of people who've written a lot of poetry and none of it was any good). I think one of the most important things in art is the art of differentiation—the art of *not copying*.

It's too easy to be cynical. Not a totally original idea but one of those that needs to be hammered out and stated all the time. You can do a Warhol which you can do at once—that period of art makes me want to chuck up. You can almost make a statement about it, that it's not art. I don't know what it is. I like the way Robert Hughes attacked that.

R/S: What did he say?

SPK: He was really sarcastic about it; he just said that it *was* public art, and that you can always take the piss out of anything. . . parody's not amusing. Warhol's like a parrot or something.

Getting back to the idea of differentiation—it's a whole recognition that art is a real sort of convulsive change, or it *can* be a convulsive change. . . .

I could ask *you* a question I've always wondered. You always talk about information, in the sense that you're researching information, trying to make it more available. What about concentrating equally as much on imagination as non-factual information?

R/S: We're always looking for suggestions, ways to *trigger the imagination*, bringing it into actual usage more and more. That's why reading even a biography of a relatively uninteresting artist may yield an account of *how* he (or she) got an idea or inspiration, and that will be more interesting than anything the artist ever created. Basically, the big goal is changing the *process* of perception, rather than selling people a set of perceptions or life 'styles' to consume—you know, this year's fashion selection. People should be able to look at *anything* themselves and make an independent judgment. And not even so much a judgment as a differentiation based on—

SPK: Taste?

R/S: In another part of this handbook, Boyd Rice talks about the necessity for *no* taste—the necessity for absolute abolishment of the whole idea of taste. I know what he's trying to get at—

SPK: I sort of know what he's trying to get at, too. It's like, as I said, the idea of (to put it blatantly) screwing a Playbody girl and screwing a Mongoloid. It's the purest idea, the idea of no taste. I wonder if it works....

R/S: I think he means a sort of all-around aesthetic cleansing process....

SPK: I think as far as taste goes, most of us just dis-

imaginative—

R/S: Or 99 percent.

SPK: But I'd like to refuse to believe that.

R/S: So would I, because—I look back on myself at certain stages and shudder.

SPK: Yeah, well I think everybody does. But we try not to fall prey to facile rationalizations like: *It's only human.* That's one of the most loaded phrases in the English language!

R/S: To deal with this problem, I usually think of Charles Fourier, who proposed that even the most *apparently* untal-

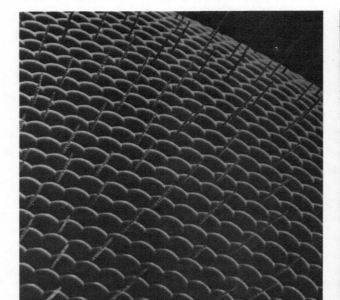

At a Neuropsychiatric Lab in San Diego, men are shown a series of gruesome films which become steadily more horrific. The trainee is forced to watch by having his head clamped so he cannot turn away, and by the use of a device which keeps his eyelids open. One of the first films shows an African youth being circumcized with a blunt knife and without anaesthetic. When the film is over, the trainee is asked questions like ''What was the motif on the knife handle?'' or, ''How many people were holding the youth down?''

criminate on the basis of originality.

R/S: Well, that's one way. I always try to find out who *did* anything first—*Where have I heard that before? Seen that before?* You can't help it. At the same time I hate to see in print comparisons—art in any form compared to other art.

SPK: That's part of the conditioning of classification—everything *has* to be classified.

R/S: Well, that's kind of the way memory works, doesn't it?

SPK How much do you actually subscribe to the old animist psychological ideas? That perception has something to do with humans all going through stages of perceptive developments: from age nought to 6 we open our eyes...after the age of 14 we develop our abstractive capabilities—things like that. I think to a large extent a debate like this is political because it is useful to those who *gain* from any justification of inequality, that suggestion that *some* of us are endowed with this capacity to be geniuses and brilliantly imaginative and perceptive, while unfortunately the majority aren't. And therefore if I happen to be one of these people who are thus endowed I can get a lot more money and become king of this state—and you shall be the serfs.

Now this is an enormous problem, I think. In some ways there is a large justification for this theory that there will always be that 90 percent of the population which is basically incapable of doing *anything*

ented of us have certain talents which usually just remain latent, but could be put to admirable use in a more enlightened society. Like, even simple-minded people might make wonderful mud sculptures that more rational people could never do.

SPK: Well, that's what *art brut's* about, in a way. You wonder what goes on in the mind of a retard, because we don't have the facilities to understand them—they don't happen to fit into our communicative structure and system. Once we have probably *the* greatest invention to ever come to mankind—the ability to actually put on a screen a dream or what is going on in another person's mind—that's *got* to happen in our lifetime. That would be *the* most important thing to happen in our lifetime. And then actually *animate* it—that's the next step. Science fiction stuff, but beautiful.

R/S: Well, computer manipulation of color graphics is getting more sophisticated. You can now bring a tree from the background to the foreground, put people in the picture who aren't there, quickly and easily.

SPK: Some holograms aren't bad, but I actually think it's still quite poor. There's a lot of things we could do so much quicker if only we didn't have a fucking capitalist motive for everything; we didn't have to make *immediate* cash out of everything. On the other hand, capitalism is probably the most efficient system we've come up with so far to develop technology. Certainly

the communists didn't develop the microchip....

R/S: I'd like to hear a bit more about your theory of the history of philosophy being the history of syphilis, which you're writing a book about?

SPK: In a way it's a book of humor, really. It's in the same vein as *any* book which questions the validity of knowledge as some kind of structured and unified theory. Just another questioning of truth, where you can look at people like—probably most of the Greeks had syphilis, what with their bestiality. The Romans as well. A little less recurrent in recent history—you have

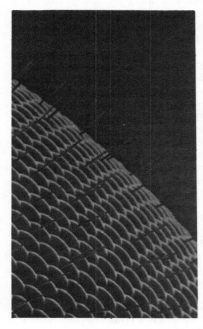

people like Nietzsche and Idi Amin—I wouldn't classify Idi Amin as a *philosopher*—

R/S: A very *practical* philosopher, actually!

SPK: Getting back, it's not so much a tongue-in-cheek laugh at philosophy and the great human knowledge, it's also an attempt to verbalize bacteria, if you like. And I think in a sense that's what *that* kind of philosophy did—it was more or less speaking for the bacterial component of the earth. And that's why I'm interested in also writing something similar about viruses. The theory of viral cancer is fascinating, especially the idea that it's in the genotype of the human population. It's in *every*body, but it's only expressed in about 10% of the cases. It's on the increase in the phenotype.

There's a theory that they actually travel in space and the earth contracted them because of the meteorites that fell onto earth. I believe satellites have seen them floating around in scans. They're quite extraordinary. They don't *need* a host, but they have a helluva lot of fun when they *find* one!

R/S: That's their art.

SPK: It's their self-expression for a bit.

R/S: Viruses from space kind of blow the old moral system out the window.

SPK: Yes. It's been quite a difficult book to write, sort of like a focus point for an idea of the human imagina-

tion as being influenced by some kind of a partnership with primitive life forms....

R/S: Why are you concerned with mutations?

SPK: They still represent the disgusting side of the society that we still live in. Why are all these mutations occurring in society at an increasing rate? It's crazy that they're all kept away from public attention—

R/S: I'm always trying to find out the *real* motivations for anything. And trying to become more scientific about death as well.

SPK: People actually believe so many different theories about life after death. Like New Guinea tribesmen have no understanding of the western idea of what life after death is. They couldn't even understand the body as a physical being in certain ways—wouldn't understand the electrical and genetic processes going on inside the body which are narrowed down to a cause-and-effect explanation. They have *no* faith in that kind of rationale.

Jean Baudrillard wrote a little book called *The Mirror of Production.* In it is a long chapter on the modern western inability to accept violent death—it has to be slow, peaceful and quiet. It seems to be a dynamic that we can't accept *anything* abrupt—it's got to be in some way cause-and-effect, an obvious, perfectly explicable decline or something like that. And even taking it down to the supposedly liberal idea of getting rid of capital punishment—maybe it's just that we can't stand the idea of violent death.

On the other hand you've got modern society where everybody delights in seeing bloody stupid TV programs with people getting shot up and killed in car crashes and things like that. But that's an attempt to make the violent thing—

R/S: Romantic?

SPK: I would have thought more a *joke!* There ought to be laugh tracks and whoopee and shouts when somebody gets killed in a cowboy movie or something like that—there's no horror involved in death whatsoever. How many people come into contact with an actual death? Very few.

The funny thing about all that is, in that sense we can almost make a claim that we are *not* sensationalists, and that we show death as *real* and in fact *not* sensational at all—those are real photos of people being shot and blood going everywhere—

R/S: I don't think many *real* images of death have been seen. In *Street Cops* there was only one photo in the whole book that affected me. It was of a guy who had just been shot by a shotgun in the stomach—there's vomit dripping everywhere, his mouth is full of vomit, and he looks sick....

SPK: In that book *Violence In Our Times,* there are photos like the one of the Jews all piled up. That's become a popular image—sensationalist in *quantity,* you know, and people've seen it 100,000 times. It's almost—respectable. But to show just one pathetic mangled body covered in vomit....

R/S: Incidentally, what ideas of yours have died on the vine, so to speak?

SPK: In our first album we tried to put a sperm capsule in every one. We lined up about five hundred capsules...and started putting the sperm in. After working hours, when we were finishing up the 500th, we noticed the first ones had almost dissolved—

101

R/S: Sperm's very acidic—

SPK: **Yes, that was a tremendous waste of energy! It was kind of corny. We weren't going to say what it was. I just wanted to see how many people would put it in their mouths.**

R/S: Of course people would—this is a pill society. People will take anything.

SPK: **It would have been funny if Customs had opened up the luggage and found this, and then run tests on it. You couldn't be prosecuted though, I think.**

R/S: It's art—Body Art, so to speak.

SPK: **What if you had any sexual disease? Could they get you for smuggling?**

R/S: Oh, like Columbus and the Indians? The Indians had syphilis, except to them it was like a cold. The white people got it by raping the Indians. It was amazing how fast it spread over Europe. Within a year it was all over Italy, down from Spain.

SPK: **Today's fashionable disease is cancer. I'm most convinced that cancer in some ways involves a faith or belief mechanism. I don't think it's purely physical— don't think *any* disease is. I think that maybe the cure even involves trying to *cooperate* in some way. . . . It's only in the last couple hundred years that we've had the conception of progress, and with that we've gotten cancer as well. I definitely think cancer is a byproduct of this civilization because it's on the increase *in spite of* how much they spend on research. It's perhaps psychosomatic in the purest sense—you can't separate the mind from the body.**

R/S: How does cancer fit into a modern mythology?

SPK: **To begin with, Durand analyzed and integrated all these symbols into massive cross-cultural myths, organizing these archetypes into:**

Heroic, i.e the sword and the spear, the penile erection, and things like that which are in some ways moving upwards. Like a cobra. . . .

Then you had the intimate images; things like digestion, or going down—the mother, water. . . .

> A technique used to exploit the *need to comply* is to spend hours asking and shouting questions to which the prisoner cannot possibly know the answer—details of atomic weaponry, etc. Many ex-prisoners spoke of the "tremendous feeling of relief you get when he finally asks something you can answer."

Then you had the great cyclical myths: Taoism, Nietzsche—more like the great cosmic circle. The ultimate in philosophy seems to be the idea of the eternal return. The yin and the yang.

But I think you can go on from that. Take the idea of *proliferation,* which seems to be extremely relevant to our society at the moment. This is the age of *everything* proliferating—information, nuclear armament, *cancer,* disease, psychosis. . . . So I really think that's worthwhile analyzing in terms of modern archetypes, and probably would be for the next few years.

After that, the idea of the *convulsion* of everything:

massive rapid changes, total upheaval, an age of extreme mutations—things like that which might come after the proliferation age. . . .

All you really need to do is look at wave forms and imagine the kind of overriding dynamics which *might* create certain eras on the earth. I think we've gone through the *progress* era—that great romantic era. We probably went through the great mystical cycle era as well very early on—pre-Christ. Maybe the Dark Ages and the Middle Ages were the great intimacy, lost-in-the-wilderness type of era. But now, *everything* is in massive expansion, moving all directions at once. And not necessarily toward apocalypse. It *seems* like that's about to happen, but that's been a popular belief for a very long time. If you read about what happened in the year 1000—there was mass hysteria all over Europe because they all thought they were in a millenial age then. We've always been in the millenial age! It's sort of natural that when you come up to the year 2000, you expect it all to happen in 1999. I don't really think we're coming into any great Nostradamus-type prophecy.

I would like to see the convulsive age. That's the one I would like to theorize. It's really the anarchist idea of total revolution—continuous revolution where everything is in constant change and you no longer need any landmarks to get a fix on. I think *that* would be the eternal return really, because everything would be happening at once. And in that sense I think we are reaching that kind of situation where it's almost impossible to keep track of what's going on.

Technology has reached an unbelievable degree of sophistication, where computers are actually designing parts of other computers. . . . But I don't think there's really anything *in* there that defies the human brain. All it is, is the number of combinations and the speed of combinations that the computer can go through; the options. There is nothing on an individual scope that the human brain does not understand. It was the one that programmed the bastard to start with—to generate those structural options. I'm afraid that I'll *always* disagree with the idea that technology is moving that fast. . . .

R/S: Technology specifically for the art of living isn't developing all that fast, but secret military innovation continues—

SPK: **There's so much going on that we won't find out about for another 10 years, if we *do* find out. For instance, the Americans have these *huge* air fields on the west coast of Australia that have been landing American Air Force planes for years and years, and the Australians have never scrutinized one of them. They've only just found out about them, because of that 5-year (or whatever) lag in information. In some way a document was "leaked" to the press that the Americans are flying B-52s in and have built some actual underground cities in the desert. But—that's only a small fraction of what's going on.**

R/S: Sometimes the information gap seems so enormous it's discouraging—trying to close up the gap. How do you keep on motivating yourselves to do more?

SPK: **Through confidence and blind optimism! All the criticism we've gotten doesn't mean anything—I always think *I know what I'm doing.* We've had a long history of being *outsiders.* . . .**

The Post-Industrial Strategy

EXPOSING THE CATHEDRAL OF DEATH

The true meaning of the slogan, *We are all German Jews,* is not solidarity but the inescapable *fact* that these people are NOT deviant phenomena. THIS SITUATION IS THE NORM. DEATH IS EVERYWHERE IN LIFE. SPK is not fetishing a situation, it is exposing this Cathedral of Death.

The strategy is not dialectical—liberation vs. *control,* unconscious vs. conscious, deviant vs. normal, sexual vs. chastity.

The strategy is CATASTROPHIC—pushing the situation to the limit.

The strategy is SYMBOLIC—using the system's own intolerable signs against it.

The strategy is ANONYMOUS—the refusal to be categorizable as another star deviant. We are the norm. We are the twilight.

THE POST-INDUSTRIAL STRATEGY
(Twilight of the Idols)

Michel Foucault in *Discipline and Punish:* the mechanism of social control has changed from liquidation or internment to *therapeutic.* Criminals or the insane are now simply recycled and turned into normalized homogeneous citizens. Both the right and the left wish to feel responsible for these problems and to reintegrate the deviant. *We must not do this.* Our interest in social deviance must be to maintain and extend the disability of the system to keep its margins under *control.*

Another fiction is the idea that by liberating the unconscious or the "psychic" we can attack the post-industrial simulacre. To begin with, the modern notion of unconscious is just another metaphysical concept. The primitives had no need of it because they had no distinction between the civilized and the savage mind. Only with emancipation or the idea of freedom did the need arise for the Master to be interiorized in us all and alienation begins. All savage, wandering and symbolic processes came to be called "unconscious" and were thereby domesticated like death. Any idea which maintains this arti-ficial separation is tragically missing the point. Furthermore it is foolish to think that a social code which created the unconscious is not able to inscribe and control it, just the same as it manipulates our conscious lives. Indeed this is the most effective method the code uses for its perpetuation. Psychic liberation is the very form of the system, not a radical solution as the drug experimentation of the Sixties showed. Changing individuals does not necessarily change societies.

THE POST-INDUSTRIAL SIMULACRE

It has been some decades since Western culture could be accurately described as Industrial. Since the under-consumption crisis of the Thirties, we have shifted entirely into a social structure dominated not by production but by reproduction, not by equivalence but by commutation, not by merchandise but by the model. We live in a post-industrial world. A world no longer where all labor is exchanged and loses its singularity but where labor and leisure become entwined. Not a culture bought and sold but one where all cultures simulate one another. Not a place where love is prostituted but one where a liberated keel sexuality is compulsory. And an era in which time is no longer accumulated like money but is broken in a confused web of nostalgia, fetishism and futurism.

SPK has always been certain to establish its separation from any label like "industrial" because it has always pursued a strategy more in keeping with an attack on a structure radically more efficient—the successor to industrial society. The realization of this difference is vital for any strategy: artistic, revolutionary, terrorist. If not, we shall only continue to confuse the symptom for the cure. . . .

If the industrial era was determined by its capitalist mode, then the post-industrial is hyper-capitalist. And in the sphere of signs the society has become indeterminate and codified. In the pre-industrial era every sign had a corresponding reality. In the industrial, every sign became equivalent to all others with money as the mode of social coherence. Now, however, all signs have become models, slightly differentiating all social reproduction—a generalized code of simulation. The real horror is that this process no longer stops at the factory gate but penetrates our homes, our loves and our minds. All our time becomes marked time. . . .

Walter Benjamin (McLuhan later) was the first to realize that technology was not a productive force but a MEDIUM—the principle—the FORM of the new society of publicity, information and communications networks. Seriality or the mechanical reproduction of exactly equivalent clones had given way to models generative of all forms according to a modulus of differences. This digitalized genetic cellule—the code—produces all questions and all possible solutions. A DNA generative of control of the social organism.

SYSTEM DEATH

The system has produced a special kind of death, a calculated system of signs. If the cemetery and the asylum are in the process of disappearing it is because death is everywhere and no longer needs to be hidden away. Today it is ethnocidal, judicial, concentrational, sensational. A complex fetishism of death as deviance—hence "star" deaths like Manson, Jones or Vietnam are just part of the system's own sensationalist fetishism. The true horror is statistical death which is the by-product of normalization and the therapeutic. Serums and laboratories are only the alibi for the prohibition of the speech of the dying.

It is quite obvious, then, why all our attention is focused on violent death, which alone manifests something like sacrifice—the transmutation of the real by the WILL of the group. All artificial death is therefore a product of a social will.

Suicide equals murder. (from the manifesto of the original *Sozialistisches Patienten Kollektiv*)

103

THE MANNEQUIN OF THE SECOND SKIN

The "sexual revolution" was nothing but a neutralization of all sexuality by its extension to all significations. It is a spectacle, an imperative, an advertisement. The fetishes are no longer private or anti-social as in de Sade—they are compulsory, they are normalized, they are transparent. Transparency is not a radical idea but a fundamental demand of the system today. Michel Foucault in *The History of Sexuality* (vol 1) shows how all sexuality including deviations are "confessed" so that the code can be total. Read *Penthouse Forum*. Every sexual possibility is catalogued in some cheap porno movie to be reproduced by us in our private lives.

The body has become entirely sexualized/but sex without qualities. Nudity is sexually redundant, the body having passed to a mannequin to focus signs—clothing, make-up, furniture, restaurant, car, etc. The body is fetishized as a manipulation of masks; the idea of the optimum body becomes nothing but the "you" of the advertisement—fragmented and reconstituted as a model.

The only possible attack on this totality is the exhibition of intolerable bodies—mutated, diseased, deformed, dead. Hence our extensive file of unacceptable flesh. This is not *our* obsession—this is merely the obverse of the obsessive code.

Marcuse called this sexual revolution "repressive desublimation." It is no longer violent and aimed at the genitals, it is more subtle and seduces us to play. Death is the only possible pornography for this system...there is no radical sexuality....

OBSESSION WITH THE NEW

To demand that information tell the truth is to revert to a pre-industrial mode. Today there is no reality, or everything is real and everything is unreal. Today the object no longer refers to the real nor to information. Both are already the result of a selection, a montage, a taking of views. The role of messages is no longer information but a *test*—of success at interpreting acording to the code for the perpetuation of the code. Thus the CONTROL problem is not one of surveillance, propaganda or paranoia. It is one of subjective influence, consent and extension to all possible spheres of life. The incorporation of the code into the corpse itself (Cf. Baudrillard: the "leucemisation" of all social substance, 103)

Modernity is not the transmutation of values—the myth of progress and change—but a commutation, combinatory and ambiguous. In this process art and reality come to simulate each other. The dichotomy between real and imaginary collapses and commerce, the political, and the scientific become immersed more in aesthetics than in reality in the old sense. Symbols everywhere—ideologies, personalities, publicity—the new form of power. In politics as in art and culture, the obsession with the "new" is always limited to the rate of change tolerable without altering the essential order. And our lives, as works of art created by this public(ity) code, participate in the same re-production.

"It remains to be seen if this operationality is not itself a myth, if DNA is not itself a myth." (Jean Baudrillard, *L'Échange symbolique et la Mort*, p94)

We are living at the beginning of an epoch which history will come to know as another Dark Age. But unlike the first one characterized by the concealment of information, we suffer from an almost opposite problem—information overload. The demand for more information is not radical—it is to demand exactly what the system already inundates us with.

THE ADMINISTRATION OF DEATH

We live entirely a fiction of evolutionism: for capitalism a belief in an eternity of accumulation and progress; for science a faith in an infinite march towards truth; for social manipulation a belief in control from cradle to grave. The profound law of the prevailing social order is therefore not economic but the progressive manipulation of life and death. From birth control to death control it's the same system of extermination. Only now there is no longer any need for actual death. The operation is realized in *forced survival* which only suicides not made of despair can breach. Society in the post-industrial era is one of slow-death where all time is marked, where all subjects are the (in)voluntary recipients of the unilateral gifts of employment, social security, material/sexual gratification and most of all the incessant bombardment of how one ought to look, think, and act. A living death.

Power always rests in the last instance on the power to put to death—actual, threatened or symbolic. And in the modern case this power operates symbolically by the naturalization, or MEDICALIZATION of life and death. "Primitive" societies treated death as a social relationship, hence the initiation ceremony or sacrificial rite was a shared or social birth and death respectively. No "individual" was ever born or put to death. This symbolic exchange ends the disjunction between life and death (a concept of naturality which is just part of our modern scientific idealism) and therefore also between real and imaginary. Instead we have autonomized death as an individual fatality, thus absolving society from most responsibility.

—SPK, 1983

≪S.P.K.≫

CHRONOLOGY

Sept 1978. Formed Sydney, Australia.

1979. Five members: EMS AKS (synthesizers, tapes, rhythm machines, vokals), Ne/H/iL (vokals, rhythm treatments), Danny Rumour (guitars), David Virgin (bass), Karmel E-Clastic (drums). Performed 3 times in Sydney. Video of performance by S. Jones.

1980-81. Four members: Operator (EMSAKS) on tapes, synthesizers, rhythms, vokals, metal; Tone Generator (synthesizers, visuals); Wilkins (guitars, bass), Mr. Clean (engineer). Performed Dec 1980 with *Throbbing Gristle* and *A Certain Ratio* in London; April 1981 with *Factrix* in San Francisco.

January-June 1982. Four members: Oblivon (Operator) on tapes, rhythms, metal, synths, vokals, electronik perkussion; Ne/H/il (rhythms, synths), Tone Generator (video, visuals), Pinker (drums, electronik perkussion). Performed twice in Sydney, Australia, including an outdoor venue at an abandoned Brickworks. Toured USA performing 11 times from San Francisco to New York.

June-December 1982. Three members: Oblivon (all kompositions and instruments), Sinan (electronik and metal perkussion), Dominik Guerin (Tone Generator) on video and visuals. Performed October with Virgin Prunes in London. Toured West Germany and Italy (Berlin, Frankfurt, Rome).

DISCOGRAPHY

1) NO MORE/KONTAKT/GERMANIK (EP, Side Effekts, deleted)

2) FAKTORY/RETARD/SLOGUN (EP, Side Effekts, deleted)

3) MEKANO/SLOGUN (45, Industrial Records)

4) INFORMATION OVERLOAD UNIT (LP, £8 from Side Effekts, 68 Bonnington Square, London SW8 UK)

5) LIVE AT THE CRYPT (cassette, £7 from Sterile Records, 90 Lilford Rd, London SE5 UK)

6) SOLIPSIK (EP, M² Records, Sydney, Australia)

7) LEICHENSCHREI (LP, $12 from Thermidor, 912 Bancroft, Berkeley CA 94710).

8) LAST ATTEMPT AT PARADISE (cassette, $11 from Fresh Sounds, PO Box 36, Lawrence KS 66044)

9) FROM SCIENCE TO RITUAL (cassette, VIVA Italy, Via Gramsci 53, 00197 Rome, Italy)

10) AUTO-DA-FE (12" 45, Walter Ulbricht, Schallfolien AG, Durchschnitt 15, 2000 Hamburg 13, W Germany)

11) DEKOMPOSITIONS (12" EP, £7 from Side Effekts, 68 Bonnington Square, London SW8 UK)

12) DESPAIR (UHS/PAL + NTSC videocassette/write Side Effekts or Fresh Sounds for availability)

REFERENCE

SOME BOOKS

ARTIFICIAL INTELLIGENCE
Machines Who Think/P McCorduck
What Computers Can't Do/H Dreyfus
Machine Intelligence (9 volume set)

ANTHROPOLOGY
Violence & The Sacred/R Girard
The Works/Claude Levi-Strauss

MILITARY
Jane's Weapon Systems (annual, London)
Improved Munitions Black Book, 2 vols,
 $20 from Desert Pubs, Cornville AZ 86325
Loompanics Catalog, $2 from PO Box 1197,
 Port Townsend WA 98368
Paladin Press Catalog, $1 from PO Box 1307,
 Boulder CO 80306

HISTORY
The Myth of The Master Race/R Cecil
International Fascism/G L Mosse
Genocide/L Kuper
Hitler: The Occult Messiah/Gerald Suster
SS & Gestapo: Rule By Terror/R Manuell
Hitler's Ideology: A Study in Psycho-
 analytic Sociology/R Koenigsberg
Hitler's Propaganda Machine/Rutherford
Nazi Cinema/Erwin Leiser

CONTROL
Physical Control of the Mind/J Delgado
The Mind Manipulators/Scheflin & Opton

MEDICINE
Wolfe Medical Atlases (£15 ea, Wolfe
 House, 3 Conway St, London W1P 6HE UK)
 Venereology; Microbiology; Forensic
 Pathology; Pediatrics; Virology
Also:
Forensic Medicine: A Study In Trauma and
 Environmental Hazards/ed Tedeschi et al
Forensic Pathology: A Handbook
 For Pathologists
Neurosurgical Treatment in Psychiatry,
 Pain & Epilepsy/ed W Sweet et al
Sudden & Unexpected Death/F Camps
Techniques of Crime Scene Investigation

SOUND
Sound, Noise & Vibration Control/Yerges
Sound & Its Medical Effects/D Crystral
Sound Research Laboratories, Basic
 Vibration Control/Bromer et al

OCCULT
The Occult & Paranormal World
Occult Guide to South America
An Occult History of the World/Brennan
History of Witchcraft, Sorcerers,
 Heretics, etc/J B Russell
Occult Philosophy/Marc E Jones
The Occult Source Book/N Perry
Ency of Occultism & Parapsychology
Maps of Consciousness/R Metzner
Superminds/J Taylor
Secret Teachings of All Ages/M P Hall
History of Magic & Experimental
 Science/8 vols, Columbia Univ, 1934
Religion & the Decline of Magic/Thomas
A Dictionary of Symbols/J E Cirlot
Mysterious Powers/Spirits & Spirit Worlds
Handbook of Parapsychology/B B Wolman
The Satanic Rituals/A S LaVey

The Alchemists/R Pearsall
The Alchemists/A J P Smith
Alchemy & Magic/S Fabricius

"ART"
Performance/R Goldberg
The Bachelor Machines (Rizzoli)
Art Brut/M Thévoz
Art Brut/ed Jean Dubuffet

PSYCHOPATHOLOGY
300 Years of Psychiatry 1535-1860
Psychology of the TV Image/Baggaley etc
Psychopathology: its causes & symptoms
Modern Psychopathology/T Millon
Human Nature & Science/S E Perry
Treatment or Torture/G S Jonas
Genetics & Mental Disorders
Russia's Political Hospitals
The Threat of Impending Disaster
The Myth of Analysis/J Hillman
Bedlam/A Masters
Works/de Sade (esp 120 Days of Sodom)

PSYCHOPHARMACOLOGY
Psychopharmacology of Aggression/Valtelli
Psychopharmacology of Depression
Psychopharmacology of Hallucinogens
Psychosexual Problems/Sidney Crown
Psychotherapy of Schizophrenia/ed Strauss
The Psychotic: Understanding Madness
The American Journal of Psychiatry

LITERATURE
The Atrocity Exhibition/J G Ballard
Crash; Hello America/J G Ballard
Myths of the Near Future/J G Ballard
Crowds & Power/Elias Canetti
Metamorphosis; The Castle/Kafka
In the Penal Colony; The Trial/ "
Ulysses/Joyce
Finnegan's Wake/Joyce
The Lost Ones/Beckett
The Unnameable/Beckett
Venus In Furs/Sacher-Masoch
Maldoror/Lautrèamont
Writings/Artaud
Works/Jorge-Luis Borges

PHILOSOPHY
Man A Machine/La Mettrie
Anti-Oedipus/Deleuze & Guattari
Rhizome/Deleuze & Guattari
Mille Plateaux/Deleuze & Guattari
Against Method/Paul Feyerabend
The Works of/Michel Foucault
Morphogenese et Imaginaire/Rene Thom
Catastrophe Theory/Rene Thom
Mirror of Production/Jean Baudrillard
L'Exchange Symbolique et la Mort/ "
Système des Objets/ "
Political Economy & the Sign/ "
The History of La Borde/F Guattari
Bruits/Jacques Attali
Libidinal Economy/Jean F Lyotard
La Condition Post-Moderne/ "
Rudiments Paiens/ "
Hermes (vol I-IV)/Michel Serres
L'Antipublicite/Jacques Fontanel
Nietzsche et Le Circle Vicieux/Klossowski
The Philosophy of No/G Bachelard
Le Normale et le Pathologique/Cariguillem
Every word of/F Nietzsche

Archetypes & The Collective
 Unconscious/Carl Jung
Symbols & Transformation/ "
Mysterium Conjunctionis/ "
Psychology & Alchemy/ "
Les Structures Anthropologiques de
 L'Imaginaire/Gilbert Durand
Passion/Jacob Boehme
Passion/Angelus Silerius
Treatises & Sermons/Meister Eckhart
Silence; Notations; M/John Cage
For The Birds/ "
Statism & Anarchism/Bakunin
 (Maximoff/Dolgoff compilations)
Ethics; Mutual Aid/Peter Kropotkin
What is Property?/Proudhon
All Situationist Texts
Mass Psychology of Fascism/W Reich
Antipsychiatry/T Szasz & D Cooper

MAGAZINES
Semiotexte
Photo (esp annual compilations)
Obliques (R Borderie, Boite postale #1,
 les Pilles, 26110 Nyons France)
des Jahres '80s (Germany)

SOME FILMS
The Golem/Paul Wegener
Nosferatu/F W Murnau
L'Age D'or; Un Chien Andalou/Buñuel
That Obscure Object of Desire; Las Hurdes/"
Dr Mabuse (series); Metropolis/Fritz Lang
Potemkin/Eisenstein
Gold; Der Tunnel/Karl Harth
Night & Fog/Alain Resnais
Psycho; The Birds/Hitchcock
Freaks/Tod Browning
Repulsion/Roman Polanski
Salo/Pasolini
Marat-Sade/Peter Brook
Eraserhead/David Lynch
The Conversation/Francis Ford Coppola
Taxi Driver/Martin Scorcese
Stalker/Andrei Tarkovski
Alphaville; Letters to Jane/Godard
Dodes'kaden/Kurosawa
Holy Mountain/Jodorowsky
Aguirre; Even Dwarfs Started Small/Herzog
Various Films/Kurt Kren (esp Action, Mama
 & Papa, Leda & the Swan w/Otto Muehl,
 Self-Mutilation, Ana—Action Brus
2001 (1st & last 5 minutes)
Sweet Movie/Makavejev
The Hill/Sidney Lumet
La Grande Bouffe/Marco Ferreri
Themroc/Claude Faraldo
Marathon Man/John Schlesinger
The Prisoner (BBC TV series)

NAZI FILMS:
Olympia/Leni Riefenstahl
Triumph of the Will/ "
The Eternal Jew/Fritz Hiffler
Jud Suss/Veit Harlan
Hitlerjunge Quaz/Hans Steinhoff
I Accuse/Wolfgang Liebeneiner

Z'EV

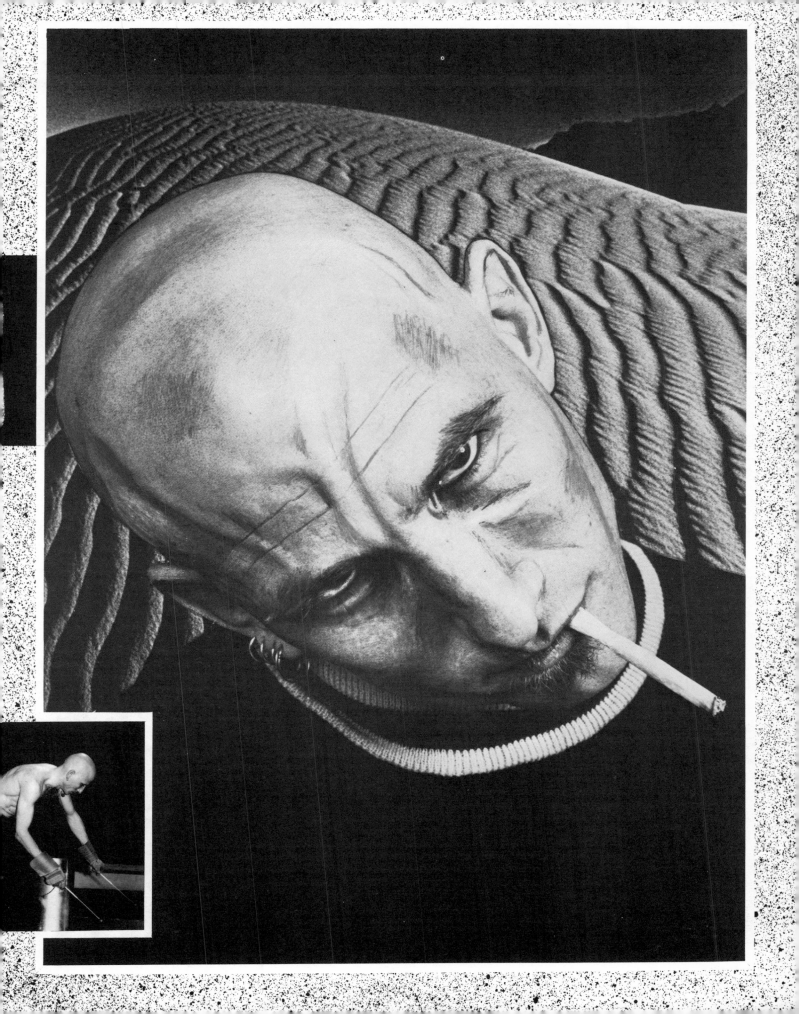

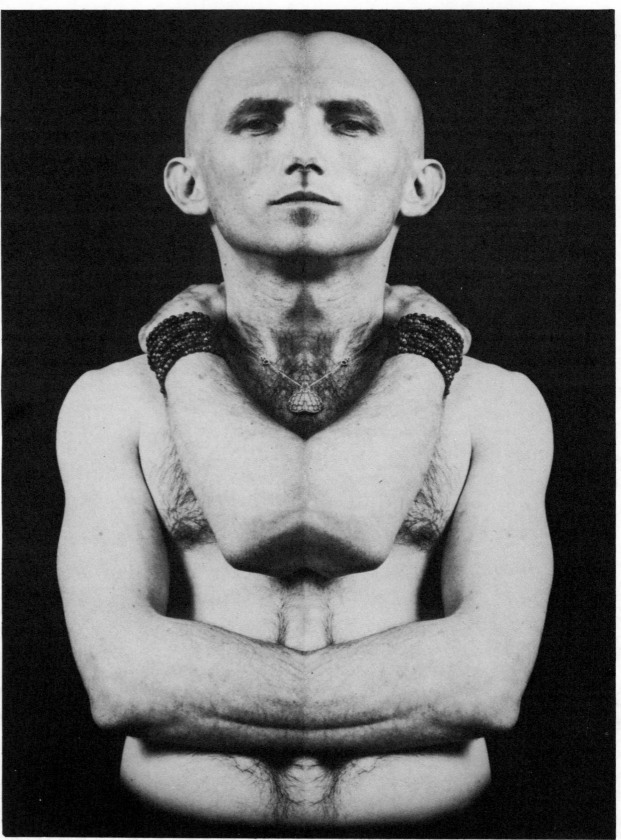

Above Z'ev portrait: Bobby Adams. Previous pages: Z'ev series by Catherine Ceresole; large portrait by Bobby Adams.

Z'ev, a constant world traveler, is a percussionist with found/assembled kinetic sculptures— metal and plastic tubes, tubs, pans, bottles, sheets, springs, strung together or not, hurtled around the stage, beat upon with mallets or sticks but orchestrated for contrasts and crescendos of rhythmic noise, in an athletic/dance feat dangerous to performer and audience alike (performer must wear knee and elbow pads).

Z'ev started out in 1978 playing countless 15-minute sets at the Mabuhay in San Francisco and getting nowhere. A turning point came in 1979 when he risked all for an East Coast tour and received serious recognition at last. Subsequently he has played countless shows in Europe and the USA, alternating between New York and Holland as bases of operation.

Z'ev, who's also known as *Yoel, Shaoul, Uns, Rax Werx, GDG, Element L, Deesse, Magneet Bond,* and *Stefan Weisser,* has released a number of records on Subterranean, Lust/Unlust, Fetish, Vinyl, and other labels.

Sidestepping his predilection for the arcane science of the Cabala, *Z'ev* reveals some of his practical prestidigitation in this interview with Andrea Juno and Vale....

R/S: What are you and people like *Mark Pauline* against?
Z'EV: Basically we're against the military-industrial complex...yet the work we're doing requires that form of economy, so you're like, *stuck!* It's fucked. It's a complete paradox: that a lot of the people that are the most politically motivated, performance-wise, use resources that are direct products of that economy.
R/S: Reagan's increased the military economy by billions under the premise that the military creates jobs, yet a recent funded investigation said that arms spending wipes out jobs....
Z'EV: Not only that, but all these new super-tech systems that they're building are broken down more than they're up. And they spend all this money training people to run them, but as soon as their term of enlistment is up they get out and go into the private sector where they make much more money. They're just always training these people—nobody sticks around! So you have complex machines that most of the time don't work, with not enough qualified people around to run them....It's amazing!
R/S: How is your politics manifested in your sound performances?
Z'EV: Through a broad definition...say, the politics of culture and consumerism. On one level it's a

double-edged sword in that you do something and somebody listens to it—it's *that* system. But *Uns,* for example, makes a music that just listening to you'd think used a huge studio, whereas it's just cassette recorders, skipping record players and an old organ. *Z'ev* uses these *metals,* and has to do with the fact that you can go out and build and create your own music— you don't have to go out to a store and buy the latest musical things. It is on one level anti-consumer technology ("to be able to do something you have to spend a certain amount of money, get the state-of-the-art this and that").

I've always been very committed to *low-tech* as opposed to high-tech! In Europe, a lot of bands are starting to use metals in percussion, to get a richness and variety of texture and timbre that one would normally go to a synthesizer for. Whereas in America there's still this concept in people's heads that a $5000 synthesizer is going to make them a better musician.
R/S: I think that even more basic than all that is the fact that what you're doing is based on stolen, recycled, discarded and re-utilized products.
Z'EV: The stealing is one aspect, the recycling is another. It involves *looking for a solution.* If I go somewhere, like to a junkyard, my sense is developed to the extent that I can look at something and have an idea what it will sound like.
R/S: Whether to take it home or leave it lying there.
Z'EV: Right. But then there's lots of pieces that I'll get that will stick around for quite a while before I figure out what the hell to do with them.
R/S: What new materials have you found recently?
Z'EV: I just got some titanium in Seattle for $3 a pound—in New York a little piece was $19. It's extremely light—I'm going to use it in my next show. It's funny stuff—the way you cut it is, you cut it for a long, long time and then suddenly you can rip it. It's so brittle that it breaks.
MATTY: That's what they use on the new hyper-velocity missiles the Army has. There's no explosive— just a big titanium tip. They go, I think, 7-8,000 ft/sec which is so fast that when they hit they'll go through 2 feet of armor plate. There's so much friction that it heats up white-hot, and melts through whatever's there. It goes through that new English tank armor and sends white-hot metal all over the guys inside. Swell way to experience a war!
You know who's the leading supplier of titanium in the world? Red China.
R/S: ...Some pieces only work as part of a greater assemblage?
Z'EV: Right, you'll have them around until enough *like* pieces get together to make an instrument. I have lots of pieces that have been around for quite a while that still have not come together, as it were.
The thievery has to do with—basically, Mercury on one level is the god of learning and *communication,* and on the other level is the god of thieves! The thievery is more of an occult situation, even though thievery is a political act on a certain level—it's shaped by certain socio-economic inequities. You know, taking from those who have, who can afford it and don't give it—forcing them to sponsor you, so to speak!
R/S: A lot of them don't even miss it, probably—

Z'ev in Holland. (Both photos: Wim Riemens)

Z'EV: No, I think a lot of them *are* starting to miss it, because since last year, when I came back, a couple of the places I went to visit that had never had burglar alarms now had them. So apparently I was making my presence felt!

But that was something that developed through childhood—first childhood crime ... subsequent crimes ... present crimes. Thievery's been completely consistent with me all of my life! Way back then I didn't have the rationalization (if that's what you want to call it) that I do now. But the thefts that I did, say in 1980, were done as *rituals.*

R/S: How were they rituals?

Z'EV: What *are* rituals? They basically have to do with 3 activities: as an act of devotion, as an act where you're going to learn something, or as an act where you're going to effect something. Overall, I don't deal that much with effect—I'm more interested in learning. It's like a conversation I had with a guy who asked, Well what *power* is this going to give you? Well, to me that's ridiculous, because all that does is give you power on the material plane—which is the last thing I'm interested in.

There's another level of working with the thievery, which has to do with the very big premium I put on *risk* in the production of works. So I feel that at the very basic beginning of the process, which means the

accumulations of the materials which are then going to get formed into instruments which are then going to get used in a performance—since the risk is such a big part in the performance aspect, I try to keep it *consistent* throughout the process! You're out there on the level of getting caught, *doing time,* as opposed to just going into a store and buying something. It's standing up for what you believe in, on a certain level.

And the risk in the performance comes from—well there's the physical threat. And then the fact that it's all improvised. The only reason I've been able to do the amount of shows that I do and work for the amount of time I've been working is—it's still growing. It might get to a small plateau, but then it goes someplace else.

If you get too used to what you're doing, too aware of what you're doing—it loses its edge. Generally the more successful an artist or act becomes, the more diluted the work, because there aren't as many risks there. They'll have the audience, and the audience comes expecting what the artist is going to give, and the artist gets into that because he starts developing a lifestyle he can't afford or doesn't want to give up. So then he does whatever is necessary to maintain that status quo...and becomes this constantly repetitious organism, kind of like a *tumor* ... that takes all the healthy cells and converts them...

R/S: You do performances as *Z'ev, Uns, Magneet Bond, Element L*—what do you think is a common inspiration?

Z'EV: The real crux of it all is—it's all coming from this basis of *poetry.* Various levels of poetry and various levels of language. Poetry encompasses all these levels, in terms of the occult situation, in terms of the cabalistic situation, in terms of the more ritual aspect of *Z'ev,* in terms of the language-and-sound aspect of *Uns,* and in terms of *Magneet Bond*—more celestial, and *Element L*—more elemental, having to do with tape processes. Having developed a relationship with phenomena/experience, all grows out of the basis of this person basically being a poet...and all these are different manifestations. That's like this missing *context*—then everything, all the connections between all of them, can be seen.

The problem with that is: in my "code of ethics" a poet is something that somebody can say about you but you can't say about yourself. I wouldn't go around proclaiming myself as one.

I came to San Francisco with some manuscripts very idealistically in 1968, and talked to some people at *City Lights.* And basically at that time (and I don't know if it's changed since then) sex and politics was the big poetry—that's all anybody was interested in publishing. Which wouldn't necessarily be bad, but sex—eroticism's a very fine line, especially for Americans—I don't think Americans are too erotic. I think mostly they get *pornographic,* or they don't really know the difference between pornography and eroticism. And they don't really get political—just these kind of hack-political, dogmatic tracts.

R/S: How do you translate your poetry into sound performance?

Z'EV: A general rock'n'roll performance is a social structure that is thrust upon people, where the music is only a part, a *soundtrack* for an experience that the people know everything about in advance—they're going to the club, they'll see people that they know.... It isn't meant to effect any change, it's not directed at the audience so they'll interpret and create a new experience from it. There's no basis for further extrapolation.

Whereas the *Z'ev* performance, at the sound level, deals with an evocative, experiential mode in the listener—the person listens and it gives him food for thought—ideally. There's a tremendous amount of calligraphic language in the instruments themselves. If you closed your ears and just watched it, there is a language almost like puppeteers'—there are these dramas that get played out with these instruments in terms of defining relationships—whole sagas and dramas get played out. And there's this intuitive feeling I get that there's an actual *calligraphic language* in that, if it were videotaped and then put into some kind of computer that took the experience and broke it down into instrumental elements and their relationships, there would be a very definite language.

R/S: At the beginning of language, in early writings like those of Homer, the poet is characterized as a storyteller—

Z'EV: —where the storyteller, in telling the story, is like this river that the people get in and swim in, and get taken along in, and this particular river has things in it that the people will use as grist for their own mill, food for their own thought.

R/S: Along with words, you also talk through the drums you've invented—

Z'EV: It's very traditional that the drum is synonymous with communication in most cultures; in Africa they say *I got it on the drum.* There is this language to rhythm where there's a meta-message occurring—almost a mathematical situation with repetition, refrain, like formulas repeated and transmuted this way and that way.

R/S: What did you have in mind when you put on a deafening sound tape and aimed that huge bank of lights at the audience for your *On Broadway* show?

Z'EV: There were two problems with that—one, when the sound person put on the tape he was supposed to cut the highs from +12 to -12 and didn't. So that's why you had these unbelievable high frequencies that drove everybody crazy. They were even difficult for *me* to take—because they weren't supposed to be there. The audience who left—I don't *blame* them, because it *was* painful.

The problem with the lights was: although they had it dark at the beginning, they couldn't take the house lights out. So the lights were flashing, but it never got to total black. But that was what was needed, because the tapes that were being played had a lot of harmelodic rhythm to them—a rhythm that comes not from a pulse or beat but from the coming in and out of various tones. And what I was basically aiming for was a real synaesthetic experience, where the rhythm coming from these randomly blinking on-and-off lights—people would have heard *that* rhythm. The two of them would have combined to where you would have been listening to the sound, hearing this rhythmic differentiation triggered by your eyes taking in pulse/ light patterns. Basically, you'd have these 2 forms of information that by themselves are too much to handle, either one, but together your processing of them would have created this *other*. But for a variety of two basic reasons it didn't happen.

That was called the *Z'ev* show even though it was really an *Element L/Magneet Bond* show. So people came expecting to see Z'ev play. That was really the first time I had dealt with the audience's expectation—where people were real aggravated that *I wasn't playing*. Even though I was presenting them with information (which is all that they should expect), it wasn't the information they wanted to see. Then you get into this "What *right* does the audience have to expect?" question. *P.I.L.* dealt with this quite a bit—they were like a one-line joke in that that was *the* most important thing for them: *dealing with the audience's expectation.*

R/S: What do you think you have in common with, say, *Mark Pauline, Non, Throbbing Gristle* or *Johanna Went?*

Z'EV: The concept of being a cultural subversive, a cultural revolutionary—more the concept of being a cultural *subversive*. Rather than some "post-industrial" context. A perfect metaphor being *TG,* at their shows, putting huge mirrors on stage so the audience would be looking at themselves. It's like that—where you're holding up this mirror to people, dealing within this sphere while breaking as many rules as it's possible to break, and you're trying to educate that audience as much as possible, and *empower* that audience. I think most of the people involved would be just as happy for the audience to get out of their apathy and start doing *something*.

In America, people have just been so demoralized to their own *power* to where they don't think their voice has any say....so they just become this consumer of whatever Nixon, Reagan, television show, pop band, new wave is around.

R/S: Have you ever considered yourself in the context of, say, those master drummers of Burundi?

Z'EV: I've studied ethnomusicology...but I wouldn't want to *call myself* a master drummer. Most of those situations where there is a master drummer—those are drumming systems where the drumming is directly related to either ritual use or communicational use, not music per se. And because that's also where I'm coming from, my performance has evolved along the same levels. Like, some drummers are somewhat annoyed by it because it's so simple. In most western drumming like in jazz or rock, there are these very nifty little patterns with a lot of fast technique—like trying to squeeze as many notes into a given space as is possible. Myself, I'm always trying to play as *little* as possible, so that the effect of what you're doing can actually sink in.

R/S: How much of what you're doing are you consciously aware of while you're drumming?

Z'EV: At the *On Broadway,* the first piece I did was about 12 minutes. I was consciously aware for maybe 3 or 4 of those minutes, and the rest of the time there was this level where I would have no idea what I was actually playing. Because you get a basic groove, as it were, and then you let that groove groove itself...show itself. And that's so the actual message of it can appear...the process of pure form.

In the summer of '80 I was working with a Haitian man, and learned quite a bit from him toward under-

Z'ev. (Two photos: Paula Court)

UNS Performance at Mabuhay. (Photo: Marion Gray)

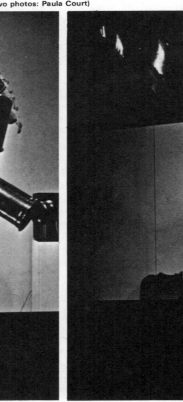

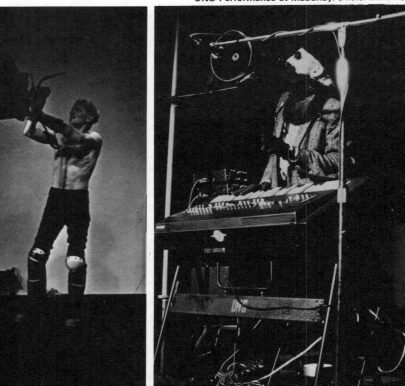

standing the Caribbean systems of voodoo drumming. In voodoo, the drum patterns are *the calls*—if there's going to be an invocation of a particular spirit-energy, it's a drum pattern that *calls* that energy. So I started learning about that—I became much more linked up to that system. I've used it subliminally, but I haven't really dealt with it that much overtly because...it's difficult to do, to keep the concentration. Because if you call an energy down, you have to be able to deal with it. And if you're doing shows night after night, for example, you have to be very centered, otherwise *the energy will not leave.* And so I'd walk off stage and *I would not be me anymore.*

R/S: You mean an entity would take you over?

Z'EV: Yeah...basically. I can deal with that in prescribed situations, but as a general performance mode that's still a few years away before I would attempt it.

R/S: That's one risk you don't want to try!

Z'EV: Yeah, because it's *foolish*...so it's not worth it. Also, on a certain level there's not really any point, because it's almost like an abuse. Because they're not going to be fed by anything other than me in that situation—none of the people in the audience are going to participate....

For example, I have very definite plans in mind for a trip through Western Africa, performing, and *there* I will do it because there is where these energies come from. So it would make real sense, because the people in the audience would recognize those energies and pay those energies proper respect, as it were.

R/S: It seems Hitler managed to pull off mass trance rituals regularly.

Z'EV: Yes, but number one—there would be extreme amounts of conjurations, before, during and after his big rallies. Number two, he was using his hands—the people did not spontaneously arrive at it, it was a form of mass hypnotism he was using. He put the image in the people. Still, it's outside the range of 99.99 percent of humanity to be able to do that to 75-100,000 people. I'm sure that, at times, all those 100,000 people were polarized. But it wasn't Hitler who was doing it, Hitler was manifesting a particular type of energy which did it. It's not within the capability of a person to do it, it is within the capability of non-material energies to do such things...coming from a certain trance inducement.

R/S: ...What soundtracks do you like? And why?

Z'EV: I think in the psychedelic era, a lot of people went to see *Juliet of the Spirits*—that was a very favorite psychedelic film. And so a lot of people then would buy the record. For a lot of people of a certain age that might have been a crucial movie in terms of the soundtrack.

I liked *The Good, The Bad and the Ugly* because ...there was a segment where this guy was being tortured. It was in a prisoner-of-war camp in the Civil War, and to cover the sound they had this prisoner's band playing. So you'd hear this *Uh! Uh!* of this guy being beat up during this very pastoral music, and then the bandleader would go, *More feeling!* Then there were tremendous amounts of explosions and gunshots—it was a very dense soundtrack, they got very carried away.

You'd have this one track of all the bird sounds in

this town; one of all these wagon wheels—ratchets turning, and all these explosions. Then all these sardonic comments, 'cause there's not a lot of dialogue in the movie. I made two different tapes of it, and I think

Z'ev battling cold steel. (Photo: Paul Velik)

I'll use both of them in a show *simultaneously* so there'll be these overlaps. As source material, I think some soundtracks can be very good.

The soundtrack to *Raging Bull* was very interesting. The dialogue was so real it was amazing. De Niro plays this absolutely insane character who'd got it in his mind that his brother had fucked his wife. And his brother wouldn't admit it; he said, "I'm not going to answer you, it's a stupid question." That fed de Niro, who was saying, "Well if you're not going to answer me it must be true." His brother said, "Fuck You!" and left. Then de Niro got on his wife about it and his wife said, "OK! I fucked your brother! Not only that, I sucked his cock!" He said, "You sucked his cock?" She said, "Yeah, I sucked his cock, and not only that, he's got a bigger cock than you." So de Niro goes and beats the shit out of his brother. It's just this amazing portrayal of this absolutely insane, paranoid person who has his mind made up and the more you try to tell them—

R/S: But how does this tie into soundtracks?

Z'EV: Well, there is a lot of conversation, and I really like that: conversation as sound. Then there's the fight scenes, and the fight scenes that are done in slow motion have real time sound—very physical sounds.

The amount of subliminal information that comes in through soundtracks—I was watching a horror movie with my niece and nephew and they started getting scared. I walked over and turned the sound down and showed them that if they just watched it, it wasn't scary what they were seeing—it was the *sound* that was scary. So for most horror films, the soundtrack is the scariest element—if you take out the sound, they lose 75% of their impact.

Basically what happens is, if you're listening to a sound, you sub-vocalize—your vocal chords follow while you're listening to music...which is why sudden changes in pitch are so emotional, causing a physical change in you because you don't realize that you're like *singing along* as it were with whatever it is.

113

When the pitch changes suddenly, your vocal chords *freak out,* causing this shock. So, a tremendous amount of the manipulation of the audience comes from the soundtrack. Also, because you're watching what's going on, you're not concentrating as much on what you're listening to, so—that's why so many pop records have a telephone bell pushed way back in the mix, because a telephone in this culture gets someone's attention immediately. Not only that, but—Eno used on a record the clinking of car keys. Try it sometime the next time you have a lot of people over—get your car keys and clink 'em around. Everyone will leave! Maybe not in San Francisco or New York, but you do it in LA or any suburban setting where people drive a lot, and the sound of keys will get people to leave.

People who are using sound to affect people's subconscious, trying to create a real effect *within* the person, are interested in soundtracks. And for me the soundtrack isn't just the music, it's also the dialogue, all the effects that are used. I think of them not as an end in themselves. They are built to get an actual psychological effect in an audience. But there are very few I would say I like, on their own . . . .

R/S: You've read the 2 volumes of *Her-Bak* about Egyptian education?

Z'EV: They're really about past-life recall even though they're works of fiction. Agricultural societies

Z'ev at On Broadway, San Francisco 1982. (Photo: Erich Mueller)

being linked up to the earth possibly are more civilized than mechanical societies.

R/S: Why?

Z'EV: Mechanical societies are man building these machines which are extensions of himself. If machines could write about man, man would be a god to these machines. Or, machines could become man's gods. Now with computers around, some people think of themselves as computers. The computers could be as significant to man as the Industrial Revolution was. Which has to do with the metaphors that people think of and deal with in themselves having to do with the machines they're creating.

But in an agricultural society you're dealing with the basic myth of dying and rebirth—winter and spring. Which may make people more civilized in their dealings with each other . . . .

R/S: Because of the underlying recognition of a common fate of death?

Z'EV: More an outlook like, you look at a plant, watch it develop and—in everything you see the *divine.*

R/S: Can you summarize the value you've gotten from reading books by Aleister Crowley?

Z'EV: I got the most use out of 777—the list of correspondences, and his number dictionary which was the only one you could buy—now Llewellyn's got a number dictionary out, I think it's called a Cabalistic Dictionary. Basically it's a copy of Crowley's plus more material like names of angels. In terms of rituals, I was never involved in any rituals that he was specifically dealing with, which were basically Egyptian rituals.

I saw some of the *Psychic Television* videos of David Tibet obviously involved in some ritual, and I don't know—I think if you did a *real* ritual nothing would show up on the videotape! Or, they might be working on some form of video ritual but it seems like a new form of carried-awayness!

One of Crowley's overall meta-perspective roles was on a large scale finding and publishing lots of information—there were lawsuits and court cases about this, brought about by The Golden Dawn. The Golden Dawn was an upper-class, very racist, *very* elitist group. Crowley was appalled by them socially, and by the fact they were elitist. His whole contention, in *Magick in Theory and Practice,* was that *anyone can do it,* and that this was the western path. And if you in fact *do* the exercises in *Magick in Theory and Practice,* eventually you would get your concentration and attention developed to the point where you would be able to capitalize on your imagination. And when you're able to capitalize on your imagination . . . !

What is referred to as imagination is your overlap with this other world. When you have your concentration to such a point that you start imagining, then you can totally get into this imaginary world. At that point you pick up your spirit guides. When you do in fact pick up your spirit guides, then you're fine. Then you can progress on certain levels.

But there's certain rituals you just can't get in a book. You have to have a teacher in a physical body correcting your ritual, because you can't know you're doing it right yourself, because you've never seen anyone do it right. And if you're not doing it right—it's not that it doesn't work—you do create a doorway between the spirit world and this world, but if your protection isn't together then what ends up happening can be basically what happened to Crowley in India. He was getting into evocations of forces that were actually more powerful than he was able to maintain a defense against, so he was attached, and that led to his senility.

R/S: What was he attached by?

Z'EV: Basically a disembodied psychic vampire. There's *bodied* psychic vampires—people who get involved in relationships with people and eat up all their psychic energy. Then you have a disembodied psychic vampire who attaches and just sucks up all the life energy.

Crowley consciously built up a stereotype of "the world's most evil man" as a type of fence around the law. So that a person had to be of a certain sophistication to not be intimidated by that facade and go after it anyway. But Crowley was really, on some levels, a very moral person, and on some levels a deeply religious person—note the *Hymns to the Star Goddess* and *The Vision and The Voice.* It's not possible for this person to be "the world's most evil man"!

R/S: What do you think Crowley achieved with his Abbey of Thelema?

Z'EV: I don't know. Possibly his notion that all magical ritual is phallic in nature! I don't know. But, his system of ceremonial magic isn't mine....

If you want to affect things on the physical plane, use voodoo. And western ceremonial black magic, put up against a South American or African black magician—I don't think it would hold up, or hold a candle. There are some people known as the Mayomberos; they're the most evil people alive on that level, although there's probably some Tibetans as well.

In the West there may be 15 or 20 real ceremonial magicians left—if that many. But I don't think there's been a western magician who could handle a malignant spirit for centuries. Some of the ones involved with the Nazis may possibly have been close— possibly. But obviously they weren't close enough, or the outcome of WWII would have been different. The Nazis had cults from Tibet working with them, etc, but obviously there was only so much they could do.

The thing about voodoo and black magic is—when the English came into Haiti, all the voodoo, gris-gris and magic against them didn't matter. The English troops just walked right past all this stuff that should have scared the shit out of any normal human beings—they did not even see it, and they wiped out all the camps and cleaned out the mountains. It just went right over their heads. So on a certain level, *ignorance is a terrific protection.*

The thing is, if you're having a fight with someone and you're using magic but they have a gun, there's no hocus-pocus that's going to keep that bullet from going through you! But on the other hand, if you could find one of these Mayomberos, you probably could kill somebody efficiently, magically. Maybe give them a heart attack with acute anxiety.

The biggest protection somebody can have is the knowledge that somebody else is trying to do magic against them. That's the opposite situation, where ignorance is *not* protection. That cuts down the efficiency tremendously—just the fact that you know....

(Photo: Erich Mueller)

ASCETIC AESTHETICS:

"Process in the pursuit of
the performance of pure form"

AXIOMS:

AS ABOVE/SO BELOW.

What things were/is more important than what things are.

We're talking perfection—if you don't gamble/you can't win.

Be prepared. Intention draws attention.

If it's worth doing, it's worth doing.

Honesty's the best policy.

A place for everything/and everything in its place.

Open doors/don't close them.

LEARNING = LIVING: the learning of a lesson is the living of that lesson.

The Axiom "As Above/So Below" is evidenced in the Basic Occult Ritual of all peoples: THE FERTILITY RITE; albeit, ANIMAL, VEGETABLE, ELEMENTAL, SPIRITUAL (comprising the 4 WORLDS of the OCCULT, based on an ordering of vibrational magnitude).

The INTENT of any individual ritual is to replicate the ARCHETYPICAL PROCESS, influencing the specific sphere of activity in question. INFLUX is the metaphor for the result of a successful ritual. At times of INFLUX the worlds are united.

PROCESS is THE Vehicle for the source and protection of experiential information/influx—situations/manifestations as performance (and yes, even entertainment) eliminating the need to create subjectively. Choosing structures from the body of invocation/evocational ritual practice and establishing an integration/integrity within one's material existence on the same order and with the same correspondence that occult existence utilizes in its relationship with divine existence.

DEVOTION THROUGH SACRIFICE the DISCIPLINE (purifying and consecrating the vessel) to translate/transpose this into a/the performance context; DOING not THINKING: invoking/evoking, by analogy, a "model" on the physical plane of the archetypical process, channeling "thought-form/energy/action(s)" into manifestation.

ASCETIC ANALOGIES. Consider spiritual energy as a light source in a room which is separated in two by a curtain. The curtain is the ego—the light ½ spirit, the dark ½ body-world. The dynamic INFLUX is created by the diminishing of the ego/curtain.

ALSO WITH REGARDS TO STARVATION: as the physical MASS diminishes in the physical FORM it is replaced/replenished by spiritual MASS.

115

Z'EV CHRONOLOGY

Born in Los Angeles, CA and given 2 names: *Stefan Joel Weisser* and *Sha'ul Z'ev*. Prior to 1978 all works were by *Stefan Weisser*. In 1978 began using different names to signify different creative *persona*, briefly as follows: *Stefan Weisser* does audio-visual-textual poetics. *Yoel* did percussion musics 1977-78. *Sha'ul Z'ev* does cabalistic studies. *Sha'ul* does musics for organ and tape. When anglicized as *Saul Zev* does words & voice for the band *UNS*. *Z'ev* is the name for kinetic movement & musics—concussion musics, movements & installations. *UNS* is a band producing "low-tech" rhythms and rants (the vocalist's name is *Saul Zev);* the band solo is *Magneet Bond*. *Element L Musics* is the name for studio tape percussion musics and stereo-sonics—it will also be the name of an ensemble utilizing transducer-amplified sculptures. *Rax Werx* is a composite of *Z'ev* percussion used in recording plus *Saul Zev* (live performance vocalist plus tapes).

1957. Studied music.

1963-66. In a variety of rock'n'roll bands in L.A.

1966-69. Leading a band, *Ariel,* with Carl Stone (kybds & electronics), James Stewart (bass & vocals). Band broke up after negotiations with Frank Zappa's *Bizarre* Records.

1969-75. Studied Ewe (pronounced A-way, Ghana tribal) music with Seth & Alfred Cadzekpo. Stopped playing music & studied concrete poetry with Emmett Williams.

1975. Moved to Bay Area, did poetry pieces & work by *Stefan Weisser*. Formed *Cellar M* with Naut & Rex from *R&N* and Will Jackson.

1976-77. *Cellar M* broke up. Band *TO* started with Will Jackson. Produced record, performed West Coast & went to Japan. *TO* broke up. At La Mamelle *Stefan Weisser* did first solo percussion show Aug 28, 1977.

1978. *Z'ev* performed monthly at Fort Mason, and at Mabuhay from March on as *Yoel* and from Sept on as *Z'ev*.

1979. Returned to L.A. Worked with *Johanna Went*. October, for first time went to East Coast—played Boston, R.I., NYC, NJ.

1980. West Coast. April-May went to NYC with *Non & Johanna Went*. Aug, played with *DNA* at Berkeley Square, then NYC & Europe. Sept, did show with *R&N* at The Compound.

1981. Feb 8, London show with *Throbbing Gristle, Clock DVA, Cabaret Voltaire* and *Non*. Feb 12, 1981, Savoy Tivoli *Z'ev* & *Uns* show (this will be released on Subterranean). Thru Dec, peformed in Holland, Belgium, Sweden, Germany, Austria, England.

1982. Jan-Feb, West Coast. Mar-Apr, France, Holland, Germany. May, NYC. June-Nov, Europe, including June *Documenta* show in Kassel, Germany and Oct *Final Academy* show in London.

1983. January, video & sound work with *R&N. Uns* collaboration with *Target Video*. Initial performances of *Element L Musics*, beginning presentations of *Z'ev* as movement. Feb-Mar, Germany & Holland. Apr-May, NYC.

1984. Re-concentration on American performances.

SOME Z'EV DATA:

Race semitic, height 5'8'', weight 135.

Father's occupation: Optometrist. Mother's occupation: Perception and learning disabilities. One sister: Faryl, born 1949.

Schools attended: Chandler Elementary, Mulholland Jr High, Birmingham High, Rexford High, California Institute of the Arts (6 mos).

Childhood obsessions: clouds and dark places. Present obsession: obsession.

Present collections: Books, masks, Ritual Objects in general, metal and plastic objects, sonic data, cassette conversations.

Childhood pets: Baron (Weimaraner), Kahara (cat—17 years old now).

Favorite Childhood TV show: *20th Century* with Walter Cronkite. After childhood no TV ever owned.

Favorite childhood expeditions: Dry gulches.

First important sexual experience: seeing aunt naked at age 17.

Present relationship: Fr. Dr. Dorothea Franck-Oberaspach.

Present social scene: As little as possible.

Ideal household: metal shop, tape/sound studio, library, 1 large "living" room.

Job history: cleaning apartments, laying carpet, furniture delivery, offset printing, managing retail store, archaeological digs, musician, hospital dishwasher, rebuilding alternators, cook & housekeeper, "prescribing" at occult shop, counseling J.D.'s, hospital cafeteria, buying and selling clothes.

Marketable occupational skills: Musician, rough carpentry, plumbing, managerial (retail).

Favorite foreign country: none yet, though Japan heads list.

Drug history: addictions to methamphetamine, alcohol, tobacco, caffein, cocaine, LSD, barbiturates, marijuana. At one time or another most every drug taken at least once. Near-fatal overdose of Belladonna at age 16. Drug use ascribed to Piscean nature.

Medical history: chronic pneumonia since 1963. Vocal chord scraping; no talking for 3 months (1974).

Sleep history: Sometimes insomnia, sometimes awake 30-40 hrs then sleep 12-18; sometimes sleep 20-48 hrs. Dream as often as possible; dreams are critically important. Sleep 5/6AM to 10AM-2PM.

Favorite foods: spicy. Mineral waters. Hate "health" foods. Prefer European eating habits.

Clothes: emphasis on function. Sometimes wear clothing of own design.

Actual library: large sci-fi, large literature, large occult and metaphysical.

Current projects: Finishing compilation of numerical dictionary. A variety of works with Fr. Dr. Dorothea Franck-Oberaspach (chairperson Dept of Rhetoric and Poetics, University of A'dam, Netherlands) in Ethnomethodology, Socio-linguistics, Conversational Analysis, and Comparative Religion. *Plus other projects.*

Z'EV RECORDS

-SALTS OF HEAVY METALS (Lust/Unlust— out of print)
-PRODUCTION & DECAY OF SPATIAL RELATIONS (Backstreet Records—out of print)
-AUF/UIT (½ of 7'' 45, Kremlin)
-WIPE OUT (½ of 7'' 45, Fetish)
-SHAKE RATTLE & ROLL (video, Fetish Mail Orders, 10 Martello St, London E8 England)
-ZONES (¼ 4x4 LP, Subterranean)
-F.F.F. (LP, Subterranean)
-3 FOR 3 (½ of LP, Zensor)
-DOCUMENTA 7 COMPILATION (Carmen Knobel, Camphansenstr 8, 4000 Dusseldorf W Germany)

Z'EV SYNESTHETICS KINETIC MUSIC AND MOVEMENTS

MUSICS: an orchestral continuum built from the following form and content:

FORM: tuned metal constructions/assemblages (modular compositional units in their own right), using 2 modes of employment: 1) percussive—'striking,' specific actions and 2) 'shaking apart,' general actions.

CONTENT: catacoustics (the study of reflected sound for the production of acoustic phenomena) AND:

NOISE: (sound you don't like) with the intent to expand the range of sounds people like, hence consider musical. ("The instruments are collections of objects...strung together on ropes and swung...at varying speeds and directions to produce a fairly astonishing range of pitches and timbres"—*NY Rocker,* July-Aug/1980).

MOVEMENTS: ("...the nature of his self-designed instruments dictates almost as much emphasis on dance as on music. And the moves...to manipulate the instruments, are for grace and athleticism...strong stuff."—*NY Rocker,* July-Aug/1980).

This physical motion of performer and instrument alike establishes a unification of sonic and visual elements into a dance/language of 'configuration.' In effect, a movement and the sound of the movement forming a discreet unit; that unit in relationship to all other such units forms these configurations which unfold in a drama of elemental energies.

STEFAN WEISSER DATA

ARCHIVES: Archives of California Art, Oakland Museum. Performance Proposal File, L.A. County Museum of Art. La Mamelle Inc Contemporary Art Archives. Archive Small Press and Communication, Belgium. Artist Book Collection, Otis Art Institute.

VISUAL PUBLICATIONS: *LAICA Journal #7.* La Mamelle #1 & #2. *Art Contemporary #2. Imagezine #3. Fanache.* Synapse. Intermedia. Dumb Ox. Contexts (limited edition). *Videozine #3.*

AUDIO PUBLICATIONS: *Audiozine #2* (Art Contemporary Publications. *Audio Editions* (Union Gallery, CSUSJ). *Blub Krad* (L.A. Free Music Society).

AUDIENCE PERFORMANCES: 1969, CSU Long Beach. 1973, Pierce Jr College (L.A.). 1974, UC Santa Barbara, Books Etc (L.A.). 1975, L.A.I.C.A., La Mamelle, Museum of Conceptual Art, Project Artaud. 1976, Beyond Baroque Foundation, Harmonia, Theatre Vanguard (Long Beach), Institute of Dance and Experimental Art (L.A.). 1977, Word Works (San Jose). 1978, SF Art Institute, Union Gallery (CSUSJ), Works (SJ), Fort Mason Center, Otis Art Institute, Vanguard Gallery (L.A.), Peace Pagoda Plaza (S.F.).

GALLERY PRESENTATIONS: 1972-1978. ONE PERSON: Beyond Baroque Foundation, Jan 1976. GROUP: CSU (Sacramento), La Mamelle (S.F.), Pierce Jr College (L.A.), And/Or (Seattle), Galerie Kontak (Antwerp), Academy (Ghent), Galerie Posada (Brussels), Rhode Island School of Design, Brown University, The Sculpture Center (Australia), Apropos Gallery (Switzerland), Union Gallery (CSUSJ).

RADIO PERFORMANCES: KPFA (Berkeley), KPOO (S.F.), KCSB (Santa Barbara).

S WEISSER AESTHETICS

AUDIO: 'Poextensions'—''pure poetry'' compositions for massed voices using tape replay and integrating the resonance, reflection, and phase relations of acoustic phenomena to create a universal, archetypical VOICE producing lingual, spacial ''fields.''

VISUAL: from ''context'' (''the weaving together of language''—Oxford English Dictionary), taken literally as the actual, physical, weaving of alphabetical representations, transforming them into glyphic, pictorial ''fields.''

TEXTUAL: images are chosen for their subjective, associative potential and are combined in varying relationships, which themselves carry a train of associations. This provides a ''oom'' (woof & warp = image & relationship) for the reader to ''weave'' their own ''history'' on. ''History'' refers to the narrative outcome of 2 elements: 1) the image associations combined/juxtaposed with the relationship associations, and 2) the meaning which arises from the totality of these individual combinations and juxtapositions. This process then can extend the notion of ''reading'' towards that of ''sounding'' (i.e. sounding the depths).

STEFAN WEISSER SOURCES

-POEXTENSIONS & CONTEXTS (Subterranean)
-INSTILL (¼ of 4x4 LP, Subterranean)
-IMAGEZINE #3 (Con-Arts Press, PO Box 3123 Rincon Annex, San Francisco CA 94119)
-AUDIOZINE #1 & #2 (Con-Arts Press)

UNS CHRONOLOGY

1980. FEBRUARY: Ist performance at The Farm. Then performances at Mabuhay, Aldo's. MARCH: Show with Factrix, Non, Mark Pauline at Studio Eremos, Project Artaud. Then East Coast Tour—all equipment stolen in NYC.

1981. FEBRUARY: Savoy Tivoli show with Z'ev.

1982. Performances in NYC (Public Theater), Holland, Zurich (Music Out of Control Festival), London (Final Academy).

UNS RECORDS/VIDEOS

-MOTHER TONGUE (LP, Subterranean, 577 Valencia, San Francisco CA 94110)
-LIFE SENTENCE (cassette, Subterranean)
-LIVE AT TARGET (¼ of LP, Subterranean)
-LIVE AT TARGET (¼ of Video by Target, 678 S Van Ness, San Francisco CA 94110)
-SAVE WHAT? (½ of cassette, Kremlin Records, c/o Dommelstrt. 2, Eindhoven 5611CK Netherlands)
-THE PAST 2 DAYS (½ of LP, Zensor Records, Beilzigerstrs 23, 1000 Berlin 62 W Germany)
-SAYS (¼ of 4x4 LP, Subterranean)
-FINAL ACADEMY COMPILATION (Crepescule)

ELEMENT L RECORDS

-½ of 7'' 45 (Kremlin 002)
-½ of 7'' 45 (Fetish FE 13)
-¼ of 4x4 LP (Subterranean)

SOME BOOKS

White Goddess/Robert Graves
Sweet Hearts/Emmett Williams
Valentine for Noel/E Williams
Collected Works of Emmett Williams (New Directions)
Divine Pymander/tr J. Everard
Book of Enoch/tr R. Laurence
Sacred Mysteries Among the Mayas & Quiches/Augustus Le Plongeon
Ancient Fragments/I P Cory
Theoretical Arithmetic of the Pythagoreans/T Taylor
Theon of Smyrna/tr R&D Lawlor
Qabbalah-Philosophical Writings of Avicebron
Dictionary of Angels/G Davidson
Holy Kaballah/A E Waite
777/Aleister Crowley
Book of Thoth/Aleister Crowley
Mudra
Fragments of a Faith Forgotten/Mead
The Way of God/M Luzzatto
Bion Experiments/Wilhelm Reich
The Murder of Christ/W Reich
The Function of the Orgasm/W Reich
Character Analysis/W Reich
Eye of the Cyclone/John Lilly
Programming & Metaprogramming the Human Biocomputer/John Lilly
Remarks on Colour/Wittgenstein
Zettel/Wittgenstein
Collected Works/Shakespeare
Inferno/Dante
Ethics of the Fathers/Philip Blackman
The Self & The Brain/Popper & Eccles
Interaction Rituals/Goffman
Behavior in Public Places/Goffman
Jewish Magic & Superstition/ Trachtenberg
Notebooks of Leonardo da Vinci
Egyptian Book of the Dead
Tibetan Book of the Dead
The First Sex/Elisabeth G Davis
On the Sensations of Tone/Helmholtz
Recognitions/W Gaddis
JR/W Gaddis
How Writing is Written/G Stein
Making of Americans/G Stein
Geography & Plays/G Stein
Lucy Church Amiably/G Stein
Calculus of Variation/D Di Prima
Collected Poems/Kenneth Patchen
Journal of Albion Moonlight
Sleepers Awake/Kenneth Patchen
9 Ways of Bon (Shambhala)
Book of 5 Rings/Musashi
The Pronouns/J MacLow
Secret Doctrine/H P Blavatsky
Isis Unveiled/H P Blavatsky
Hebraic Tongue Restored/ Fabre d'Olivet
Golden Verses of Pythagoras/ Fabre d'Olivet
Adam & the Kabalistic Tree/Levi
Exodus/Levi
Meditation & The Bible/Areya Kaplan
Meditation & The Kabalah/A Kaplan
Book of Tokens/Paul Foster Case
Sefer Yetzirah/tr P Mordell

Jewish Mystical Testimonies/ ed L Jacobs
Her-Bak: Living Face of Ancient Egypt/Isha Schwaller de Lubicz
Her-Bak: Egyptian Initiate/ Isha Schwaller de Lubicz
The Opening of the Way/ R A Schwaller de Lubicz
Blast Power & Ballistics/ Jack Lindsay
Dada Painters & Poets/ ed R Motherwell & B Karpel
Futurist Manifestos/ed Umberto Apollonio
Adventures in the Skin Trade/ Dylan Thomas
The Sword of Gnosis/ed Needleman
Stand on Zanzibar/John Brunner
Dosadi Experiment/Frank Herbert
Whipping Star/Frank Herbert
Short Stories/Philip K Dick

SOME MOVIES

Performance/Nicholas Roeg
Pound/Robert Downey
Greasers Palace/   ''
Invasion of the Body Snatchers (1956 Don Siegel version)
Golddigger Series/Busby Berkeley (esp Lullaby on Broadway, & We're In The Money in pig latin)
Stage Door/Gregory La Cava
In the Realm of the Senses/Oshima
Kwaidan/Misuki Kobayashi
Kuroneko/Kaneto Shindo
Werewolf of London/Henry Hull
Night Porter/Liliana Cavani
Pork Chop Hill/Lewis Milestone
Persona/Ingmar Bergman
Hour of the Wolf/I Bergman
Cries & Whispers/I Bergman
Woman Under The Influence/ John Cassavetes
Husbands/J Cassavetes
Coconuts/Marx Bros
Night at the Opera/Marx Bros
Horsefeathers/Marx Bros
Duck Soup/Marx Bros
Animal Crackers/Marx Bros

SOME RECORDS

Greatest Hits/Otis Redding
By Tim Buckley:
    Goodbye & Hello   Star Sailor
    Happy Sad   Lorca
    Welcome to LA
Sun, Moon & Herbs/Dr John
Gris-Gris/Dr John
American Indian Anthology (In fact, most Everest LPs)
Tibetan, Balinese, Javanese & African LPs (on Nonesuch label)
Astral Weeks/Van Morrison
Highway 61/Bob Dylan
Country/Tracy Nelson
Love Like Anthrax/Gang of Four
Sister Ray/Velvet Underground
Velvet Underground/V U
Motorhead/Motorhead
Salisbury Hill/Peter Gabriel
Trout Mask Replica/Capt Beefheart

JOHANNA WENT

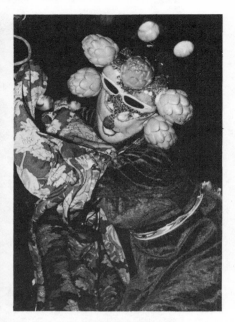

Above photo: Siegfried. Previous pages: serial photos by Peggy Photo; large photo by Ana Barrado. All Johanna Went serial photographs by Peggy Photo.

In Seattle, Johanna Went grew up in a housing project; it would have been easy to succumb to her poor white trash milieu and become a welfare mother with five children. A chance 1974 encounter with theater innovator Tom Murrin resulted in several years' involvement in street theater, including a 1978 tour of Europe and America. In the summer of 1979 she did her first solo show at the Hong Kong Cafe in Los Angeles.

Out of dreams and endless foraging in thrift stores and garbage bins, Johanna has created by sewing, gluing, collaging, and painting, the vivid props and dolls for her shows—all of which involve sex, food, liquids, meat, meat by-products, and destruction. The constant theme in her shows is *transformation*—from birth (or abortion) to death....

Set against a background of very loud noise/rhythm, Johanna's show is more a furiously energetic trance-state than the performance of a rational being. Then again, this is not real time — a slow-motion drug would be needed to comprehend all the images, symbols, details, and gestures crammed into the 15 or 20 minutes of a Johanna Went show. Definitely not for the cleanliness-and-order set, this is sheer fun and black humor masquerading as modern art....

Johanna Went has a 45 available on Boyd Rice's Graybeat Records, *Slave Beyond The Grave/NO U NO*, and a new album, *Hyena*....

R/S: How do you prepare for each show? I get the impression it takes months....

JOHANNA: It doesn't take that long. It depends. I gather up a lot of stuff, things, junk, articles, just items. You know: styrofoam, plastic, cardboard, clothes, shoes, food things—anything you can think of. Kotex, sandwiches, tools—anything. And then I just kind of think about different things: what I dream about, what I see everyday, or somebody I'll be fascinated with, and somehow I'll use them in my show. Or a movie that I saw—all these kinds of things *affect* me.

And then when I put together my show, I try not to think a lot. I just glue things together and paint things and make things look like something that I like! Then I take all of these things to where I'm going to do a show, and the musicians come and play whatever it is they want to play, and then I sing anything that comes out of my mouth. There's lots of blood and messy things and then I fall down and it's all over.

R/S: Well, you pay a lot of attention to details—I remember at one show, you had a little naked baby doll (it was just a small part of your costume)—you couldn't even really see it across the stage, yet you'd glued pubic hair on it.

JOHANNA: You *saw* it! That was just a little joke for myself. I like to give myself little jokes; I like to entertain myself.

R/S: At the On Broadway show, you became a huge Statue of Liberty...that suddenly started to spew blood all over the audience—

JOHANNA: That was a really hard show for me—

R/S: Oh yes, your sister had suddenly died.

JOHANNA: I'd made the Statue of Liberty, the whole costume, and when I brought it up to San Francisco I asked Mark Pauline if he could do something to it to make it spit blood. He hooked up this pump and it was really great—I wasn't sure if it was going to work and then all of a sudden it started squirting blood into the audience—I couldn't believe it. It worked really good! Just what I wanted.

I love violence in movies. I like that safe atmosphere where I can sit there and watch violence—I like the color, I like things exploding, and I like fires, I like blood, I like guts. Sometimes it's so ridiculous I can't believe people look away from it! But personally, I prefer not to be involved in violent situations.

R/S: I got some on my coat and it wouldn't come off. Was it stage blood?

JOHANNA: It's a secret old family recipe. Sometimes if you wash things it comes out but sometimes it doesn't. I can't help it. One time somebody asked me to pay their cleaning bill, but I just said Fuck you.

> If I don't do shows for awhile I get weird, I get crazy, I get strange and I know that I need to do a show....

R/S: What was the most extreme performance you ever did?

JOHANNA: Most extreme? I don't know—I used to do a lot of street performances that in a way were more extreme than what I do now, just because of the different environments. Probably the most extreme—at least the one that everybody always talks about—was when I did a performance with a dead cat. Probably because the cat was dead and people were upset because they thought I killed it. Which I didn't—*I do not kill cats*. But I don't know, because I have trouble remembering performances....

R/S: Because you kind of go into a trance during them?

JOHANNA: Right after the performances I can't remember anything, and then I ask what happened—people tell me different things that happened. Sometimes when I clean up the stuff I can *kind of* remember. It's really hard to remember.

R/S: Well, what happened with the dead cat on stage?

JOHANNA: It was on a really small stage at Vinyl Fetish (an L.A. record store) when they first opened. There were a lot of people packed into such a small area so they had to really look at it.

R/S: They were forced to be really close to you—

JOHANNA: I just poked it a little bit with a knife—you know, threw it around a little bit. I didn't kill it, it died a natural cat death.

R/S: How many abortions have you had?

JOHANNA: What? This month? I've had a few.

R/S: At the On Broadway show you had a birth.

JOHANNA: It was a baby devil—it came out of the devil; that wasn't *me*. The devil gave birth to the baby devil. He was the devil sleeping in his bed, and he woke up—he had a bad stomach ache—there was a baby inside of his stomach. What a surprise, right? And the baby had a whole bunch of stuff over him—

afterbirth, or something. It was silly, wasn't it? I can't stand the devil—so silly-looking with those horns.

R/S: ...What's your latest dream?

JOHANNA: I just recently dreamed that my friend—see, I've been working 2 jobs recently.

R/S: Why, for money?

JOHANNA: Yeah, I'm really broke. Long hours—I leave one job and go to the other job. For a long time I've been working 7 days a week, and it's really been getting to me—I've been getting crazy. But it's really good for me because I need to keep busy because I've just been really unhappy—I've just been depressed about my sister. You know those things take a long time to get over, so I thought I should work.

Anyway, I had this dream that my friend called me up and said, "Johanna! I got this great job for you! Well, it's not a very good job but it pays good." So I meet her downtown...in the sewers, but the sewers are all done up real gothic-looking like a vampire would live there. And then she gives me this bat...and these rats come running out of this hole and we have to bash them with the bat. I started laughing, and she said, "Well, it's not such a great job but it pays pretty good." So then we're bashing all these rats and all of a sudden this little rat comes up and she says, "Oh look at this one, it's so cute!" and I say, "Mary, you have to *kill* it!" and she says, "No no no, I don't want to kill it." "Come on Mary." "No no, I don't want to kill it." So I go chasing after the rat and she goes chasing after me and we go down this long, long ways and all of a sudden we hear this door shut—SLAM! And then we realize that we have to stay there until we kill all the rats. I woke up laughing; I thought it was really funny. But I think it was from working too many hours.

R/S: What was your favorite costume at the Ed Mock show?

JOHANNA: There was this costume that I never got to see again. I had this yellow hat with all these yellow flowers on top, with some kind of veil on it. It looked like some weird missionary. Then I had this yellow dress that had this black stuff on it—it had these glasses that went around and around and around. It was all yellow, yellow, yellow. The costume got wrecked and I threw it away—that was the only time I ever wore it. If somebody has a picture of it I'd like to see it again.

R/S: How many costumes did you get ready for your last show?

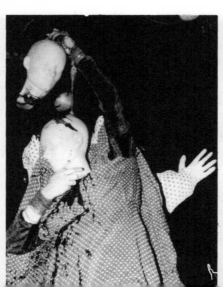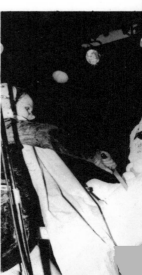

JOHANNA: My last show I think I had 9 costumes. I had my wedding costume with the 2 faces, 2 white faces one on top of the other, and then it had a veil and a plastic wedding-cake decoration like a bride-and-groom only it was a devil. Then there was the wedding dress with bloody kotexes on it, and a big yellow kind-of-face in the middle of it. Then it had two little plastic tits on the outside and—*Mark Pauline* sent me a really pretty color picture where I'm holding the baby devil with all this red stuff coming out of my mouth. That was one of my favorite costumes.

Then I made a costume that was black with a whole bunch of white faces on it, with blood on them. Then it had black curly hair, with voodoo dolls sticking out of the faces.

The one with the baby doll with the pubic hair on it—I can't even describe it. It was kind of a red shiny vest with a long arm that sticks out of the head, that has some kind of yarn on it, and has a hand on it, and you can kind of hold the hand and dance with it if you want. And it has a purple face with little plastic yellow circles around the eyes and the mouth. It looks to me like an African kind of costume. I just like it because you can dance with yourself when you wear it. You can hold the hand and dance around.

I like anything that's little and then looks really big. I like things that take on a life of their own, that move by themselves, that seem to have some kind of spirit to them. And that change shape.

I didn't kill it, it died a natural cat death.

My record's out—it has a picture of a hyena mask that I made—half is the hyena mask and half is my face. A video's out as well (for info on both LP and videocassette write PO Box 291071, Los Angeles CA 90029). I might work with Shirley Clarke—do you know her?

R/S: I've seen her film, *The Cool World.*

JOHANNA: *The Cool World* is a great movie. I like that black kid in the movie—his face is so cool. Every different way you look at his face, the way the camera looks at it—he looks like another person. His face just takes all these different shapes. One time I looked at his face and I thought he was a mountain or some kind of cliff. Another time, his eyes were like lime. I just

thought he was so handsome and his lips were really beautiful.

And the best thing I liked about the movie was when everybody talked. That was exciting to me, because when people talked you realized that they were people with a past and a future, that they were real human beings living in time. Sometimes when you watch somebody like Harrison Ford on the screen, you have a feeling that they only exist for like a second, or maybe that they're like Bugs Bunny—somebody drew them and then that's it. Like they don't shit, or they don't eat, or go to the store, or anything. But these people—you knew that they had problems they had to take care of after they went home at night. I liked it a lot. Shirley said she used real gang kids.

I just saw her films and I couldn't believe it, I was really impressed. I'm really glad because I just feel she's somebody I can get along with. Because most people really want to direct you and make you say all these things that you don't want to say. Especially me—I hate to have somebody telling me what to say...*or do.* "Wear this dress and say this and walk over there!" I really have problems with that.

R/S: Do you watch much TV?

JOHANNA: Right now I'm watching *Dynasty,* and on my TV *they're* watching something on TV too! This show's really silly. Everyone that I work with watches it. I think this old woman that's on now is a psychic....

R/S: Have you ever visited a psychic?

JOHANNA: When I was in New Orleans I went to this guy who read my cards. He was real interesting. He was this kid who was 17 years old but he looked like he was 40 years old. I went into this house and there was this picture of this 17th century guy, like a Frenchman, on the wall. All of a sudden this guy walks out and here he is—and he's 17 years old. He's kind of paunchy-looking, kind of balding—he looks like the same guy, he even has a little pony tail. Then he starts playing this harpsichord that he made himself (this other guy told me he writes in this strange script from that time period). And he had this crippled father that lives in the back room—when I went to go to the bathroom his father grabbed my hand and kept looking at me.

I was really impressed when he read my cards—he told me things that would happen, that did happen. He told me things that had happened that I didn't think he would have any way of knowing. I thought it was

interesting—I'd go back and see him again. Plus I just liked his whole style—I like people that have *some* kind of style. I mean it could get boring if I had to hang around with him too much, I'm sure, but to just be visiting in New Orleans it was all right.

One time in Montreal I was at this French/African restaurant, and I don't speak any French. There were beaded paintings on the wall; they had heavy food like beans and bread. We were sitting there eating this dinner, thinking about getting ready to leave. There was hardly anybody there except for these women. All of a sudden this man comes rushing into the restaurant and he said something really loud to this woman in French. And I don't know French. My friend Tom asked, "What did he say?" and I said, "Oh, he said there was a dead man in the parking lot." So then everybody ran outside, and there was this man lying in the parking lot with his wrists all sliced up. Somehow I *knew*. . . .

R/S: Did you visit those famous graveyards in New Orleans?
JOHANNA: I don't know how famous they were; I went to some graveyards. We just laid on the tombstones because it was really, really hot at night. It was a full moon and we were lying on this cool, cool marble. They bury everyone above the ground because of floods, so all the tombs are high and you can climb on top of them. There's a lot of them around, really old ones, very interesting-looking. I love New Orleans; people like to party and there were a lot of parties and I liked the people on the streets a lot. I'd like to go there for Mardi Gras.

R/S: What are you making for your Halloween show?
JOHANNA: I made some day-glo green ghosts, and I have this huge Wolfman poster. I think I'm going to do something to the Wolfman, and use the hyena mask somehow. And I made a couple of monster costumes that I like a lot. I'm just putting stuff together right now, but I'm excited about it. I've been exercising a lot.

R/S: Hey, are you watching TV now?
JOHANNA: Yeah—they just showed Edith Massey for a second. I sent Edith Massey a fan letter because I had this dream that she was on *The Love Boat* with Divine. I thought that was perfect so I wrote her a letter, because one time when I was in Baltimore I saw her in a thrift shop and I really liked her a lot. Plus I really like her in the movies—so wonderful. She sent me a postcard back and told me when she was going to be in L.A.

R/S: Do you have any tattoos?
JOHANNA: I'd love to get another tattoo. I have a little tattoo—just a dumb little bird. A long time ago I got it. It's cute though, I like it.

> I trust myself. I trust myself that I'm never gonna kill somebody by accident or set the stage on fire. . . .

Everybody always says, "Oh god, you get a tattoo and then you'll hate it," but I like it still. I like tattoos, I like the whole idea, I don't care if it's dumb. In fact I wish I had a couple more. But I'm glad I didn't get the Zig-Zag Man tattooed on my forehead. I mean I do think you can really start to hate something after awhile.

See, my dad always had a tattoo and so I always wanted one, ever since I was a little kid. He had something like a heart and scroll with my mom's name. She died, but he didn't get it erased. I don't think I'm going to get anybody's name tattooed on me. I'd like some kind of Japanese tattoo or something. I just have to find the right one.

When I got this one, it was just a choice out of what was there. I went to this woman named Madame Lazonga in Seattle; I got a cheap tattoo. I got what I could get for 20 bucks—there were like 3 choices or 10 choices—I can't remember.

Madame Lazonga has, like, 1,000 tattoos; she was the youngest tattoo artist in Seattle then. She used to wear these big glasses with rhinestones all over them, and I thought she was really cool. She has "sleeves" tattooed on her arms, like lace. . .and tattoos on her back and stomach and legs. I'm really impressed with that!

You know tattoos hurt, too. They hurt more than I thought they would.

R/S: Tattoos seem to be much more popular now. People never used to talk about them.
JOHANNA: Well, when there were hippies, everybody got hippie tattoos. Now people get skulls and bats and snakes and devils and things like that. I have two friends that are married and they have matches on their butts. I think it's some kind of joke but I can't remember.

R/S: What are you the most scared of?

JOHANNA: I think I'm really scared of being trapped in some kind of boring life where there's no outlet, where you can't get away from the boredom, where you can't *not* think about it. I guess I really wouldn't want to be in prison. I think of that as being really, really dull...and not having control over how bored you can be. Not that I'm sure there aren't exciting moments, but that kind of lack of control I really don't care to think about happening to me.

R/S: Well, you know how paranoid New York City can make people.

JOHANNA: I hate to hear those stories. Like there was this couple visiting from Belgium. They were in town one or two days and the wife, downtown, gets offered a ride. And she goes with them and then they rape her. And it's really shitty, because—if I went to Belgium, it probably wouldn't happen to me there.

It really pisses me off. I get tired of this really personal violence; I think it's so silly when people are taking their frustrations out on people who don't have it any better than they do. It just seems like they should be more cunning, and really evil, genuinely evil, and do something really horrendous. Or else just admit that you're a fuck-up, you're impotent, rather than beat up on somebody that's worse off than you, or as bad. Go after the assholes who have all the power and the money, or else...just swim around in the gutter!

R/S: That's funny, because it seems like there's a lot of violence in your shows.

JOHANNA: It does seem that way, doesn't it? Funny you should mention that. I don't know where it all comes from. Sometimes people think things are more violent than I think they are. I don't know, but sometimes people who don't know me are afraid to invite me over to their house or anything. You know I'm a polite person, I never go over and bust up anybody's house or anything...unless they ask me to.

Sometimes I feel really violent, and sometimes I'm really angry. Sometimes I feel real anger and real emotions during a show. Other times I'll be doing something that I don't particularly think is violent, but I'll just feel these intense feelings and get involved in the movement or the action of whatever I'm doing and it *appears* to be extremely violent to someone, whereas maybe I'm thinking it's something different, you know? That happens a lot.

Just like the blood that I use—I really think that I've gotten past the point of it being that *symbolic*, to *me* anyway. It's like when I go to horror movies, I never can really get scared anymore. But I can remember that at one time I could get so scared I'd sleep with the lights on. And I kinda lost that, you know—it's kind of like losing your virginity or something—you forget what it was like. And so, I always *wanted* to feel that feeling again; I always *hoped* for it, and yet I don't feel it anymore. Movies don't scare me anymore, at least not monster movies.

R/S: Some people think your shows arouse strong fears—emotions related to birth or abortion traumas, with all the liquids and afterbirth, etc.

JOHANNA: I don't know. I go through phases, like sometimes the only thing I'm interested in my whole show is the colors...or form, or sometimes it'll be things that crunch a lot—that make crunching sounds. I get into these phases—I get into a lot of color phases where I'm really affected by certain colors. Like right now I'm using a lot of this day-glo green-green color, and it kind of makes me shaky—maybe it's the spray cans! But there's something about this color—if you look at it a long time, other colors all look pink. I just feel this real kind of nervous, edgy feeling from this color. And other colors make me feel different ways. Sometimes the same color makes me feel different at different times, but I'm really affected by color, and I really think that color could be like a whole form of communication by itself, and I always wonder how come it's not used that way, more.

I also like liquids a lot—they change their color and shape, plus they have a life of their own. They can move by themselves, and you don't *know* what they're going to do—they're unpredictable. I mean, sometimes they won't come out of their container. Sometimes they'll be really thicker than you thought—they just go plop! plop! plop! Other times they'll *spray* out. And you just have more of a feeling that it's not an inanimate object; you have the feeling of it being another *force* that you have to deal with.

Plus, liquid has a color. Sometimes it's translucent, sometimes it's opaque—there's all kinds of things about it. Especially for me, because I make a lot of my stuff on my own, so I don't know how it's going to look

125

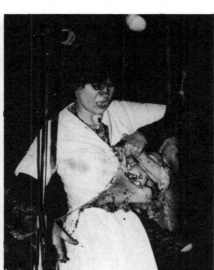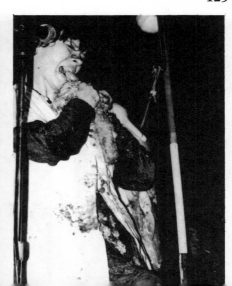

later. Because if I pack it away into my prop, sometimes it changes—it changes color, it changes shape; because it's been put away for awhile it gets thick or something. And sometimes it really stinks, and I didn't think it was going to stink—

R/S: That's right; at the On Broadway show you used aged meat—

JOHANNA: Oh yeah, those were especially weird sausages. I made them myself—homemade guts. They were pretty good—weren't they real-looking?

R/S: Yes, what were they?

JOHANNA: I can't tell.

R/S: Didn't you use a pig's head once?

JOHANNA: I like pigs' heads a lot, because they're so funny. I like goats' heads—I like any kind of meat, bones, things like that. Sometimes they smell bad—I like that. I like liver—liver's really good.

The thing is that people react to these things—I cannot believe how people react to things. I cannot believe that people are disgusted by certain things. I just can't! Sometimes it just amazes me—the things that people are upset by. And then when I think about it, I think about things that I'm upset by, things that I don't like. Then I realize that. . .I'm just different.

R/S: These same people will eat steak or liver or brains in their scrambled eggs and not think about it—

JOHANNA: A lot of people won't eat brains. I'd eat brains. But I won't eat steak. Steak tastes like sweat. Don't you think? It tastes like sweat, take my word for it. Whereas liver, and organ meats, have *flavor,* because they have a blood taste. Muscle meat tastes like sweat, whereas liver—you feel like you're eating something flesh-like—you can rip it with your teeth really good.

See, the thing I don't understand about meat-eaters is: I don't understand how these same people that eat meat are repulsed at the idea of killing an animal. But a lot of them are really upset at the idea. Whereas I understand: if you want to eat some meat, you take the animal, kill it, then make some little earmuffs out of its coat—there sure would be a lot of people with earmuffs if they had to wear all these animals they ate. God, when I drive up to San Francisco and pass all these cows—I can't believe Cowtown. Have you ever driven by there when there's like a zillion billion cows, all standing right next to each other. And you see them for like miles?

R/S: And you can smell them too.

JOHANNA: I don't get it—how come they don't figure it out and go after these people? Fight back! How did they ever get into this sorry state? They're pretty big. . .and there's a bunch of them. . . .

R/S: "Attack of the Killer Cows." Do you ever worry about people misinterpreting your shows?

JOHANNA: Nobody is ever going to think what I think about my shows. I'm so transient, I change my mind from minute to minute, that *I* don't even know what I think about them.

First of all, I hate anybody telling me anything; I hate getting messages, through art, films, all that stuff—I don't think that anybody needs to tell me anything. And I'm not going to tell anybody—I'm not trying to *make* anybody feel anything or think anything. But. . .I think that my shows affect people on a real gut level. . .for reasons other than the guts! To me, the things that people probably think are the most sensational about myself are things that I really think are kind of fluff, things to entertain *me,* that I like to play with or be silly with. But I really don't think that people should be shocked by these things.

I don't use *anything* that people can't see all the time! I mean, I didn't invent *any* of these things—pigsheads, dildoes—I never even had a dildo before I did shows! I never even thought about it. But now that I have an opportunity to show them off, I have quite a few. (God they're so stupid, they're even dumber than the cows.)

Sometimes I just can't believe that people really do react to things that they react to.

R/S: Well, I reacted the first time I saw you come out with a dildo on—

JOHANNA: I think it's funny. But see, I think that my shows are a lot funnier—that's what I don't understand, why people don't laugh more. I almost laugh during the whole show. And most of the things that I use in the show I think are funny. I think they're *really* funny.

R/S: I think you've broken some kind of taboo about *dry* performing. . . .

JOHANNA: Also, a certain amount of it has to do with the fact that I'm a woman doing what I do, too. And I think that more and more, younger women performers are getting tougher and tougher, they're getting more to the point where they want to do whatever it is that they want to do. They're getting stronger, which I really like. They're sick of what they're all supposed to pretend; that's part of it.

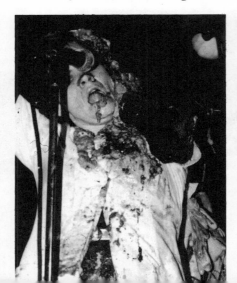

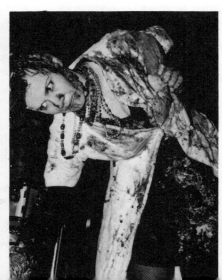

Johanna Went on top of garbage bin full of discarded costumes after her performance at the Ed Mock Dance Studio, San Francisco 1981. (Photo: Vale)

R/S: What do you think about pornography? At one show you had a huge collage/costume made out of hundreds of color photos from porno magazines.

JOHANNA: See, I think that genitals are interesting for a lot of different reasons. I've always been curious at opportunities to see other naked people. But I think that pornography definitely is not interesting to most women, because it really is insulting to women. Most pornography places women in the position of—well, placing them in positions! Which is dull—I'm not interested in that at all.

I get a little pissed off at the women for allowing themselves to be used that way for money. And at the same time I understand; I know what it's like to be broke. I know when people get broke, it's hard.

I have real mixed feelings about pornography. I always have mixed feelings about saying *This shouldn't be allowed,* yet at the same time I have feelings where I just say, *How come people are so stupid? How can they buy this stuff? How can they keep continuing on with it?*

Also, I find a lot of pornography really humorless. I guess I really like things that are funny. And anything's funny. I really liked The Tylenol Murders—I just loved the name. I mean it's really horrible when you think it could be you—that you just take a little aspirin or something and then you're dead—but at the same time it seems so funny, all of it on TV—it seems like a cartoon. I think this is how things get out of hand—

pretty soon *everything seems like a cartoon, or else it seems like it's on TV.*

R/S: Then you have the Tylenol imitations—

JOHANNA: Now they call them *The Copycat Killers.* I love all these silly words, like Copycat—that almost sounds like Krazy Kat, one of those cartoon characters.

R/S: The mass media are responsible for this copycat phenomena—

JOHANNA: They are; they love these ideas of these murderers, and then they really build it up and people get all excited....It's sad! but true.

R/S: Most of these murderers turn out to be men; women are a bit behind on that avenue of human progress....

JOHANNA (sadly): I know, I know. I had hopes when that little girl in San Diego shot all those people— Brenda Spencer. I really had hopes; I thought, "This is a good sign: young, smart girl...."

R/S: She hated Mondays—

JOHANNA: That's what you read in the paper. I'm sure if you talked with her, she'd give you a whole list of things she hated, and her dad was probably right up at the top, with the principal.

R/S: Well, she got the principal.

JOHANNA: She did? Well...I just can't believe that there aren't more sex-mutilation murders done by women to men, kind of random ones. Like a lot of ones.

R/S: Well—maybe women are too smart to do things like that?

JOHANNA: Well, they really have to think about a lot more things just to survive, I think. It's just that—if you, all the time, have to worry about if somebody's gonna try and rape you, or beat the shit out of you, or take your money; or that somebody makes more money than you, or you're poor, whatever—if you have to think about these things all the time, it's harder to plan these other things out! Whereas, if you have a certain amount of safety in your life just by the fact that you're a man—you *definitely* have a certain amount more: you can move easier at night...different things that you don't even have to *think* about. So you just have more time to think about doing other things that you want to do. I mean I definitely think there could be as many murders done by women; I think about this all the time. I haven't come up with an answer why.

Also, I've always felt that it's really bad that women don't go into the army and learn how to use guns, and actually have to *think* about and realize that you could kill somebody with your bare hands. Probably a lot of women get raped by men that have been in the service, who have learned real killing techniques, fighting techniques, and yet these women didn't get the same training...for a lot of reasons. It's really bad that they don't.

I think that women should be given Killing Classes— not just fighting classes, but Killing Classes. How To Kill. How to kill so that you *know* that you can kill. So that you know that you can do it. *How to kill someone with your hands, with yourself, with your body.* So that you really got the feeling for *what you could do.* And a small person can kill a big person—the possibilities are endless. I just really think that women should be trained to kill. And if that happened, I think that would make a real *positive* change—more than anything! More than anything else that I can think of....

R&N

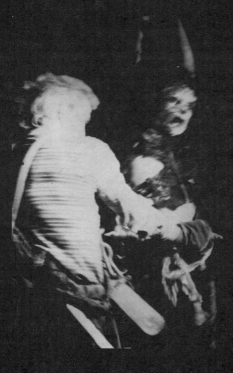

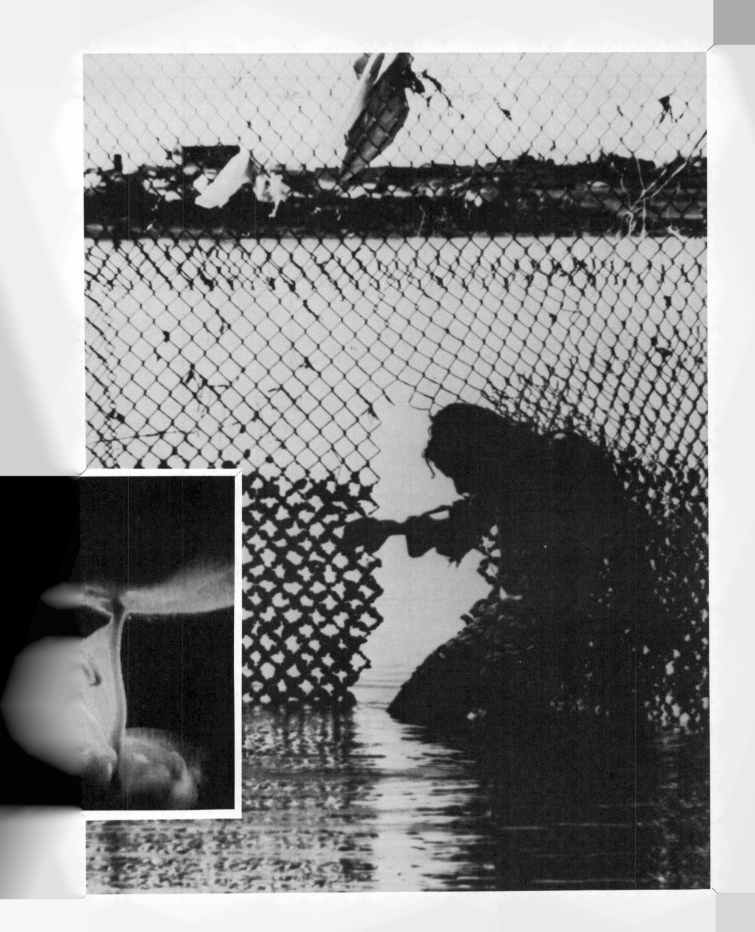

DON GEREUX – NIK FAULT ©1982

All R&N photos throughout by Polyploid Sam.

Underground since 1969, *Rhythm & Noise (R&N)* is pioneering high-tech, *live* computer-interactive video-and-sound presentations. Which means they can improvise and cut-up *interactively* between electronic image and sound at any given point—they're not just replaying prerecorded video. They see their role as propagandists against misinformation and the control process.

Visual content of the 1980 Compound shows included war documentation, weapons technology, lobotomy footage, neo-Pavlovian animal experimentation, whale butchery, post-holocaust survivalism, and other examples of 20th century progress, surrounded by a 360° force field of *loud* multi-dimensional (psychedelic?) rhythms & sounds. All 4 shows were different; all 4 were sold out.

Some minimal background: one of the personnel studied with Nam June Paik and currently works for Sam Peckinpah; the other has designed his own computerized synthesizer system. They're currently setting up an affordable public-access video editing facility while planning a series of appearances over the next 24 months, video collaborations with *Z'ev,* narrowcast TV programs, and automated installations....

R/S: Do you have a conscious philosophy about what you're doing?

R&N: *Subconscious,* yes. We're making conscious attempts to alter established information channels closed in the subconscious, where a lot of the "control" mechanisms are triggered via "real world" activities. Not *subverting* but *diverting,* rearranging those paths to consider alternatives to what is generally conceived of as the real world. By and large what we're after is hitting the 2 centers that seem to be the most susceptible to that kind of rechanneling or redirecting—sound and vision. That's what *vaudeo* is.

R/S: Vaudeo?

R&N: It's a neologism—we invented it. It's just a catchword for our synthesis of technology and ideas, based on how to get our ideas across. Basically we're involved in psychoactive processing.

R/S: Vaudeo implies greater emphasis on sound—most people think of video more in terms of images. They normally don't experience video plus extremely loud sound.

R&N: High resolution sound and high resolution graphics. It also implies a kind of integration of the two mediums. The sound component might be louder and *physically* more moving, while the video component is more cerebral. The 2 together create almost a sensorial saturation.

R/S: What was significant about your 1980 performances?

They weren't just prerecorded videos played at immense volumes?

R&N: They were the outcome of 10 years' experimentation in real-time, sound-synchro, locked video via computerized interaction, and viewed on large video projections. We really did have it "locked" to the point where certain sounds did trigger certain events, and certain images did trigger certain sounds. The performances were our testing grounds. We can show whole blocks of images in any given order, or overlapping, or sequence of overlappings, within a certain phrase list a few seconds long to many minutes long. Those become modular units you can throw into a plot line or narrative form to change the actual ideas. One night A-B-C-D, another night A-C-B-D, etc. Sometimes they link through plot lines or surrealistic dream state notions, or sometimes things don't link at all—then it's up to the spectator to put his own ends together.

R/S: Does this consciously relate to Burroughs' Cut-up ideas?

R&N: Definitely. We have a lot of relationship to the Cut-up technique, specifically. And we are going to be doing something along the lines of Brion Gysin's Dreamachine in our next show. We will be penetrating the informational, ideological shell which is imposed on us, constructed and reconstructed throughout the day, and getting to the nirvana, trance state where you're really witnessing the process of information transfer within the overall context of the mind.

R/S: Integrating dream and imagination processes while remaining conscious?

R&N: What the Cut-up does for me is—it really destroys a lot of the established patterns. By using a lot of those images which can be considered more "subconscious" or "surreal" and integrating them into a sound-electronic image package, you can in fact create that real dream space.

R/S: What content are you providing?

R&N: Without giving anything away—plots, involving a mixture of suppressed sex transmitted into violent action, etc. Plus, in terms of the overall stage presence, there will be virtually no personalities involved. Visually there will be a character who goes through various states of mind while getting from one place to another—meta-states, unconscious states, waking states, shock states, non-linearly. You'll walk away with a sense of having gone through some kind of journey, but it's not segmented like a film is. Television has always been victimized by its own history as *television,* not video—its worst mistake was to be a *passive medium* or voice for film, theater or stage. That's not what we're going to be doing, at all.

R/S: Would you say you have an apocalyptic mentality?

R&N: Do we think things are getting worse? Definitely. What interests us is *how* they're getting worse, and the techniques that someone, something, is using to make it worse. The problem rests with people not having adequate information to wade through the bulk of essentially *useless* information. At best it's useless, at the worst it's debilitating and destructive. There needs to be some kind of new guidance system by which we can get through the bulk of ideas that have so far controlled civilization which are worn out, obsolete and essentially useless. Because none of them are

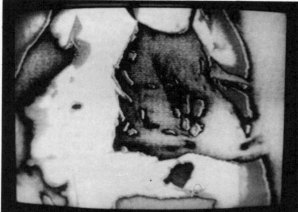

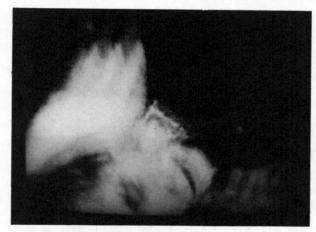

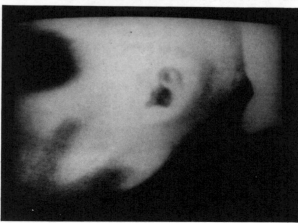

made to deal with the *process* of integrating information at such a rapid rate.

R/S: Yes, it's amazing how many media celebrities still proclaim their belief in God and the Church—

R&N: Going to church and God are essentially therapy for a lot of people who really feel insecure about what they do, while they continue to create obsolete systems in a highly interactive information environment. They put out lots of bad information. It doesn't matter how good their intentions are—they're unaware of what they're doing.

Certain people are really aware—people who monopolize the airwaves under the guise of making them controlled by the private sector—which is to say, you and I. What they really mean is that only the people who have the money and technology get access, while other people who have ideas but not the power and the bucks never get their say.

R/S: Can you say a little more about the *de-control* process?

R&N: The de-control process is pretty simple—when things are going *one way,* ideas become ideologies, and the first duty of an ideology is to defend itself, and essentially to shunt any information entering from outside the system that will take it in another direction.

By defocusing the internal eye on linear structure; creating more of an environmental impact with information rather than an architectural construct that you have to follow along to see the whole thing— defocusing makes you much freer to see the processes that go on in the subconscious world, breaking down the conscious control patterns.

R/S: On a daytime TV serial the real message will not be linear plot (which you already know but follow anyway), but *Buy the osterizer in the background.*

R&N: You have to realize that commercial TV is not advertising 6 minutes an hour, it's advertising 24 hours a day. It's advertising lifestyles, it's advertising social mores, it's advertising behavioral patterns; it's reinforcing certain ways of behaving which become to the viewer the proper way to be. And so it creates those patterns of behavior and reinforces them on a daily basis. We need other types of behavior! Where's the *other* channel?

That's subliminal programming, but to actually get inside your own mind is a much more difficult task, especially if most of your time is taken up reacting to this conditioning and superficial programming— superficial ideas that you're being bombarded with on a day-to-day basis. So the idea is to get inside that whole mechanism and then put something else there, or at least open it up so you can see whatever is there yourself and then make a conscious decision about what it is you really want to do. Rather than being told what to do.

R/S: How can you do anti-consumerism video?

R&N: The problem with that is that most people end up doing satire or some kind of take-off on commercial TV, but all they're doing is taking a different slant— they're turning the coin over, but it's the same coin. Most "funny" or "hip" TV programs just reinforce the popular "alternative" lifestyles, rather than creating a *real alternative of thinking about ideas*....

REFERENCE

CHRONOLOGY

SCRAPE. An original audience abduction and mobilization event. Participants were moved from trailers into barrels. L.A., 1969.

DANCING ON DEAD ROCK. Darkness/deprivation weather chamber featured ravaged terrain and sonic incisions. Version #2 performed in underground city sector collapsed since 1889. Seattle. 1969.

CRASH PROGRAM. Arrivals fastened into view-slit packing crates which are lifted, hammered and moved down an industrial assembly line. Packages are then shipped several blocks. L.A., 1970.

ROLLER WRESTLE. Sparring match on skates for rink, restaurant and record players. L.A., 1970.

XIXIZXIZIZ. Twelve trucks and 2 boats transport hundreds of spectators to 12 simultaneous locations, each of which is rotated hourly until all vehicles reconverge at dawn. L.A., 1970.

CHRYPILTDESTINY. A 9,000 hour mining construction project within an academic facility, aborted midstream as authorities confronted bulldozers bearing tree stumps. L.A., 1971.

PALUS SOMNORIUM. First installation to include audio and video synthesizer link-ups. L.A., 1971.

SMELL OF THE VESTURE. Glorifying the massacre of media rites by antiseptic distortion. L.A., 1972.

FATHOM VOID ENLARGED. A library of early electronic abrasives is recorded in abandoned breweries and the Mojave desert. 1972.

CHALLUS EPIDAUREM. Spectator stretchers are carried to a krypton laser scaffold which pierces a movie screen. L.A., 1973.

HYDROSIFLESH. An on-camera examination of the excavation of a 300 lb. ice block with picks, axes and torches. L.A., 1973.

CELLAR M. Hearings featuring Stefan Weisser's pre-*Z'ev* acoustic percussion interfaced to the ongoing electronic framework. Uneasy listening. L.A.-S.F., 1974-75.

1976-77. Vaudeo sortie signals the push into research and development of group-designed tools. S.F.

RHYTHM & NOISE becomes the moniker for the Humon/Fault/Probe configuration. Machine prototypes continue development. S.F., 1978-79.

CRISIS DATA TRANSFER sneak previews. Live testing of systems and ideas through a segmented, cinematic display. Some sections sung: *Stuck On The Front, Half Life Housewife, Alizarin K, and Atomcraft*. S.F., 1980.

1981-82. Equipment and personnel are stripped down, updated and reconditioned. A business base is established, facilitating long-term goals of product and performance. S.F.

SOME BOOKS

Section 605 of the
  Communications Act (FCC)
Formalized Music/Xenakis
Video & Videology/Paik
Through the Vanishing Point/McLuhan
Theatre & Its Double/Artaud
Human Use of Human Beings/Weiner
Network Project
Radical Software
Maldoror/Lautréamont
Gravity's Rainbow/Pynchon
Will To Power/Nietzsche
Messengers of Deception/Vallée
My Secret Life/Dali
Last Aid/Chivian, et al
The Day After Midnight/Riordan, ed
A Heritage of Stone/Garrison

SOME RECORDS

Persepolis/Iannis Xenakis
Electro-Acoustic Music/ ''
Hymnen/Karlheinz Stockhausen
Kurzwellen/ ''
Wings of the Delirious Demon/
  Ilhan Mimaroglu
Quarter Mass/Todd Dockstader
Luna Park/ ''
Le Voyage/Pierre Henry
Variations for a Door & Sigh/
  Pierre Henry
Dresden Interleaf/Gordon Mumma
Megaton/ ''
Pandemonium/Jean Baptiste Barriere
Omnicircus/Frank Garvey
Computer Pieces from IRCAM/
  Jean Risset
Terminal Music from Stanford/
  John Chowning
American Time Capsule 1967/
  Alvin Lucier
L'arbre et caetera/Alain Savouret
Immersion/Michel Redolfi
De Natura Sonorum/Bernard Parmegiani
Brand Polyphonie/Francois Bayle
Requiem/Michel Chion
Granulations/Guy Reikel

SOME FILMS

Greed/von Stroheim
Foolish Wives/von Stroheim
Anaemic Cinema/Duchamp
Ballet Mécanique/Leger
Entr'acte/Clair
Ghosts Before Breakfast/Richter
Rhythmus 21/Richter
Return to Reason/Man Ray
Emak Bakia/Man Ray
Uberfall/Metzner
In the Tombs/Edison
An Execution by Hanging/Edison
Electrocution of an Elephant/Edison
Witchcraft Through the Ages/
  Christensen (W S Burroughs narr)
Passion of Joan of Arc/Dreyer
Vampyr/Dreyer
The Phantom Chariot/Sjöström
The Man with the Movie Camera/Vertov
10 Days That Shook The World/
  Eisenstein
Metropolis/Lang
Spies/Lang
Woman in the Moon/Lang
The Last Laugh/Murnau
Nosferatu/Murnau
The Monster/Mélies
The Red Spector/Fréres
Electronic Opera #1 & #2/
  Nam June Paik
Variations on Johnny Carson vs.
  Charlotte Moorman/Nam June Paik

SOURCES

Trashola c/o Jim Morton
Suite 583, 109 Minna St
San Francisco CA 94105
($3.50 for 1 yr's postage)

Armada International
Holliger + Partner AG
Postfach CH-8035
Zurich, Switzerland
($70/yr & worthwhile)

Loompanics
PO Box 1197
Port Townsend WA 98368
(book catalog, $2)

Desert Publications
Cornville AZ 86325
(book catalog, $1)

Survival Books
11106 Magnolia Blvd
No Hollywood CA 91601
(213) 763-0804
(book catalog, $2)

SIMCO Media/Pistolero etc
1421 Tower Square
Ventura CA 93003
(sub, $15 for next 3 books)

Shotgun News
PO Box 669
Hastings NE 68901
($15/yr—indispensable)

City Lights Mail Orders
261 Columbus
San Francisco CA 94133
(for every in-print book by
W.S. Burroughs, Brion Gysin
and J.G. Ballard, etc.)

John Lyle Books
Harpford, Sidmouth
Devon EX10 ONH U.K.
(surrealist bk catalog, £1)

Blackwell's
Broad Street
Oxford, U.K. OX1 3BQ
(book search service)

Pociao's
Aloys Schulte Str. 15
D5300 Bonn 1
West Germany
(send 4 IRCs for catalog)

Tattootime
PO Box 890
Forked River NJ 08731
(subscription, $17)

THE PUBLIC LIBRARY
Reader's Guide to Periodicals
Medical Books & Journals
Psychology Books & Jrnls
Occult, War, Sci-fi, etc
The Economist; Fortune

Rough Trade Record Dist.
326 6th St
San Francisco CA 94103
(415) 621-4045
(50¢ for catalog)

Giorno Poetry Systems
222 Bowery
NYC NY 10012

CLEM (Elec Music Guide)
PO Box 86010
No Vancouver B.C.
Canada V7L 4J5
($7/yr; $12 air foreign)

Sordide Sentimental
B.P. 534
76005 Rouen Cedex
France

Sexy Politzei (9x12'' book)
Bruno Richard
7, rue de Bourg-l'Abbé
Paris 75003 France
(send 150 Fr. Francs)

OP (monthly record guide)
PO Box 2391
Olympia WA 98507
(subscription, $8)

Paladin Press
PO Box 1307
Boulder CO 80306
(book catalog, $1)

SOME FORTHCOMING RE/SEARCH PROJECTS:

☐ A comprehensive *Re/Search* special on J.G. Ballard
☐ A *Re/Search* special on Paul Bowles and friends
☐ *Re/Search*: Sex & Control
☐ *The Alternative Scouting Manual* by William S. Burroughs, illustrated by Jim and Dan Osborne
☐ A Guide to *Incredibly Strange Films* by Jim Morton (of *Trashola*) and Boyd Rice
☐ *Pranks.* Ingenious tales of malicious wit from Boyd Rice, Mark Pauline, Frank Discussion & other enemies of the conditioned reflex.
☐ *Power, Sex and Magick:* a history of *Coum Transmissions* by Gray Watson
☐ Bruno Richard: Sex/Play of an Obsessive Graphiste
☐ Brion Gysin Interviewed by Jon Savage, Genesis P-Orridge & Peter Christopherson
☐ Modern Primitivism: A Survey
☐ Situationism: Selected Graphic-Texts
☐ Surrealism: Neglected Writings
☐ Diary of a Teenage Girl Runaway